The Jewish Heritage

Dan Cohn-Sherbok

Basil Blackwell

First published 1988

Basil Blackwell Ltd
108 Cowley Road, Oxford, OX4 1JF, UK

Basil Blackwell Inc.
432 Park Avenue South, Suite 1503
New York, NY 10016, USA

British Library Cataloguing in Publication Data

Cohn-Sherbok, Dan
  The Jewish heritage.
  1. Jews—History
  I. Title
  909'.04924   DS117
  ISBN 0–631–15413–2
  ISBN 0–631–15414–0 Pbk

Library of Congress Cataloging in Publication Data

Cohn-Sherbok, Dan.
  The Jewish heritage/Dan Cohn-Sherbok.
    p.   cm.
    ISBN 0–631–15413–2 ISBN 0–631–15414–0 (pbk.)
    1. Judaism—History. 2. Jews—History. I. Title.
  BM155.2.C64 1988
  296'.09—dc19

Typeset in 10½ on 12 pt Sabon
by Cambrian Typesetters, Frimley, Surrey
Printed in Great Britain by
T J Press Ltd, Padstow

The Jewish Heritage

For Lavinia, Herod and Dido

Contents

Acknowledgements and a Note on Dates

In writing this study I am particularly indebted to a number of helpful works from which I have obtained information and maps: Robert M. Seltzer, *Jewish People, Jewish Thought: The Jewish Experience in History* (Macmillan, 1980); John Drane, *The Old Testament Story* (Lion, 1983); G. W. Anderson, *The History and Religion of Israel* (Oxford University Press, 1966); Michael Grant, *The History of Ancient Israel* (Charles Scribner's Sons, 1984); Herbert G. May, *Oxford Bible Atlas* (Oxford University Press, 1962); Isaac Husik, *A History of Medieval Jewish Philosophy* (Harper and Row, 1966); H. H. Ben-Sasson (ed.), *A History of the Jewish People* (Harvard University Press, 1976); Paul Johnson, *A History of the Jews* (Weidenfeld and Nicolson, 1987); H. M. Sacher, *The Course of Modern Jewish History* (Delta Publishing Company, 1958). I would also like to thank Stephan Chambers of Basil Blackwell for his encouragement and Janice Newton for her patience in typing the manuscript.

A note on dates: In the case of rulers, all dates refer to the years of their reign; dates for other individuals indicate life-spans. In chapters 1–5, dates are either BC or AD; from chapter 6 all dates are AD. (I have used this terminology rather than B.C.E. and C.E. since it is more familiar.)

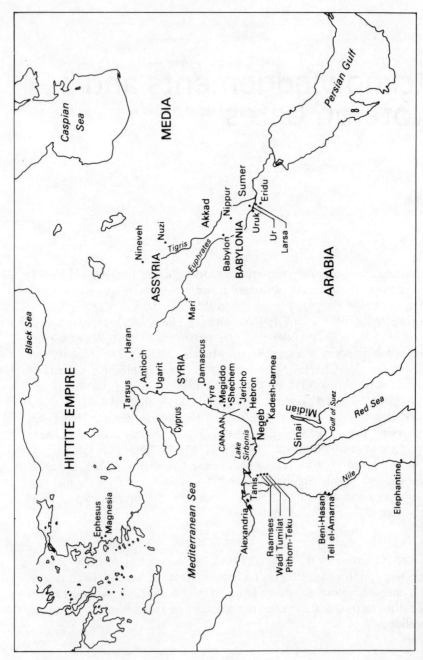

Map 1 The ancient Near East

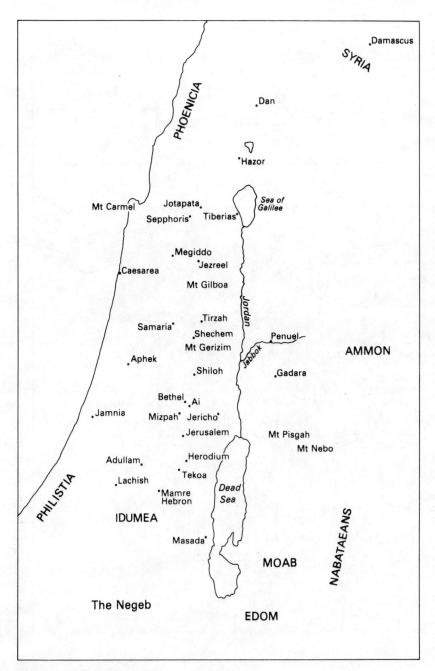

Map 2 Ancient Israel

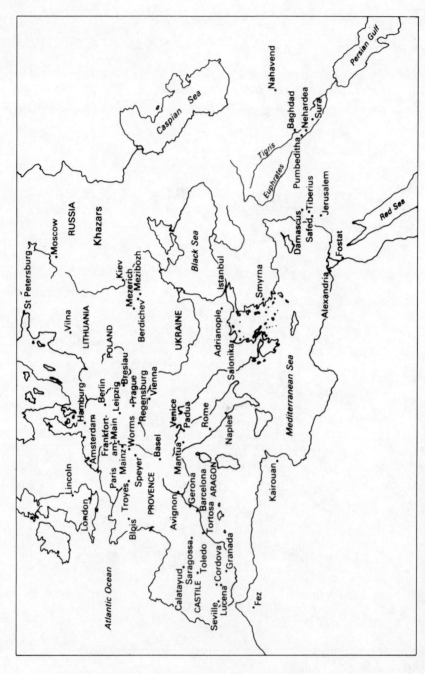

Map 3 Medieval and modern Jewry

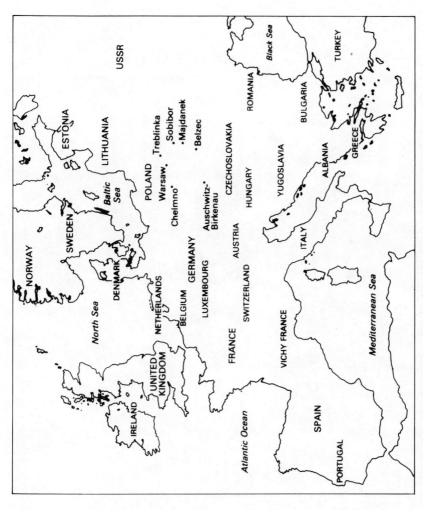

Map 4 European Jewry and the death camps under the Nazis

1

The Ancient Near Eastern Background

The story of the Jewish people begins in the fertile lowlands alongside the Tigris and Euphrates rivers. It was here in Mesopotamia that successive empires of the ancient world flourished and decayed before the Jews emerged as a separate people. The culture of these civilizations had a profound impact on the Hebrew religion: ancient Near Eastern myths and traditions were filtered and refashioned to serve the needs of the faith of the Jewish nation. The Hebrew Scriptures are thus an amalgam of elements from neighbouring peoples, and modern archaeology provides a vast array of literary documents preserved on stone and clay tablets which shed light on this development. These sources give an account of the rise and fall of states and empires and the spread of religious ideas, and although only referring to Israel they indirectly help to clarify the intellectual and religious milieu in which the Bible was formed.

Ancient Mesopotamian civilization

The rise of ancient Mesopotamian civilization occurred at the end of the fourth millennium in southern Mesopotamia where the Sumerians created city states, each with its local god. In Uruk, which is the best known from excavations by archaeologists, there were two main temples: one was for Anu, the supreme god of heaven; the other was for Inanna, the mother goddess of fertility, love and war. Besides these two gods, additional deities were worshipped at other sites – Enlil, lord of the atmosphere, was worshipped at Nippur; Enki, ruler of the fresh waters beneath the earth, at Eridu; Utu, the sun god, at Larsa; Nanna, the moon god, at Ur. Each principal god had a family and servants who were also worshipped at various shrines. The temple itself was placed on a high platform and housed in a holy room a statue of the god, who was washed, dressed and fed each day. Throughout the centuries, Sumerian priests told stories about these gods, whose actions were restricted to specific spheres of influence – frequently they were depicted as quarrelling over their areas of power, engaging in trickery and showing every kind of human emotion and vice. In addition, the Sumerian legends contain accounts of creation: Enlil separated heaven from earth, and Enki created man to grow food for himself and the gods.

During the third millennium, waves of Semitic peoples settled amidst the Sumerians, adopting their writing and culture. From 2300 BC when Sargon of Akkad set up the first Semitic empire, they dominated Mesopotamia. At this time the Sumerian stories were written in the Semitic language, Akkadian (rather than Sumerian cuneiform script). These Semites identified some of their gods with the Sumerian ones: Anu was equated with El (the chief god); Inanna with Ishtar; Enki with Ea. In Akkadian schools epics of the gods were recorded. The Gilgamesh epic, for example, tells of King Gilgamesh who ruled Uruk in about 2700 BC. Gilgamesh set out on a quest for immortality, and eventually encountered an old man Ut-napishtim who told Gilgamesh how he had become immortal. The gods, he explained, created man, but were disturbed by his noise. Unable to quell this tumult, they decided to destroy man by a great flood. Enki, who had made man in the first place, told Ut-napishtim to build a large boat in which he could escape. After the flood, the boat was grounded on a mountain, and the gods rewarded Ut-napishtim with immortality. Ut-napishtim told Gilgamesh to get a plant that could make him young again. Although Gilgamesh found it, he put it on the ground when he went for a swim; it was eventually eaten by a snake and Gilgamesh returned home empty-handed.

For the Sumerians and Akkadians, life was under the control of the gods. To obtain happiness, it was essential to keep the gods in a good humour through worship and sacrifice. Yet the gods were un-predictable, and this gave rise to the use of reading omens. In the birth of monstrosities, in the movements of animals, in the shapes of cracks in the wall and in oil poured into a cup of water these ancient peoples saw the fingers of the gods pointing to the future. Thus, if a man wanted to marry, or a king desired to go to war, they would consult omens. One common practice was to examine the liver of a sacrificed animal, and a special class of priests was trained to interpret such signs.

At its height the empire of Sargon and his descendants stretched from the Persian coast to the Syrian shores of the Mediterranean, but this empire collapsed in about 2200 BC through invasion and internal conflict. Among the new arrivals in Mesopotamia were the Amorites who settled in Mesopotamian cities such as Mari and Babylon where they were integrated into Sumero-Akkadian civilization. Other Amorites penetrated into the Syria–Palestine area (ancient Canaan) where they retained their separate tribal structure. The breakdown of the Akkadian empire was followed by a Sumerian revival in the Third Dynasty of Ur (2060–1950 BC). One of the greatest subsequent rulers was Hammurabi of Babylon who reigned from 1792 to 1750 BC; in his honour the Babylonian creation story ('Enuma Elish') was written. Several centuries later (in about 1400 BC) the state of Assyria grew strong in northern Mesopotamia, and after an interval became the dominant power in the Near East. The Assyrian kings copied the Babylonians: they worshipped the same gods, but their chief god, identified with Enlil, was Ashur. When the Assyrians went to battle, it was at Ashur's command and it was to defend or expand his frontiers that they fought.

In the second millennium, the inhabitants of Canaan were a mixture of races largely of Semitic origin. Excavations have unearthed the remains of small temples in Canaanite towns which housed cultic statues in niches opposite doorways. Where temples had courtyards, it appears that worshippers stood outside while the priests entered the sanctuary. A large altar was probably placed in the courtyard with a smaller one inside the temple, and animal remains suggest that sacrifices consisted mainly of lambs and kids. Liquid offerings of wine and oil were also made and incense was burned. In some temples, stone pillars stood as memorials to the dead; other pillars were symbols of gods. Statues of gods and goddesses were carved in stone or moulded in metal overlaid with gold, dressed in expensive clothes and decorated with valuable jewellery. To the north of ancient Canaan, excavations of the city of Ugarit have provided more information about the local religion. The texts of Ugarit illustrate that the gods of Canaan were like many others of the ancient Near East: they were powers of the natural world. El was the father of gods and men. His wife was Asherah, the mother goddess. El had a daughter Anat who personified war and love and is described in some accounts as the lover of her brother, Baal, the god of weather. The texts of Ugarit describe Baal's victory over Yam (the sea) and against Mot (the god of death). Other gods include Shapash, the sun goddess; Yarikh, the moon god; Eshmun, the healer. This Canaanite religious structure as well as the earlier Sumerian and Akkadian civilizations set the backdrop for the emergence of the religion of the Jewish people. The earliest stories in the Pentateuch (Genesis, Exodus, Leviticus, Numbers and Deuteronomy) contain centuries-old legends written in the light of Mesopotamian myth. Jewish civilization did not emerge in a vacuum, but was forged out of the essential elements of an extensive Mesopotamian cultural inheritance.

Ancient Near Eastern literature and the Bible

From what is known of Mesopotamian civilization, we can see that the Bible reflects various aspects of this cultural milieu. The physical structure of the universe as outlined in Genesis parallels what is found in Near Eastern literature: the earth is conceived of as a thin disk floating in the surrounding ocean; the heavens are a dome holding back the upper waters; under the earth is the abode of the dead. Like the gods of ancient literatures, the God of Israel is understood anthropomorphically. As with other peoples, the Israelites (the descendants of the Biblical patriarchs) accepted magical procedures (Exodus 7:11–12), recognized the power of blessings and curses (Numbers 22–4), and believed that God's will can be known through dreams, dice and oracles. Furthermore, as in other cultures, holy men, kings and priests were revered, and there was a preoccupation with ritual uncleanliness and purity as well as priestly rites.

In addition to these similarities, there are strong parallels between the Bible and the literature of the ancient Near East: Genesis appears to borrow details from the Mesopotamian epic of Gilgamesh in connection with the legend of the flood; Biblical law bears a striking resemblance to ancient legal codes, in particular the Assyrian treaties between a king and his vassals which are very like the covenantal relationship between God and Israel. Yet despite such parallels, Israelite monotheism radically transformed these mythological features: themes retained in the Bible (such as the marriage of divine beings with women) are only briefly mentioned; Biblical heroes are not worshipped; nor is the underworld a subject for speculation. The cult is free of rites to placate ghosts and demons; there is no ancestor worship; divination (such as investigating the livers of sacrificial animals) is forbidden. In essence, the Biblical narratives are simplified and demythologized. There are no myths of the birth of gods, their rivalries, sexual relations or accounts of death and resurrection. Moreover, there is no mention of fate to which both men and gods are subject. Instead, the Bible concentrates on the moral condition of mankind within the context of divine providence.

Such demythologization is a particular feature of Biblical narratives. According to modern scholarship, the priestly editors composed a creation account (Genesis 1–2:4) markedly different from the Babylonian narrative. In the 'Enuma Elish', which is a reworking of old Sumerian themes, the primordial power Tiamat (salt water) and Apsu (sweet water) gave birth to a pair of forces which engendered other gods such as Anu (the god of heaven) and Ea (the god of running waters). Apsu plots the destruction of the gods but is prevented by Ea. Later Tiamat with her second husband and an army of gods and monsters attack the younger gods. Marduk (the god of Babylonia), however, slaughters Tiamat and from her corpse fashions the cosmos and from the blood of her consort Ea makes man. Though there are echoes of this mythology in the Bible, Genesis decrees that God formed the universe without any struggle against other gods. The entities created by God's fiat have no divine aspect. Further, the abyss (in Hebrew *tehom* which is etymologically related to Tiamat) simply refers to the original state of the universe after a primary substance – an unformed and watery chaos – came into existence. Turning to the flood story – a central element of Mesopotamian myth – the Bible ignores such details as the gods' terror at the cataclysms accompanying the flood. In the epic of Gilgamesh the flood is seen as the god Enil's remedy to reduce the level of human noise in the world. The Bible, however, proclaims that man's wickedness is its cause; and when the flood comes, God gives laws to restrain future human evil and promises that this devastation will never happen again. A comparison of texts from the Babylonian flood-story and the Bible forcefully illustrates the demythologizing intention of the Biblical authors:

Gilgamesh epic (eleventh canto)	*Genesis 8*
I sent forth a dove and let her go, The dove went to and fro, But there was no resting place, and she returned. Then I sent forth a raven and let her go. The raven flew away, she beheld the abatement of waters, And she came near, wading and croaking, but did not return.	Then he sent forth a dove from him to see if the waters had subsided from the face of the ground; but the dove found no place to set her foot, and she returned to him . . . He waited another seven days, and sent forth the dove: and she did not return to him any more . . .

Then I sent everything forth to the four quarters of heaven, I offered sacrifice,
I made a libation on the peak of the mountain.
By sevens I set out the vessels,
Under them I heaped up reed and cedarwood and myrtle,
The gods smelt the savour,
The gods smelt the sweet savour,
The gods gathered like flies about him that offered up the sacrifice.

So Noah went forth, and his sons and his wife and his sons wife went with him. And every beast, every creeping thing, and every bird, everything that moves upon the earth, went forth by families out of the ark.
Then Noah built up an altar to the Lord, and took of every clean animal and of every clean bird, and offered burnt offerings on the altar.
And when the Lord smelled the pleasing odour, the Lord said in his heart, I will never again curse the ground because of man, for the imagination of man's heart is evil from his youth; neither will I ever again destroy every living creature as I have done.

In these passages the Hebrew writer has reshaped this story to emphasize God's dominion over the cosmos as well as his concern for human morality. By refashioning the myths of the Near East, the ancient Israelites proclaimed the God of Israel as the creator and ruler of all things.

Israelite monotheism

The belief in one God is perhaps the greatest contribution of the Jews to western civilization. How did such a religious view arise? According to some scholars, the beginnings of Israelite monotheism stemmed from a disillusionment with Mesopotamian religion in the second millennium. These scholars attribute this radical break to Abraham's discovery that the concept of universal justice must rest on the belief in one supreme God. Other scholars see Moses as the principal architect of Israelite monotheism. Such scholars point out that before Moses there was evidence of monotheistic belief in the religious reforms of the Egyptian Pharaoh Akhenaton in the fourteenth century BC; in this light Moses is seen as following the path of this Egyptian revolutionary figure. There are other scholars, however, who contend that it is unlikely that monotheism can be attributed to Abraham or Moses. Such a view, they believe, conflicts with the Biblical narratives of the tribal and monarchical periods that give evidence of a struggle on the part of some Israelites to remain faithful to God in the face of competing deities. For these writers, monotheism should be understood as the result of a clash of cults and religious concepts over the centuries.

According to this latter view, ancient Israelite religion was not monotheism but monolatry: the worship of one God despite the admitted existence of other gods. Arguably this may have been the meaning of Deuteronomy 6:4: 'Hear, O Israel: the Lord our God is one Lord.' With this view, the God of Israel was understood as the Divine Being who revealed His will to Israel, inspired its leaders, protected the Israelites in their wanderings, and led them to the Promised Land. The worship of any other deity was, according to Exodus 20:3, betrayal and blasphemy: 'You shall have no other gods before me'. The God of Israel was not like any other gods of Mesopotamia, Egypt or Canaan, and it was forbidden to make an image of Him: 'You shall not make for yourself a graven image, or any likeness of anything that is in Heaven above, or that is in the earth beneath, or that is in the water under the earth' (Exodus 20:4). Instead of symbolizing the cycle of nature like the Canaanite deities, the Israelite God was a redeemer who liberated His people from slavery: 'I am the Lord your God who brought you out of the land of Egypt, out of the house of bondage' (Exodus 20:2). It was this God, not the Canaanite El, who was the creator of heaven and earth; He, not Baal, was the source of rain and agricultural fertility; through His action, rather than that of Asshur or Marduk, the Assyrian and Babylonian conquest took place.

Monotheism was thus a later development in the history of Israel; it took place when foreign gods were seen as simply the work of men's hands. Possibly this was the view of Elijah in the ninth century BC when confronting the prophets of Baal; he declared: 'The Lord He is God; the Lord He is God' (1 Kings 18:39). But certainly by the time of Jeremiah (several decades before the Babylonian exile) monotheism appears to have taken a firm hold on the Israelite community. In the words of Jeremiah: 'Their idols are like scarecrows in a cucumber field, and they cannot speak; they have to be carried for they cannot walk. Be not afraid of them, for they cannot do evil, neither is it in them to do good' (Jeremiah 10.5). According to some scholars, Psalm 82 gives evidence of this transition from monolatry to monotheism; here the psalmist declares that God rebukes the other gods for their injustice and deprives them of divine status and immortality.

God has taken his place in the divine council;
In the midst of the gods he holds judgment;
How long will you judge unjustly,
and show partiality to the wicked? Selah.
Give justice to the weak and the fatherless;
maintain the right of the afflicted and the destitute.
Rescue the weak and the needy;
deliver them from the hand of the wicked –
They have neither knowledge, nor understanding, they walk about in
darkness;
all the foundations of the earth are shaken –
I say, "You are gods,
sons of the Most High, all of you;
nevertheless you shall die like men,
and fall like any prince".
Arise, O god, judge the earth,
for to thee belong all the nations!

The God of Israel is the true God, the creator of all things, who guides history and will eventually be recognized by all.

Biblical law

Recently scholars have become increasingly aware of the degree to which the Biblical writers utilized ancient Near Eastern treaties as models for legal codes. Israel's Covenant with God, for example, has been traced back to king–vassal treaties of the Hittites in the second millennium BC and of the Assyrians in the first millennium BC. These political documents usually include a historical prologue describing the benevolent acts of the rulers, the stipulations that the vassal accepts, the provision for the deposit of the treaty in a sanctuary, an agreement about its periodic recitation, and an indication of punishments if the agreement is broken and of rewards if it is kept. As Biblical scholars emphasize, such features are also present to some degree in the central collections of law in the Pentateuch.

The oldest corpus of Pentateuchal law is found in the Book of the Covenant (Exodus 20–3). God's speech in Exodus 19:4–6 serves as an introduction; the specific laws which follow are the covenantal stipulations that Israel agrees to follow; the sacrificial meal of Exodus 24:9–11 is a ceremony of acceptance; Deuteronomy 12–26 is the second collection of law, and is largely a revision of the Book of the Covenant. The law is presented as a speech by Moses to the people on the plains of Moab just before his death. It is prefaced by a review of what God has done for Israel, and followed by a list of blessings and curses which will befall the people for their loyalty or disobedience to God's commands. The third corpus of law is the priestly material (Exodus 25 to Numbers 10) which contains the Holiness Code (Leviticus 17–26).

Despite differences in detail, these three legal collections have much in common: all condemn murder, robbery, incest and adultery; each requires respect for parents and strict justice in the courts; the laws protect the rights of the stranger and the impoverished; there is provision made for a liberation of slaves and rest for the soil; certain locations are set aside as refuges for those who unintentionally committed manslaughter; destruction of idols and a ban on divination are stipulated; observance of the Passover and festivals are required; tithes are to be given to priests and Levites; the first-born of animals and men belong to God but may be redeemed. As scholars have demonstrated, this compilation of moral, civil and criminal law draws extensively on ancient Near Eastern precedent in various spheres. First, the civil and criminal code borrows from Mesopotamian legislation, reshaping laws according to the characteristic features of the religion of ancient Israel. *Lex Talionis* (an eye for an eye, etc.) for example – which in Mesopotamia was a legal protection only for freemen – was extended by the Biblical writers to all groups in society. In other areas, too, Biblical legislation treated all equally: judgements were to be the same regardless of the wealth or poverty of plaintiffs; bribery of judges was forbidden; the defenceless (such as widows, orphans and slaves) were to be protected; and the same ruling was to apply to the native resident and the resident alien. A second feature of the Mesopotamian law code – the protection of the dignity and purity of the family – was also a central feature of Biblical legislation. Severe punishments were enjoined against acts that undermine family life (such as incest, sodomy and bestiality).

A third area of borrowing from Near Eastern culture deals with the dichotomy between the holy and the profane. All Near Eastern cultures subscribed to the belief that the sacred is a source of danger; and Biblical writers similarly believed that supernatural danger stems from God. 1 and 2 Samuel, for example, emphasize the power inherent in the Ark of the Covenant (a portable chest symbolizing God's presence); the Pentateuch focuses on dangers faced by the priests in handling holy objects in the sanctuary; diseases and plagues are brought about by God. In priestly law there is a contaminating substance that adheres to things and people, and can only be eliminated through religious rites; the main sources of impurity are:

the dead carcasses of impure animals, human corpses, leprosy, and male and female sexual emissions. The impure must be kept from contact with sanctuary vessels, offerings, priests, the holy city and the holy land, yet through the passage of time and immersion in water such pollution can be removed.

The sacrificial system is a fourth area of borrowing from the ancient Near East. Yet unlike the myths of Mesopotamia, God in the Bible is not dependent on nourishment from sacrifices. Instead sacrifice is a concrete means by which the Israelites were able to establish a relationship with their God. Some offerings expressed thanksgiving, gratitude and reverence whereas others effected expiation through blood poured on the altar. Since blood was understood as the principle of life, the blood of an actual victim symbolized atonement for the guilt of the offerer. Unless such offerings were made, the wrath of God could be kindled with terrible consequences for the people, and thus the task of ensuring the ritual purity of the nation was a central priestly task.

A final sphere of borrowing concerned the major festivals. All the Israelites' agricultural celebrations seem to have been adopted from Canaanite practices and transformed into occasions of pilgrimage to God's sanctuary in order to celebrate His role in bestowing fertility on nature.

From this survey it is clear the Pentateuchal law was drawn and modified from the legal collections and political treaties of their neighbours. The Biblical writers utilized concepts of election and covenant to give authority to the legal system: God was conceived as supreme and worthy of worship – Israel was therefore obligated to serve Him with fidelity. In such a context, justice was a cardinal obligation imposed on the leaders of the people and Israelite society as a whole as a result of their relationship with God. Law in ancient Israel was not simply the concern of the elite as in the ancient Near East; instead legal obligations were at the centre of public life. In numerous cases no reasons were given why laws should be observed; they were simply decrees to be followed by all. As a consequence, the study and interpretation of law came to be a central preoccupation of the religious life in the history of the nation.

Authorship of the Pentateuch

According to traditional Judaism, the Five Books of Moses were dictated by God to Moses on Mt Sinai. This doctrine implies that the entire text – including precepts, theology and history – is of divine origin; all of its contents are inerrent. Such a belief guarantees the validity of the legal system, the Jewish view of God, and the concept of Israel's pre-eminence among the nations. In the modern period, however, it has become increasingly difficult to sustain this concept of Scripture in the light of scholarly investigation and discovery. As early as the sixteenth century, scholars pointed out that the Five Books of Moses appear to be composed of different sources. In the middle of the nineteenth century sustained investigation by two German scholars, Karl Heinrich Graf and Julius Wellhausen, concluded that the Five Books of Moses are composed of four main documents which once existed separately but were later combined by a series of editors or redactors. The first document, J, dating from the ninth century BC attributes the most anthropomorphic character to God, referred to by the four Hebrew letters YHWH. The second source, E, stemming from the eighth century BC, is less anthropomorphic and utilizes the divine name Elohim. In the seventh century BC the D source was written, concentrating on religious purity and the priesthood. Finally the P source from the fifth century BC, which has a more transcendental view of God, emphasizes the importance of the sacrificial cult.

By utilizing this framework, Graf and Wellhausen maintained that it is possible to account for the manifold problems and discrepancies in the Biblical text: for example, there are two creation accounts in Genesis; the appointment of a king is sanctioned in Deuteronomy but opposed in 1 Samuel; Isaac appears to have spent eighty years on his death bed; camels bearing loads are mentioned in the narratives even though they were not domesticated until much later; the centralization of worship in Deuteronomy was unknown in prophetic times. These are only a few illustrations of textual difficulties which can be resolved by seeing the Five Books as the result of the weaving together of source material from different periods in the history of ancient Israel. The Graf–Wellhausen hypothesis was however modified by subsequent writers. Some scholars have preferred not to speak of separate sources, but of circles of tradition. On this view, J, E, P and D represent oral traditions rather than written documents. Further, these scholars stress that the separate traditions themselves contain early material; thus it is a mistake to think they originated in their entirety at particular periods. Other scholars reject the theory of separate sources altogether; they argue that oral traditions were modified throughout the history of ancient Israel and only eventually were compiled into a single narrative. Yet despite these different theories, there is a general recognition among modern Biblical critics that the Pentateuch was not written by Moses; rather, it is seen as a collection of traditions originating at different times in ancient Israel.

In addition to Biblical criticism, textual studies of ancient manuscripts highlight the improbability of the traditional view of the Scriptures. According to tradition, the Hebrew text of the Five Books of Moses used in synagogues today (the Masoretic text) is the same as that given to Moses. Yet it is widely accepted among scholars that the script of contemporary Torah scrolls is not the same as that which was current in ancient Israel from the time of the monarchy until the sixth century BC. It was only later, possibly under Aramaic influence, that the square script was adopted as the standard for Hebrew writing. Furthermore the fact that ancient translations of the Hebrew Bible into languages such as Syriac and Greek contain variant readings from the Masoretic text suggests that the Hebrew text of the Pentateuch now in use is not entirely free from error. A final aspect of modern studies which bears on the question of Mosaic authorship concerns the influence of the ancient Near East on the Bible. According to Orthodoxy, the Five Books of Moses were essentially created out of nothing. But, as we have seen, there are strong parallels in the Bible to laws, stories and myths found throughout the ancient Near East. It is unlikely that this is simply a coincidence – the similarities offer compelling evidence that the Five Books of Moses emerged in a specific social and cultural context. The authors of the Biblical period shared much of the same world view as their neighbours and no doubt transformed this framework to fit their own religious notions. In this light, most modern Biblical scholars would find it impossible to reconcile the traditional conceptions of Mosaic authorship of the Five Books of Moses with the findings of modern Biblical scholarship and scientific discovery.

2
Patriarchy to Monarchy

Scholars generally consider that the Jews emerged as a separate people between the nineteenth and sixteenth centuries BC. Some writers maintain that the patriarchs (Abraham, Isaac and Jacob) were real persons – chiefs or founders of tribal units; others argue that the names of the patriarchs refer not to individuals but to families, clans or tribes. In either case, these ancestors of the Jewish nation appear to have been part of a wave of north-western Semitic-speaking peoples who moved into Canaan in the second millennium BC. They and their descendants were semi-nomadic groups with small bands of sheep and goats coming from the desert in search of pasture and intermingling with the local inhabitants. It has been suggested that these immigrants and sojourners were part of a larger social stratum living on the fringes of settled society referred to in Near Eastern sources as *Habiru* – a term which resembles the Biblical word 'Hebrew'. The patriarchal clans may have been part of this *Habiru* element in ancient Canaan.

The patriarchs

According to the Biblical narrative in Genesis, Abraham was the father of the Jewish nation. Originally known as Abram, he came from Ur of the Chaldaeans – a Sumerian city of Mesopotamia near the head of the Persian Gulf. Together with his father Terah, his wife Sarai, and his nephew Lot, he travelled to Haran, a trading centre in northern Syria. There his father died, and God called upon him to go to Canaan: 'Go from your country and your kindred and your father's house to the land I will show you. And I will make of you a great nation' (Genesis 12:1–2). During a famine in Canaan, he went first to Egypt and then proceeded to the Negeb, finally settling in the plain near Hebron. Here he experienced a revelation which confirmed that his deliverance from Ur was an act of providence: 'I am the Lord who brought you from Ur of the Chaldaeans to give you this land to possess' (Genesis 15:7).

Since Sarai had not given birth to children, Abram had relations with her servant girl, Hagar, who bore Ishmael. But when Abram was ninety-nine and Sarai ninety, God granted them a son, Isaac. It was then that Abram was given his new name Abraham ('the father of a multitude'), and Sarai was renamed Sarah ('princess'). When Isaac was born, Abraham sent Hagar and Ishmael away at Sarah's request. During this time God made a covenant with Abraham symbolized by an act of circumcision: 'You shall be circumcised in the flesh of your foreskins, and it shall be a sign of the covenant between me and you' (Genesis 17:11). Later God tested Abraham's dedication by ordering him to sacrifice Isaac, only telling him at the last moment to refrain. When Isaac became older, Abraham sent a servant to his kinsfolk in Hebron to find a wife, and the messenger returned with Rebecca. After many years, God answered Isaac's prayers for a son, and twins – Esau and Jacob – were born. Jacob bought his brother's birthright for food, and with his mother's help secured Isaac's blessing thereby incurring Esau's wrath. Fleeing from his brother, Jacob travelled northwards towards Haran; en route he had a vision of a ladder rising to heaven and heard God speak to him promising that his offspring would inherit the land and fill the earth:

> And he dreamed that there was a ladder set up on the earth, and the top of it reached to heaven; and behold, the angels of God were ascending and descending on it! And behold, the Lord stood above it and said, 'I am the Lord, the God of Abraham your father and the god of Isaac; the land on which you lie I will give to you and to your descendants; and your descendants shall be like the dust of the earth.' (Genesis 28:12–14)

After arriving in Haran, Jacob worked for twenty years as a shepherd for his uncle Laban. There he married Laban's daughters, Rachel and Leah, and they and their maids (Bilhah and Zilpah) bore twelve sons and a daughter. When he eventually returned to Canaan, Jacob wrestled with a mysterious stranger in the gorge of the Jabbok river, a tributary of the Jordan, where God bestowed upon him the new name 'Israel':

> When the man saw that he did not prevail against Jacob, he touched the hollow of his thigh; and Jacob's thigh was put out of joint as he

wrestled with him. Then he said, 'Let me go, for the day is breaking'. But Jacob said, 'I will not let you go, unless you bless me.' And he said to him, 'What is your name?' And he said, 'Jacob.' Then he said, 'Your name shall no more be called Jacob, but Israel, for you have striven with God and with men and have prevailed.' (Genesis 32:25–8)

Jacob was welcomed by Essau in Edom, but then the brothers parted. Jacob lived in Canaan until one of his sons, Joseph, invited him to settle in Egypt where he died at the age of 147.

For some time scholars have attempted to relate these patriarchal stories to Old Testament times. In particular they have emphasized, on the basis of ancient documents found at the Mesopotamian sites of Mari and Nuzi, that the accounts of the Hebrew patriarchs accurately reflect the conditions of the Middle Bronze Age period (2000–1500 BC). Names like Abraham, Isaac and Jacob, for example, have been found in numerous texts – they appear to have been especially popular among the Amorites. Other names from Genesis as well (such as Terah and Ishmael) were also widely used. Furthermore these ancient documents illustrate that the wandering of the patriarchs mirrors what is known of life in the early part of the second millennium BC. The legal documents found at Nuzi also help to explain patriarchal customs. For example the story of Sarai presenting Abraham with a slave girl by whom to have a child is paralleled by a text from Nuzi which explains how in certain marriage contracts a childless wife could be required to provide her husband with a substitute. Again, Nuzi law stipulates that childless couples could ensure the continuation of their family by adopting a slave who would take the place of a son. This child would then inherit their property, but if a natural son were eventually born the slave son would lose his inheritance rights. Such a law is paralleled by Genesis 15:1–4 where Abraham expresses a fear that his slave Eliezer could succeed him. Though these Mari and Nuzi texts do not specifically refer to the patriarchs themselves, we can see that the Genesis legends are largely in accord with the laws and customs of the second millennium BC. Thus there is good reason to believe that the Genesis narrative preserved a broadly accurate picture of the earliest ancestors of the Jewish people.

Joseph

This history of the three patriarchs is followed by the cycle of stories about Jacob's son Joseph. As a young boy, Joseph was presented with a special coat (or a long-sleeved robe) of many colours as a sign that he was his father's favourite. When he was in Shechem helping his brothers tend his family's flocks, he angered them by recounting dreams in which they bowed down before him. They reacted by plotting his death, but one of the brothers (Reuben) persuaded them to wait, and another (Judah) suggested that they should sell him as a slave rather that kill him. Eventually Joseph was taken to Egypt; his brothers dipped his coat in a kid's blood and declared to their father that he had been mauled by a wild animal. In Egypt Joseph served in the house of Potiphar but was falsely accused by Potiphar's wife of rape and incarcerated in prison. Some time later he was set free by the reigning pharaoh to interpret his dreams and subsequently became chief minister of the land. After a famine, he made the country rich and later encountered his brothers who came before him to buy grain. Movingly he revealed to them his true identity, and God's providential care: 'I am your brother Joseph', he declared, 'whom you sold into Egypt. And now do not be distressed, or angry with yourselves, because you sold me here; for God sent me before you to preserve life' (Genesis 45:4–5). Joseph died when he was 110, and his family remained and flourished in Egypt. But with the reign of a new pharaoh 'who did not know Joseph' (Exodus 1:8) the Jewish people were oppressed and persecuted and forced to work as slaves on the construction of the royal cities of Pithom and Raamses. Finally the pharaoh declared that all male offspring should be killed at birth: 'Every son that is born to the Hebrews – you shall cast into the Nile, but you shall let every daughter live' (Exodus 1:22).

Scholars point out that the Joseph legends consist of a collection of stories which were woven together into a complex form. Yet it is recognized that Semitic-speaking groups had for centuries been emigrating into Egypt to escape the adverse conditions in the north as well as to find food and engage in trade. The tomb-paintings of 1900–1890 BC at Beni-Hasan (250 miles up the Nile), for example, portray a group of such aliens led by Ibsha (or Abishar) and accompanied by donkeys bringing lead sulphide from the Red Sea. From the later eighteenth century BC onwards such immigration appears to have been widespread as is evidenced by the Canaanite influence on Egyptian culture and ritual. It is possible that the Joseph legends derive from such a pattern of immigration. Some scholars have pointed out that if the story of Joseph took place in the time of the Hyskos empire in Egypt (1720–1580/1567 BC), it is possible that these non-Egyptian Semitic-speaking rulers were more likely to appoint an alien like Joseph to a position of authority. The new king who did not know Joseph might have been a native Egyptian pharaoh who came to power after the Hyskos had been overthrown.

Other scholars date the Joseph story much later; they suggest that the ancient Hebrew may have migrated to Egypt during the reign of the Pharaoh Seti I (1304–1290 BC) the son of Rameses I (the founder of the Nineteenth Dynasty). Seti I re-established Egyptian dominance over Canaan; it was he who moved his capital to Tanis in the eastern delta where according to the Psalms Joseph and his followers resided, 'in the land of Zoan' (Psalm 78:12, 43). In either case, the pharaoh who 'did not know Joseph' may have been Rameses II (1290–1224 BC) of the Nineteenth Dynasty who, scholars believe, built the cities of Pithom and Raamses where it is recorded the Jewish people worked as slaves. Pithom (-Teku) at the mouth of the Wadi Tumilat near the Salt Lakes contained granaries; in all likelihood it was in their construction that the Israelites were employed. The location of Raamses is uncertain, but it may have been the new designation of the city of Avaris, reconstructed as part of a great urban palace and storage complex fifteen miles from Tunis. The successor of Rameses II was Merneptah (1224–1211 BC). On a large black granite stele of Merneptah is inscribed an account of an alleged military victory mentioning Israel: 'Israel is laid waste; its [grain] seed is not.' The word 'Israel' is here written with an inflexion denoting 'people' rather than 'country' – in such a case it is possible that this inscription provides historical corroboration for the existence of the House of Joseph in Egypt at this time.

The Exodus

The Biblical narrative continues with an account of the deliverance of the Jews from Egyptian bondage. Exodus relates that a son had been born to Amram of the House of Levi and his wife Jochebed. When he was three months old his parents concealed him among the reeds growing on the banks of the Nile to save him from Pharaoh's decree. Pharaoh's daughter found the child and adopted him as her son, Moses. When he became older, he attacked and killed a taskmaster who was oppressing a Hebrew slave, and fled to the desert. There he dwelt with Jethro (a priest of Midian) and married his daughter, Zipporah. Eventually God revealed Himself to Moses, commanding that he deliver the chosen people from Pharaoh's harsh bondage: 'I am the God of your father, the God of Abraham, the God of Isaac, and the God of Jacob . . . I have seen the affliction of my people who are in Egypt, and have heard their cry because of their taskmasters. I know their sufferings . . . Come, I will send you to Pharaoh that you may bring forth my people, the sons of Israel, out of Egypt' (Exodus 3:6–7, 10).

To persuade Pharaoh that he should let the Jewish people go, God inflicted ten plagues on the Egyptians culminating in the slaying of every Egyptian first-born son. The first-born of the Israelites were spared as each family slaughtered a lamb and smeared its blood on the doorposts. Seeing this, the Angel of Death passed over that household. After this final plague, Pharaoh released the Israelites, and they fled without even waiting for their bread to rise. However the perils were not over; Pharaoh changed his mind and sent his forces in pursuit. When the Israelites came to an expanse of water, it seemed they were trapped. Miraculously it was converted to dry land by a strong wind so they were able to escape. The Egyptians however were drowned as they chased after them: 'The Egyptians pursued, and went in after them into the midst of the sea, all Pharaoh's horses, his chariots, and his horsemen . . . The waters returned and covered the chariots and the horsemen and all the host of Pharaoh that had followed them into the sea; not so much as one of them remained' (Exodus 14:23,28).

The band of free people entered the wilderness of Sinai where Moses performed miracles to provide them with food and water (Exodus 16–17). After travelling for about ninety days, they encamped before Mt Sinai. God called Moses up to the top of the mountain and told him that if his people would listen to him and keep His covenant, they would become God's special people. They were commanded to wash and purify themselves for two days; on the third day they came to the foot of the mountain amongst thunder, lightning and the sound of a ram's horn to hear God's voice. Alone Moses climbed the mountain again where he remained for forty days. At the end of this period, he returned with two tablets of stone on which were inscribed God's laws. But on his return, Moses found the people had forsaken him and their God, and in anger he smashed the tablets of stone (only later carving new ones). Subsequently the Jews moved on and came to Kadesh-barnea (near the border of Canaan). There Moses saw the Promised Land from a distance: 'And Moses went up from the plains of Moab to the top of Pisgah, which is opposite Jericho. And the Lord showed him all the land . . . And the Lord said to him, "This is the land of which I swore to Abraham, to Isaac, and to Jacob, 'I will give it to your descendants.' I have let you see it with your eyes, but you shall not go over there" ' (Deuteronomy 34:1,4).

From a geographical standpoint, there is considerable uncertainty about the details of this narrative account of the Exodus. Some scholars have suggested that the crossing of the Red Sea (or Reed Sea) took place, not at the head of the Gulf of Suez which is a long way from the Israelites' point of departure, but at one of the lakes now joined by the Suez Canal. Other suggestions include the head of the Gulf of Aqaba or alternatively Lake Sirbonis. The mountain where God revealed Himself to Moses has traditionally been identified with Jebel Musa in the south of Sinai, but it has been objected that such a location would have taken the Israelites dangerously near the route the Egyptians used to reach copper and turquoise mines in that area. Another suggestion is that the occurrences on the mountain suggest volcanic activity: since no mountain in the Sinai peninsula is volcanic, it has been advanced that the site was in north-western Arabia, east of the Gulf of Aqaba. The Bible thus does not enable us to trace the route of the Jews in the wilderness. Regarding the date of the Exodus, 1 Kings 6:1 states that it took place 480 years before Solomon founded the Temple (in the fourth year of his reign). Assuming Solomon came to the throne in 961 BC, the Exodus would have taken place in 1438 BC. But, as we have seen, if the Israelites laboured at Pithom and Raamses as Scripture relates, the Exodus would have taken place much later. Thus it can be seen that from a historical viewpoint, the Exodus narrative poses a number of serious difficulties.

Conquest and settlement

After Moses died, Joshua the son of Nun was commanded by God to lead the children of Israel into the Promised Land. After crossing the Jordan, he captured Jericho and went on to take Ai (near Bethel). Subsequently he defeated both southern and northern kings. The second part of the Book of Joshua begins with a list of areas which had not as yet been conquered in the plain and valley regions as well as on the coast. To encourage the people, Joshua delivered speeches enjoining them to remain steadfast in their faith: recalling God's past mercies, he ordered them to be obedient to the Covenant. After Joshua's death at the age of 110, the people began to form separate groups. At first there were twelve tribes named after the sons of Jacob: Joseph and Benjamin (the sons of Rachel); Levi, Simeon, Reuben, Judah, Issachar and Zebulun (the sons of Leah); Dan and Naphtali (the sons of Bilhah); and Gad and Asher (the sons of Zilpah). When Levi became a special priestly group excluded from this territorial division, the tribe of Joseph was divided into two named after his sons, Ephraim and Manasseh.

The Book of Judges also tells the story of the twelve national heroes who served as judges of the nation after Joshua's death. The sagas of six major judges – Othniel, Ehud, Deborah, Gideon, Jephthah and Samson – are recounted at length. The judges were tribal rulers attached to particular regions; their fragmented reign continued for more than 150 years during the twelfth and eleventh centuries BC. During quiet periods, the tribes were governed by councils of elders; it was only at times of emergency that the judges took control. From a religious perspective, the era of the judges was of central significance in the life of the people. The Covenant between God and the Israelites – first formulated by Moses – was repeatedly proclaimed at gatherings in such national shrines as Shechem. Such an emphasis on covenantal obligation reinforced the belief that the Jews were the recipients of God's loving kindness: they were his chosen people, a dedicated and separate nation.

In a more settled existence, the Covenant expanded to include additional legislation. Mosaic law was largely apodeictic in character, comprising unconditional statements of principle, but as time passed casuistic provisions for every kind of situation were included within the system. Many of these provisions were needed for an agricultural community, and seem to date back to the time of the judges. It also became clear to the Jewish nation that the God of the Covenant directed human history: the Exodus and the entry into the Promised Land were seen as the unfolding of a divine plan. Unlike their Canaanite neighbours who worshipped local gods, the people of Israel stressed their detachment from place-related ties by revering a mobile shrine which they carried from place to place. In all likelihood this tent or tabernacle was the repository of the sacred Ark.

The rejection of Canaanite religions was reinforced by the Israelite disapproval of such rites as magic fertility rituals (such as boiling a kid in its mother's milk); making images of the gods (like the figurines of the Canaanite goddess Ashtoreth); temple prostitution such as existed in Canaanite cults, and the human sacrifice of children. However, the Israelites adapted the three Canaanite agricultural festivals to suit their own religious aims. The spring festival was transformed into Pesach (Passover) to commemorate the Exodus from Egypt. The autumn festival became Succot (Booths), a celebration of the dwelling in tents during the sojourn in the desert. The early summer festival was changed to Shavuot (Weeks) to bear witness to the giving of the law on Mt Sinai. These three festivals eventually became occurrences of pilgrimage to remind the Jewish nation of their former suffering, liberation and dedication to the Covenant, but they had their origins in the Canaanite agricultural rhythms.

Though the results of archaeological investigation do not conclusively demonstrate the accuracy of the account of the conquest as portrayed in the Book of Joshua, archaeological findings do cast light on certain features of this period. The Tell-el-Amarna letters dating from the early fourteenth century, which were written by various rulers in Canaan and Syria to the Pharaoh Amenhotep III (1398–1361 BC) and his successor Akhen-aten (1369–1353 BC) complain of the activities of groups of raiders (*Habiru*) who caused havoc in the countryside. Previously scholars identified the *Habiru* with the Hebrew nation and equated the invasions into southern Canaan with Joshua's incursions. Nowadays this is thought to be too neat a theory; it is argued instead that these letters reflect a more generalized migration of foreign peoples into Canaan. It is possible to see the Israelites as part of this movement, although this would imply a very early date for the Exodus and conquest. However there is the possibility that some of the Israelites settled in Canaan prior to the liberation from Egyptian bondage.

Regarding the Biblical claim that Joshua conquered several Canaanite cities, an excavation of Jericho carried out this century was thought to prove that the city was in fact captured by the Israelites: the walls appeared to have collapsed and there was evidence of considerable destruction by fire. Investigations by later archaeologists, however, cast serious doubt on this theory – the remains have been shown to have been at a lower level and to date from the latter part of the third millennium BC. On the other hand, evidence from different sites such as the city of Hazor shows that there was widespread devastation during the thirteenth century BC. Some scholars argue that this had nothing to do with Joshua; they believe it was the result of feuding between Canaanite city states. Others maintain that this destruction was caused by foreign invaders such as Philistines and Amorites. Nevertheless, the fact that parts of Canaan were destroyed during this period provides some corroboration for the accuracy of the Joshua account.

Archaeological evidence has cast considerable light on Canaanite religion. The tell of Ras-esh-Shamra on the coast of Syria was the site of the citadel of Ugarit which flourished in the fifteenth and fourteenth centuries BC. In an annexe to the temple, archaeologists discovered a collection of thirteenth-century clay tablets describing the exploits of Baal and other Canaanite gods and goddesses. El is portrayed as chief of the gods with his female consort Asherah, but they appear to be subservient to Baal, the weather god, and his lover, Anat. One story relates that Baal was attacked by Mot, the god of barrenness and sterility: he was overcome and his body scattered to the four corners of the earth. But Anat took her revenge:

> She seizes Mot, the son of El
> with the knife she cuts him
> with the shovel she winnows him,
> with the fire she burns him,
> with millstones she grinds him,
> on the field she throws him.
> The birds eat his remains,
> The feathered ones make an end to what is left over.

Baal's power returned when he engaged in sexual relations with Anat; this ensured the fertility of the earth. In Canaanite religion this was crucial since rainfall was vital for agriculture. Some scholars believe that the story of Baal's revival was the high point of the autumn New Year Festival – the King and a temple prostitute would act out the story of Baal and Anat. Such a mixture of sexual activity and fertility presented a major challenge to the Israelite concept of a God who demands moral and ritual obedience to His decree.

The rise of monarchy

During the period of the judges, God was conceived of as the supreme monarch. When some tribes suggested to Gideon that he deserved a formal position of power, he declared it was impossible for the nation to be ruled by both God and a human king (Judges 8:22–3). The political associations of the Israelites have been described as an amphictyony – a loose confederation united for common welfare. During Samuel's lifetime, however, the people found tribal alliance and simple trust in God's power inadequate. Politically and militarily Israel was less well organized than the Philistines (who occupied southern Canaan) and could offer no effective resistance to invading armies. After a defeat at Aphek, the leaders of the nation realized they were powerless and decided to make certain God would be with them in battle: 'Let us bring the ark of the covenant of the Lord here from Shiloh', they declared, 'that he may come among us and save us from the power of our enemies' (1 Samuel 4:3). This plan was unsuccessful: the Ark was captured, its shrine at Shiloh demolished and the Israelite army overcome. Though the Ark was later returned, this defeat crushed the people's confidence. The Israelites needed a king, but in the chapters which describe Saul's election to kingship (1 Samuel 8–12), there appear to be at least two strands of tradition. The first (1 Samuel 9:1–10:16) represents Saul as God's instrument for deliverance as evidenced by his leadership of the Israelite army against the Ammonites who had threatened Jabesh-Gilead. As a mark of his office, he was anointed by Samuel and was filled with God's power. The other strand (1 Samuel 8:10–17, 12), however, presents the people's desire for a king as a rejection of God's authority. According to this account, the king was selected by means of a sacred lot at a national assembly convened by Samuel; it is in this context that Samuel's warning against the dangers of kingship was expressed:

> And now behold the king whom you have chosen, for whom you have asked; behold, the Lord has set a king over you. If you will fear the Lord and serve him and hearken to his voice and not rebel against the commandment of the Lord, and if both you and the king who reigns over you will follow the Lord your God, it will be well; but if you will not hearken to the voice of the Lord, but rebel against the commandment of the Lord, then the hand of the Lord will be against you and your king. (1 Samuel 12:13–15)

Samuel's forebodings proved to be correct: Saul's reign was plagued by a number of difficulties. His first problem was that he soon lost the support of Samuel. When Saul was instructed to take neither prisoners nor spoil in a campaign against the Amalekites, these instructions were not strictly followed. As a consequence, Samuel denounced the King and declared he had been rejected by God (1 Samuel 15). The second problem concerned Saul's moods of gloom and violence. After his anointing, God's spirit came upon Saul and imparted to him prophetic frenzy so that he could lead Israel to victory. As is known from the eighteenth-century-BC letters from Mari, prophetic ecstasy linked with military triumph was a feature of the ancient Near East. But for Saul such emotional activity took a toll on his mental state. To relieve him from depression, David joined his retinue so that he might bring relief through music. Yet this was no solution. Saul became jealous of David's popularity and success. Much of the account of Saul's reign is concerned with the deteriorating relationship between the two men. Saul's reign thus began with a successful military action reminiscent of the exploits of the judges, but it ended in madness and defeat.

3
Kings and Prophets

After a long period of tribal unity, the Israelite nation divided into two kingdoms. This separation was a reflection of an ideological division which had existed for much longer. The northern tribes led by Ephraim and the southern tribes led by Judah had only been united by their allegiance to David. But when Solomon and his son Rehoboam violated many of the ancient traditions, the northern tribes revolted. The reason they gave for this rebellion was the injustice of the kings, but in fact they sought to recapture the simpler ways of the generation that had escaped from Egypt. Then there had been no monarch, and leadership was exercised on the basis of charisma. What the north looked for was allegiance and loyalty to the King of Kings who had brought them from Egyptian bondage into the Promised Land. It was against this background that the pre-exilic prophets endeavoured to bring the nation back to the true worship of God. Righteousness, they declared, is the standard by which all people are to be judged, especially kings and rulers.

Prophecy was not a phenomenon unique to the Israelites. There are records of prophets of other Near Eastern religions such as that of the Phoenician Baal. Like them, the official Israelite cult employed prophets, or prophetic bands known as sons of the prophets, to predict the outcome of battles and to serve near the shrines. Scholars have not determined the exact relationship between these official prophets and the solitary prophets whose words are recorded in the Scriptures. It used to be thought that the Biblical prophets were separate from and indeed stood against the cult prophets. Now it is recognized that there was probably a closer connection between the two groups. In any case, throughout the pre-exilic period the Biblical prophets provided a commentary on the historical events of their day, and continually reminded the kings that they were only rulers under God.

David and Solomon

After joining Saul's entourage, David (1010–970 BC) quickly gained a reputation as a successful warrior as is reflected in the account of his victory over the giant Goliath. Later he married Saul's daughter Michal, buying her hand with the foreskins of a hundred slaughtered Philistines. But David's military exploits and general popularity evoked Saul's anger. On the advice of Saul's son Jonathan, David fled for safety to the cave of Adullam in the southern wilderness. When Saul, along with his son Jonathan, was killed at Mt Gilboa, David became the leader of the southern tribes; at Hebron he was anointed King of Judah. In the north, Saul's son Ishbaal was appointed king. Later however David supplanted Ishbaal and became king over the entire country.

One of David's first victories was over the Jebusites in Jerusalem which he declared the new capital. Very little exists of the Jerusalem of David's reign, but there is no question that David transformed the city into a major administrative centre. Employing foreign craftsmen, he built new fortifications and a palace. To Jerusalem he also brought the Ark of the Covenant, and by this act symbolically transferred power away from the tribes.

Despite his glory as a conquerer and leader, Scripture bemoans David's moral failings. After he had committed adultery with Bathsheba and caused the death of her husband Uriah, the court prophet Nathan denounced David and demanded repentance – even the King was subject to God's moral dictates. Yet for all his immorality, David was assured that his dynasty would continue. As God declared: 'When your days are fulfilled and you lie down with your fathers, I will raise up your offspring after you, who shall come forth from your body, and I will establish his Kingdom. He shall build a house for my name, and I will establish the throne of his Kingdom for ever' (2 Samuel 7:12–14).

Towards the end of David's life, rivals for the throne battled against one another. Revolts led by his son Absalom and by Sheba from the tribe of Benjamin were suppressed; by the time of David's death, his son Adonijah seemed the likely successor. Although Adonijah was supported by the priest Abiathar and the army-general Joab, another son, Solomon (970–930 BC), had still more powerful allies. Solomon's mother, Bathsheba, had been David's favourite wife, and was supported by the prophet Nathan, Zadok the priest and Benaiah, another army commander. Eventually Solomon was victorious – Adonijah and his supporters were killed and Abiathar was exiled. But unlike David, Solomon was concerned more with his own security than the defence of the nation. Enormous resources were directed into a personal army consisting of 12,000 men and horses and 1,400 chariots.

In foreign affairs Solomon traded with Phoenicia, Arabia and Syria, Cilicia and probably with north and east Africa as well. By marrying an Egyptian princess he linked himself with Egypt. One of Solomon's close contacts was with Hiram, King of Tyre. The Phoenicians had extensive trading links in the Mediterranean, and through this alliance Solomon was able to develop his own trade in the Red Sea and the Indian Ocean. In all likelihood the Phoenicians also helped him build and operate his copper refineries on the Gulf of Aqaba. In addition, it appears that Solomon traded horses with the Egyptians in the south and the Hittites in the north.

As a result of this activity, Solomon was able to build a new palace for himself, another for his Egyptian wife, a hall for state occasions, a judgement chamber and, most importantly, the Temple. Originally David wanted to build a temple to house the Ark of the Covenant, but this became Solomon's greatest triumph. The best material was transported (such as timber from the King of Tyre), and skilled craftsmen from Phoenicia were employed. Scholars have pointed out that the actual plan of the Temple was identical to the temples of Baal which have been discovered by archaeologists, and they note that the Jerusalem Temple was consecrated at exactly the same time in the year as the Baal temple at Ugarit (before the autumn rains). Yet whether or not Solomon attempted to initiate Canaanite worship, he did play an active part in the Israelite cult, offering sacrifices and blessing the people – actions Saul and David had been expressly forbidden from performing.

In addition to his architectural achievements, Solomon was universally recognized as a wise ruler. In the words of 1 Kings: 'Solomon's wisdom surpassed the wisdom of all the people of the east, and all the wisdom of Egypt' (1 Kings 4:30). According to tradition, he was able to recite 'three thousand proverbs; and his songs were a thousand and five. He spoke of trees, from the cedar that is in Lebanon to the hyssop that grows out of the wall; he spoke also of beasts, and of birds, and of reptiles, and of fish' (1 Kings 4:32–3). Scholars have recognized that such wisdom was part of an intellectual movement of the time, and Solomon's achievement is akin to the pursuits of kings and philosophers in ancient Egypt and Mesopotamia. It has been argued that it was as a reaction to such artistic and cultural interests that scribes during Solomon's reign wove together Israel's early history. Their purpose was to point out that heroes such as Abraham and Moses prospered as a result of God's grace and loving kindness, not because of their own efforts.

To support Solomon's many projects, an elaborate system of taxation had been developed: each of the twelve districts of the territory was obligated to support the court for one month a year. Not surprisingly, this taxation evoked a strong reaction. The notion of a privileged elite supported by the general population conflicted with the egalitarian tribal organization. In place of twelve tribes serving God, twelve districts served the king. Moreover, the fact that the Canaanites adopted a similar financial system emphasized the foreignness of this arrangement. But even such taxation was insufficient to support Solomon's projects; to meet his expenses he instituted forced labour. This provision provoked a revolt led by the northern army leader Jeroboam, but his plot was uncovered and he fled to Egypt. The northern tribes remained dissatisfied, but the southern tribes were loyal to the house of David. Not only were David and his son southerners by birth, they also favoured the southern tribes: Judah and Benjamin seem to have been excluded from the taxation burden.

The two kingdoms

After Solomon's death, his son Rehoboam (930–908 BC) became king and sought the allegiance of the northern tribes. When he went to Shechem from Jerusalem to meet them, they outlined the terms on which they would accept the monarchy. Rehoboam refused to listen and arrogantly proclaimed, 'My father made your yoke heavy, but I will add to your yoke; my father chastised you with whips, but I will chastise you with scorpions' (1 Kings 12:14). As a consequence of Rehoboam's policies the northern tribes revolted against him and chose instead Jeroboam I (930–910 BC) as their monarch: 'When all Israel heard that Jeroboam had returned, they sent and called him to the assembly and made him king over all Israel' (1 Kings 12:20). Shechem initially served as Jeroboam's administrative centre, but he later made Tirzah his capital. No major battle appears to have taken place between the northern kingdom (Israel) and the southern kingdom (Judah), but border clashes resulted from Judah's retention of the territory of Benjamin.

As the kingdoms divided, the aggressor who threatened the nation was Shoshenk I (945–924 BC), the first pharaoh of the Twenty-Second Dynasty who invaded the land and forced Rehoboam to pay tribute. An inscription in the Temple of Amun at Thebes refers to this conquest. Shoshenk does not mention any towns in Judah being captured, but he does refer to some cities in the northern kingdom. Another inscription found at Megiddo suggests that the Egyptian incursion must have enveloped most of the territory. In the north the external danger was matched by an internal threat – the tribes keenly felt the loss of the Temple and desired to make pilgrimage to Jerusalem. To stem such disloyalty, Jeroboam I set up alternative shrines at old centres of Canaanite worship, Dan and Bethel. There he placed golden bulls in an attempt to reconcile the faith of Israel with features of Canaanite belief, a policy which he believed to be necessary since there was a sizeable Canaanite population within his territory: the Canaanite elements would have no difficulty in associating these idols with their own god Baal (who was often represented as a bull); the Israelites could regard them as thrones for their God (like the throne in the Temple).

Jeroboam I's successor was his son Nadab (910–909 BC) who was followed by Baasha (909–886 BC). Like Jeroboam I, he encouraged a mixture of Canaanite and Israelite religions or, as the Biblical writers put it, he 'made Israel to sin'. (1 Kings 15:34) When he died his son Elah (886 BC) attempted to succeed him, but was assassinated and Zimri the army commander (886 BC) usurped the throne. Zimri's reign lasted only seven days; he was followed by another general, Omri (885–874 BC) and his son Ahab (874–852 BC). Under the rule of these later two kings, the position of the northern kingdom was greatly strengthened. They ended the conflict with Judah, and the alliance of the kingdoms was sealed by the marriage of Ahab's daughter, Athaliah, to Jehoram (851–842 BC), the son of Jehoshaphat (875–851 BC), King of Judah. Israel also made peace with the powerful kingdom of Phoenicia and Ahab himself married the Phoenician princess, Jezebel. Further, Omri gained control over Moab. This victory is mentioned in a large stone inscription erected by King Mesha of Moab after he had released his kingdom from Israel's grasp after Ahab's death. Much of the inscription concerns Mesha's victory, but the text states 'Omri, King of Israel, humbled Moab for many years'. To solidify his position, Omri built a new administrative centre and shrine in Samaria. Like Jeroboam, Ahab incorporated Canaanite religious features. He provided for the worship of Baal, and thereby incurred the condemnation of Scripture: 'He did evil in the sight of the Lord more than all that were before him. And as if it had been a light thing for him to walk in the sins of Jeroboam . . . and went and served Baal and worshipped him' (1 Kings 16:31).

Such idolatrous practice was encouraged by Jezebel who wanted Baal to become the god of Israel. To combat this threat, the prophet Elijah was determined to prove the God of Israel was supreme. Thus he challenged 450 prophets of Baal and 400 prophets of Asherah to a contest on Mt Carmel, near Phonician territory. This had once been the site of an altar to the Israelite God, but it had been displaced by a shrine to Baal. There he and the Canaanite prophets prepared sacrifices and prayed to their respective gods to send fire from Heaven to ignite the offerings. Although the prophets of Baal and Asherah cried aloud in ecstatic frenzy and cut themselves with swords, no answer was forthcoming. But Elijah's supplication was successful: 'the fire of the Lord fell, and consumed the burnt offering, and the wood and the stones, and the dust and licked up the water that was in the trench. And when all the people saw it, they fell on their faces; and they said, 'The Lord, he is God; the Lord, he is God' (1 Kings 18:38–9). Despite Elijah's victory, Jezebel encouraged Ahab to follow Phoenician customs. She regarded the life and property of every subject as belonging to the King, and so had no hesitation in having the Israelite Naboth killed in order that Ahab could take possession of his property. But Elijah denounced the foreign queen, just as Nathan had previously rebuked David for similar unscrupulousness. For these early prophets, religion was bound up with life and politics, and not even the royal couple were above God's law.

Ahab was succeeded by his two sons, Ahaziah (852–850 BC) and Joram (850–842 BC), but it was not long before those loyal to the faith of Israel rebelled. These devotees, inspired by the prophet Elisha, Elijah's successor, chose an army officer Jehu (842–815 BC) to be the next king of Israel. During a battle between Israel and Syria, Joram was wounded and returned to recuperate in Jezreel. Jehu followed him there where he discovered Ahaziah (842 BC), King of Judah, who was paying a visit. Jehu assassinated both kings as well as Jezebel, the queen mother, and appealed to the city rulers of Samaria to pay allegiance to him. This they did by presenting him with the heads of seventy members of Ahab's family. But Jehu was less successful politically. Since he had killed the Phoenician princess Jezebel, he could no longer rely on the support of a Phoenician alliance. And by killing the King of Judah, he also lost the loyalty of the southern kingdom. In Judah Athaliah, Ahab's sister (842–837 BC), seized control and murdered all claimants for the throne except for one child, Joash (837–800 BC), who was rescued by the priest Jehoiada. Athaliah reigned for six years, but was deposed in a coup led by Jehoiada. Joash was then installed as King.

During this period the Syrians had been engaged in war with the Assyrian King Shalmaneser III (859–824 BC) who was intent on expanding his empire. After Jehu came to power, Shalmaneser invaded Syria and besieged Damascus; Phoenicia and Israel were forced to pay tribute so as to avoid being conquered by Assyria. On the Black Obelisk of Shalmaneser III, Jehu is depicted as a leader of a vassal state paying tribute (this is the first known portrait of a Biblical figure). At the end of Shalmaneser III's reign, a revolt took place in Nineveh which weakened the Assyrian empire and gave the King of Damascus, Hazael (843–796 BC), an opportunity to invade Israel. Under Jehu's son Jehoahaz (815–801 BC), Israel became almost a province of Syria. The entire country east of the Jordan was occupied, and the Syrians continued their attack into Judah. But Joash offered Hazael treasure from the Temple to dissuade him from invading Jerusalem.

By the time Jehu's grandson Jehoash (801–786 BC) became king, Assyria had grown in power under Shalmaneser's grandson, Adad-Nirari III (810–783 BC). According to Assyrian records, Israel was forced to pay tribute to Assyria along with the Edomites and Philistines. Damascus was devastated by the Assyrian advance. When Scripture states 'The Lord gave Israel a saviour so that they escaped from the hand of the Syrians' (2 Kings 13:5), some scholars contend that this refers to Adad-Nirari. The Assyrian attack on Syria gave Jehoash the opportunity to recover Israel's lost territory; Amaziah the king of Judah (800–783 BC) similarly captured his land from the Edomites. At this stage Amaziah declared war also on the northern kingdom, but Judah was defeated and Jehoash raided Jerusalem. As a consequence, Amaziah lost favour and was assassinated, to be succeeded by his son Uzziah (783–742 BC).

Jeroboam II to the fall of the northern kingdom

Under Uzziah in Judah and Jeroboam II (786–746 BC) in Israel, the nation prospered for the next forty years. Uzziah repaired the fortifications in Jerusalem, reorganized the army, and equipped it with new weapons. He also instituted new agricultural methods and reopened parts of Solomon's copper refineries on the Gulf of Aqabah. In the northern kingdom Jeroboam II constructed new buildings and engaged in international trade. As the nation grew richer, the people became more religious – they believed their wealth was a sign of God's favour. Yet some dissenters thought that the quest for riches was incompatible with God's Covenant. According to some scholars, a new edition of Israel's early history was written at this time as a reaction against such high living. This reflected northern traditions and emphasized the role of Moses. Many of these stories, they believe, came to form a part of the Bible, particularly the books of Genesis and Exodus.

Towards the end of Jeroboam II's reign, Amos, a shepherd from Tekoa who firmly differentiated himself from the official cultic prophets, expressed his dissatisfaction; he proclaimed that Israelite society had become morally corrupt. Many Israelites had become rich, but at the expense of the poor. Israel had sinned, he declared,

> because they sell the righteous for silver
> and the needy for a pair of shoes –
> they that trample the head of the poor
> into the dust of the earth,
> and turn aside the way of the afflicted.
> (Amos 2:6–7)

Shrines like Bethel were full of worshippers, but such ritual was empty. The 'day of the Lord', Amos announced, would be a time of punishment for the nation's sinfulness:

> Woe to you who desire the day of the Lord . . .
> It is darkness and not light . . .
> I hate, I despise your feasts, and I take no delight in your solemn
>   assemblies.
> Even though you offer me your burnt offerings and cereal offerings,
> I will not accept them . . .
> Therefore I will take you into exile beyond Damascus, says the Lord,
>   whose name is the God of Hosts.
> (Amos 5:18, 21–2, 27)

His later contemporary, the prophet Hosea, echoed these dire predictions. Israel had gone astray and would be punished. Yet through personal tragedy – the infidelity of his wife Gomer – Hosea was able to offer words of consolation and hope. Just as his love for his wife had been rejected, so God's love for Israel had been despised. But despite the coming devastation, God would not cease to love his chosen people. Just as Hosea could not give up his wife, God could not abandon Israel: 'How can I hand you over, O Israel! . . . My heart recoils within me, my compassion grows warm and tender' (Hosea 11:8).

It was not long before these prophecies of destruction were fulfilled. The Assyrian King Tiglath-Pileser III (745–727 BC) embarked on a policy of expansion during the reign of Menahem, King of Israel (746–738 BC). Israel's government was unstable at the time anyway. Menahem's son Pekahiah (738–737 BC) held his throne for two years by paying tribute to the Assyrian king, but was overthrown by his rival Pekah (737–732 BC). The new Israelite king formed an alliance with the King of Syria against the Assyrians. Together they attempted to persuade Jotham, King of Judah (742–735 BC), to join them; when he refused, they declared war on Judah. In face of this danger, the southern prophet Isaiah declared to Ahaz (735–715 BC), Jotham's successor, that this threat would come to naught: both Israel and Syria would collapse. But Ahaz was unconvinced. He attempted to placate the Assyrians and went to Damascus (which the Assyrians had just conquered) to pay homage to Tiglath-Pileser III. He returned with the plans for an altar to be erected in the Temple as a sign of Judah's submission.

In the northern kingdom, Pekah's position was weakened as the Assyrians pressed forward, and he was assassinated by Hoshea (732–722 BC) who surrendered to the Assyrians. When Shalmaneser V (727–732 BC) replaced Tiglath-Pileser III, Egyptian forces were powerless to help, and Shalmaneser V conquered Israel's capital, Samaria, after a seige of two years. The annals of Shalmaneser's successor Sargon II (722–705 BC) record that 27,290 Israelites were deported as a result of this conquest. This marked the end of the kingdom of Israel.

Ahaz and Hezekiah

With the collapse of the northern kingdom, Judah was under threat. To avoid a similar fate in the south, King Ahaz (735–715 BC) continued to pay tribute to Assyria and to encourage the nation to worship Assyrian gods. However the prophet Isaiah was deeply concerned about such idolatrous practices. He believed that the collapse of Israel was God's punishment for sinfulness, and he foresaw a similar fate for Judah. Echoing the words of Amos, Isaiah warned his countrymen that God was not satisfied with empty ritual:

> What to me is the multitude of your
> sacrifices? says the Lord.
> I have had enough of burnt offerings of rams
> and the fat of fed beasts;
> I do not delight in the blood of bulls,
> or of lambs, or of he-goats.
>
> (Isaiah 10:11)

A contemporary of Isaiah, the prophet Micah, also criticized the people for their iniquity and foretold destruction:

> Hear this, you heads of the house of Jacob
> and rulers of the house of Israel,
> who abhor justice and pervert all equity . . .
> because of you Zion shall be plowed as a field;
> Jerusalem shall become a heap of ruins.
>
> (Micah 3:9, 12)

Ahaz refused to listen to these words; trusting in his own political alliances, he believed his kingdom was secure.

By the time Hezekiah (715–687 BC) succeeded Ahaz, the Assyrian king, Sargon II, had turned his attention to problems in other parts of the empire. This gave Egypt and Philistia an opportunity to join ranks to throw off Assyrian domination. Seeking the help of Judah, the Philistine ambassadors tried to secure Hezekiah's support. But the prophet Isaiah warned that such an alliance would be of no avail. Assyria could not be stopped, and to dramatize the inevitable devastation, Isaiah walked naked around Jerusalem. 'So', he said, 'shall the king of Assyria lead away the Egyptian captives, and the Ethiopian exiles, both the young and the old, naked and barefoot, with buttocks uncovered, to the shame of Egypt' (Isaiah 20:4). Fortunately Hezekiah heeded Isaiah's prediction. Assyria quickly conquered the Philistine and Egyptian nations.

After this conquest Hezekiah attempted to establish his independence from Assyrian domination by reforming the religious practices of the people. As well as removing the altar to Assyrian gods in the temple which his father Ahaz had erected, he tried to close down local shrines in order to centralize the cult in Jerusalem. Further, he sent a message to those who remained in the former northern kingdom urging them to come south to worship. Hezekiah also prepared his kingdom for an Assyrian onslaught: he created new defences, restructured the army, established new store cities, and rationalized the civil service. In Jerusalem he built the Siloam Tunnel to ensure that the city would have a water supply if it were beseiged. A surviving Hebrew inscription from this period etched on this tunnel describes its construction.

After the death of Sargon II, the kings of Babylon and Egypt asked Hezekiah to help overthrow the Assyrians. Isaiah cautioned against joining such an alliance, but Hezekiah took no notice. Sargon's successor Sennacherib (705–681 BC) quickly acted to suppress this revolt. He subdued Babylon, Phoenicia and Philistia, and then moved against the kingdom of Judah in 701 BC. According to an account of this assault in the annals of Sennacherib, the Assyrian army besieged and captured forty-six of Hezekiah's 'strong walled cities as well as the small cities in their neighbourhood'. Though the Assyrian records do not list the names of these places, the defeat of Lachish was depicted by Assyrian royal artists and placed in Sennacherib's palace at Nineveh. These surviving reliefs carved on stone portray the attack on Lachish and its eventual conquest.

The next step in the Assyrian campaign was the assault on Jerusalem. According to Sennacherib's records, Hezekiah was shut up in the city like a bird in a cage. Seeing no way of escape, he sent gold and silver as tribute to Sennacherib who was encamped at Lachish. It is unclear what events occurred next. 2 Kings contains an account of a seige of Jerusalem which ended in failure: the Assyrian army camped outside the city, but just as their victory seemed imminent the Assyrians withdrew. Many soldiers seem to have died. Though there are scholars who accept this story as authentic, they disagree about its dating. Some believe it was part of Sennacherib's invasion; others contend it refers to a second Assyrian campaign, since the narrative mentions King Tirhakah of Sudan who ruled in Egypt from about 689 BC. Sennacherib's annals, however, contain no mention of this defeat – thus this Biblical account may be no more than a pious legend.

From Manasseh to Babylonian captivity

Following the invasion of Judah, Sennacherib was murdered. He was succeeded by Esarhaddon (681–669 BC) who was a successful ruler. When he died the empire was divided between his two sons: Ashur-bani-pal (669–627 BC) who reigned in Nineveh, and Shamash-

Shanakin who had headquarters in Babylon. During this period Assyria was victorious against the Egyptians and became the dominant force in Mesopotamia. Under Ashbur-bani-pal Nineveh emerged as a cultural centre; here artists produced works of great merit and scribes collected together the literary treasures of Mesopotamian culture. In the kingdom of Judah, Hezekiah's successor Manasseh (687–642 BC) was completely under Assyrian domination. The nation's faith was neglected, and pagan ceremonies again became prevalent. Like Ahaz, Manasseh was forced to worship Assyrian gods as a sign of submission, and his son and successor Amon (642–640 BC) continued his father's policies.

Despite its prominence, Assyria came under increasing threat from the kingdom of Lydia in the north-west, the Medes in the east and the Scythians in the north. This weakening of the Assyrian empire brought about a nationalistic revival in Judah.

The prophet Jeremiah warned that the southern kingdom would eventually be devastated by foreign powers. The new king, Josiah (640–609 BC), believed he could restore Judah to its former glory through territorial expansion, and religious reform. Josiah banned the symbols of Assyrian domination in the former northern kingdom, destroyed the sanctuary at Bethel established by Jeroboam I and removed many local shrines and their priests. Most importantly, there was found in the Temple a forgotten book – in all likelihood the Book of Deuteronomy – which asserted that a single God should be worshipped in a central place by a united people. Some scholars argue that this text was not discovered but was commissioned by Josiah to support his policies. In any event it had a profound effect on the nation. In a solemn ceremony, the people pledged their allegiance to God: 'And the king stood by the pillar and made a covenant before the Lord, to walk after the Lord and to keep his commandments and his testimonies and his statutes, with all his heart and all his soul, to perform the words of this covenant that were written in this book; and all the people joined in the covenant' (2 Kings 23:3).

While these events took place in Judah, the Babylonians advanced against Assyria and captured all its main cities. Some years after Josiah's reform, in 609 BC the Assyrians made a final attempt to regain the town of Harran. Embroiling himself in this struggle, Josiah tried to halt the Egyptian army which had been summoned by the Assyrians to come to their aid. In the ensuing battle Josiah was mortally wounded, and Judah came under the domination of Egypt. Eventually, however, the Assyrian empire collapsed and the Babylonians succeeded in conquering the Egyptians at Carchemish in

605 BC. At this King Jehoiakim (609–598 BC), who had been put in power by the Egyptians, transferred his allegiance to King Nebuchadnezzar II of Babylon (605–562 BC). During the reign of Jehoiakim, Jeremiah continued to prophesy disaster: Jerusalem and the Temple itself, he declared, would be destroyed. His contemporary the prophet Habakkuk echoed the prediction that God would use foreign nations as instruments of his wrath. Jehoiakim was undeterred by this message; he believed he could eventually assert his independence from foreign rule.

When Babylon was defeated by Egypt several years later, Jehoaikim decided the time was ripe for rebellion. Nebuchadnezzar however quickly responded by invading the country and conquering Jerusalem. In this siege Jehoiakim was killed and replaced by his son Jehoiachin (597 BC) who was captured. Along with other important citizens he was led into captivity, and the treasures of the palace and Temple were plundered. A new king, Zedekiah (597–586 BC), was placed on the throne by Nebuchadnezzar in 597 BC. Jeremiah counselled the king to accept Babylonian domination, but he was persuaded to join a rebellion led by Egypt. After a seige of eighteen months, Jerusalem was conquered in 586 BC; all the main buildings were destroyed, and Zedekiah was blinded and exiled to Babylon. The last days of Judah just before the conquest of Jerusalem are described in a collection of potsherds (*ostraca*) written by Hoshayahu, who appears to have been the officer in charge of a military outpost to the north of Lachish. These fragments were addressed to Yaush, who was probably the military commander of Lachish. The value of these records is the insight they give into the reaction of the inhabitants of the land as they faced the end of their kingdom at the hands of the Babylonian army.

4
Captivity and Return

During the first millennium BC the Jews watched their country emerge as a powerful state only to see it sink into spiritual and moral decay. Following the Babylonian conquest, they despaired of their fate – the Temple lay in ruins and Jerusalem was demolished. This was God's punishment for their iniquity which the prophets had predicted. Yet despite defeat and exile, the nation rose anew phoenix-like from the ashes of the old kingdoms. In the centuries which followed, the Jewish people continued their religious traditions and communal life. Though they had lost their independence, their devotion to God and His law sustained them through suffering and hardship and inspired them to new heights of creativity. In Babylonia the exiles flourished, keeping their religion alive in the synagogues. These institutions were founded so that Jews could meet together for worship and study; no sacrifices were offered since that was the prerogative of the Jerusalem Temple. When in 538 BC King Cyrus of Persia permitted the Jews to return to their former home, the nation underwent a transformation. The Temple was rebuilt and religious reforms were enacted. This return to the land of their fathers led to national restoration and a renaissance of Jewish life which was to last until the first century AD when the Temple was destroyed a second time by the Romans.

Aftermath of the fall of Judah

The anguish of the people facing the tragedy of Babylonian conquest and captivity is reflected in the Book of Lamentations. Here the author bemoans the plight of Jerusalem:

How lonely sits the city that was full of people!
How like a widow she has become,
She that was great among the nations! . . .
The roads to Zion mourn,
for none come to the appointed feasts;
all her gates are desolate,
her priests groan;
her maidens have been dragged away
and she herself suffers bitterly.

(Lamentations 1:1,4)

In 586 BC Gedaliah, a palace official, was made governor of Judah with his capital at Mizpah. This appointment, however, aroused fierce opposition and Gedaliah was assassinated by Ishmael, a member of the former royal family. Fearing Babylonian vengeance, those who supported this rebellion fled to Egypt taking the prophet Jeremiah with them against his will. In exile these rebels believed that the Babylonian invasion had been the fault of prophets like Jeremiah who had discouraged the people from worshipping foreign gods. The way to renewed prosperity, they were convinced, consisted in a return to the religion of Baal. 'But we will do everything that we have vowed', they declared, 'burn incense to the queen of heaven and pour out libations to her . . . since we left off burning incense to the queen of heaven and pouring out libations to her, we have lacked everything and have been consumed by the sword and the famine' (Jeremiah 44:17–18). For Jeremiah such a view was utter blasphemy; it was just such worship that brought about the downfall of Judah. Eventually Jeremiah's view became the basis for restructuring Jewish life, and some scholars argue that the books of Deuteronomy, Joshua, Judges, Samuel and Kings were gathered together at this time to form an epic history of Israel based on this vision of God's dealings with His people.

Those exiles who settled in Babylon appear to have established a relatively prosperous community, keeping their faith alive in the synagogues. According to Scripture, the Babylonian king Nebuchadnezzar's successor Amel-Marduk (562–560 BC) released Jehoiachin from prison in Babylon and offered him a position in the Babylonian court. Yet despite their affluence, the exiles lamented the loss of their homeland as Psalm 137 records:

By the waters of Babylon, there we sat down and wept,
When we remembered Zion . . . How shall we sing the
Lord's song in a foreign land?

(Psalm 137:1,4)

The prophet Ezekiel, however, counselled those in Babylon not to despair. God, he believed, would restore the fallen nation. Though they were scattered, He would gather them up again:

I will rescue them from all places where they have been scattered on a day of clouds and thick darkness. And I will bring them out from the peoples, and gather them from the countries, and will bring them into their own land.

(Ezekiel 34:12–13)

During the decades that followed, Babylonia was ruled by a succession of weak and inept rulers. The Bible records that this was a difficult period for the Jewish community. The Book of Daniel, for example, relates how Daniel and his friends were subject to harsh treatment by Belshazzar, the King of Babylon. Such persecution is found also in the books of Judith and Tobit.

As the Babylonian empire began to disintegrate, the kingdom of Persia grew in strength. In 539 BC Cyrus of Persia (539–530 BC) conquered Babylon and set about rebuilding the city. Though he himself worshipped the god Marduk, Cyrus believed that all peoples should be free to worship their own gods and live where they wished – the surviving Cyrus cylinder depicts this religious innovation. As far as the Jews were concerned, the Book of Ezra records Cyrus's pronouncement allowing them to return to their homeland:

Concerning the house of God at Jerusalem, let the house be rebuilt, the place where sacrifices are offered and burnt offerings are brought . . . let the gold and silver vessels of the house of God which Nebuchadnezzar took out of the Temple that is in Jerusalem and brought to Babylon, be restored and brought back to the Temple which is in Jerusalem . . . let the governor of the Jews and the elders of the Jews rebuild this house of God on its site.

(Ezra 6:3–7)

In the latter part of the Book of Isaiah (which scholars attribute to a second Isaiah), this return is described as leading to a universal redemption for all people in which Israel would have a special role: 'I will give you as a light to the nations, that my salvation may reach to the end of the earth' (Isaiah 49:6).

Return and restoration

To implement their policy of repatriation, the Persians appointed Shesbazzar as governor of Judah. Other returning exiles included

Joshua the priest and Zerubbabel, the grandson of Jehoiachin, who supervised the repair and restoration of the Temple. According to the Book of Jeremiah, after Nebuchadnezzar's invasion worshippers continued to make a pilgrimage to the Temple site. These Jews offered their assistance to Zerubbabel but he refused since he did not regard them as real Jews: they were of uncertain racial origins and their worship was suspect. These Judaean inhabitants and the people of Samaria recognized that the returning exiles were intent on forming a state in which they would have no place. Having their offer of co-operation rejected, they persuaded the Persian officials responsible for the western empire that the plans of restoration were illegal, thereby delaying work on the Temple for ten years or more. This was the start of the enmity between the Jewish and Samaritan peoples which continued for many hundreds of years and is reflected in the New Testament.

Zerubbabel and Joshua were encouraged in their labours by the prophets Haggai and Zechariah. During the early part of the reign of the Persian king, Darius I (522–486 BC), Haggai urged the people to make the rebuilding of the Temple a major priority. Once the Temple was restored, he proclaimed, a new era in Jewish history would dawn. Zerubbabel was God's chosen ruler in this task of rebuilding: 'On that day, says the Lord of Hosts, I will take you, O Zerubbabel, my servant, the son of Shealtiel, . . . , and make you like a signet-ring; for I have chosen you.' (Haggai 2:23). At the same time the prophet Zechariah encouraged the completion of the Temple. He too stressed that God was with Zerubbabel: 'Moreover the word of the Lord came to me, saying, "The hands of Zerubbabel have laid the foundation of this house: his hands shall also complete it. Then you will know that the Lord of Hosts has sent me to you." ' (Zechariah 4:8–9).

In 515 BC the Temple was completed, but little is known about the period from 515 to 444 BC. The Book of Malachi, however, does depict a widespread disregard for Temple worship. The priests appear to have been negligent in their duties, and the faith of Israel seems to have been polluted by magical practices. In addition, social evil had become rampant; according to Malachi, God would eventually judge those who were corrupt. Malachi also complained that Jewish men were marrying women who belonged to the racially mixed population of the country. By the middle of the fifth century BC important steps were taken by Nehemiah and Ezra to reform the life of the Jewish community. According to modern scholars it is difficult to determine the chronological sequence of their activity; it may be that the Biblical order should be reversed and that Ezra should be placed after Nehemiah. In any case, it appears that Nehemiah was appointed by the Persian king Artaxerxes I (464–423 BC) as governor of Judah. Previous governors had been more concerned with their own comfort than with the welfare of the people, but Nehemiah was dedicated to the well-being of all. When he arrived from Persia, he discovered that Jews had intermarried with peoples of other races and that the rich were exploiting the poor. To combat such laxity, Nehemiah asserted that the community must purify itself by concentrating Jewish life within the confines of Jerusalem, and he initiated a policy of rebuilding and fortification. Such plans were opposed by Sanballat (the governor of Samaria), Tobiah (a prominent Ammonite) and others who feared that Israelites of mixed stock would be excluded from such plans. Despite this opposition, Nehemiah prevailed and Jerusalem was restored, kindling a new sense of religious identity.

In this policy of reform and renewal, Nehemiah was joined by the priest Ezra. Like Nehemiah, Ezra was a Persian state official who had come to Judah with royal authorization to reorganize religious affairs. Accompanied by other exiles (who carried with them substantial financial contributions to the Temple), Ezra was determined to bring the people back to the Covenant. For the exiles, the covenantal law had taken on supreme importance, but this was not so in Judah. Traditional worship was frequently neglected. To remedy this situation, Ezra insisted on reading the law to the people, translated by the priests; this was necessary because the law was written in Hebrew but the inhabitants of the land spoke only Aramaic, the official language of the Persian empire. It is not clear exactly what this law was, but probably it was an early version of the Pentateuch as we know it today and included the priestly codes of Leviticus. When the nation heard these words, they were profoundly moved and vowed to observe the religious practices and festivals of their ancestors as recorded in Scripture, such as the pilgrim festivals (Pesach, Shauvuot and Sukkot), the New Year celebration (Rosh Hashanah) and the Day of Atonement (Yom Kippur). The pilgrim festivals in particular provided a reason for the Jews who lived outside the land of Israel to visit Jerusalem regularly and regard it as their spiritual home.

During this period Jews lived in many parts of the world other than Judah and Babylonia where they asserted their religious identity in the synagogues. The story of Esther, which is recited every spring at the festival of Lots (Purim), provides a vivid picture of the Jewish community in Persia during this period. A number of Aramaic documents discovered at the island of Elephantine also illustrate the habits of another Jewish group settled in Egypt. Like Judah, Egypt was then part of the Persian empire, and it appears that a Jewish military force was sent to Elephantine to guard the southern frontier. In this collection of papyrus documents there are deeds of property, marriage contracts and accounts of religious practices. Despite the Deuteronomic law forbidding sacrificial worship outside Jerusalem, there was a Jewish temple on this island where sacrifices were offered. Here the priests were neither Levites nor did they seem to be knowledgeable about Jewish law. Furthermore, though this temple was dedicated to the God of Israel, other gods and goddesses were part of the cult. Though scholars disagree about the origins of this group, it is clear that these Jews believed it was possible to be pious without following the strict guidelines being established in Jerusalem.

In the years following Ezra's intrusion, the inhabitants of Judah seem to have carried out his reforms, although some scholars believe the books of Ruth and Jonah were written as propaganda against his xenophobic policies. In contrast the books of Chronicles seem to support Jewish nationalism. They look back to the reigns of David and Solomon as a golden era and blame the subsequent disasters on the corruption of later kings, particularly on their neglect of temple worship. These books may be seen against the reforming background of the post-exilic period. The peoples of Samaria on the other hand came to realize that they would not be allowed to worship God in Jerusalem. As a consequence they developed their own beliefs and culture, built their own temple on Mt Gerizim, and eventually established a strong national identity. In 333 BC the Persian king, Darius III Codomannus (336–331 BC), was defeated in battle by Alexander the Great (331–323 BC) from Macedonia. After this victory Alexander progressed towards Egypt, but the Egyptians did not attempt to repulse Alexander's advance. He subsequently founded the city of Alexandria on the Nile delta, and died in 323 BC of a fever. After a power struggle among his generals, both Egypt and Judah (by then called Judaea) came under the jurisdiction of the Ptolemaic dynasty which lasted from 320 BC until 198 BC. During this period the Ptolemies were generally tolerant of the Jewish population, and it was at this stage that the Septuagint, the Greek translation of the Torah, was made.

The Seleucids and the rise of Hellenism

Though Ptolemy was victorious in securing Judaea, another of Alexander's generals, Seleucus, was dissatisfied with this outcome. Throughout the third century BC his successors were involved in a series of battles to determine sovereignty over the country. In 198 BC the issue was settled when the Seleucid king, Antiochus III (223–187 BC), defeated Scopus, the general of the Egyptian king, Ptolemy V. Initially Antiochus III had a positive attitude toward the Jews – he reduced their taxes and made a donation to the Temple. In time he reversed these policies, but in 190 BC he was defeated in a battle against the Romans at Magnesia near Ephesus. In the peace treaty he was forced to hand over his territory in Asia Minor, the richest part of the empire. A year later Antiochus III was killed while robbing a temple to increase his revenue, and was succeeded by his son, Seleucus IV (187–175 BC), who dispatched his chancellor Heliodorus to plunder the Jerusalem Temple.

During the reign of the Seleucids in the second century, two families engaged as rivals in the Judaean Jewish community: the Tobiads and the Oniads. When Seleucus IV was murdered in 175 BC and succeeded by Antiochus IV Epiphanes (175–163 BC), Jason, a member of the Oniad family, bribed Antiochus IV to make him High Priest in place of his brother Onias. When he was appointed to this position, Jason attempted to Hellenize Jerusalem. This involved the introduction of Greek games in which the athletes competed naked – a sight shocking to traditional sensibilities. Many Jews found these changes abhorrent, and Jason was deposed from the throne and replaced by Menelaus, a member of the Tobiad family.

While this internal conflict took place in Judaea, Antiochus IV advanced against Egypt and defeated the Egyptian king, Ptolemy VI; on his return he robbed the Jerusalem Temple. In 168 BC Antiochus IV again invaded Egypt, but this time he encountered the Romans who drove back his onslaught. In Jerusalem it was rumoured that Antiochus IV had been killed, and Jason quickly tried to remove Menelaus. Antiochus IV however acted speedily to crush this rebellion. He conquered Jerusalem and led off some of the people as slaves. In addition he banned circumcision, sabbath observance and the reading of the Torah. He also decreed that the Temple should be dedicated to the worship of the Greek god Zeus, that pigs should be sacrificed on the altar, and that all people, including non-Jews, should be allowed to worship there. Hellenism which was previously encouraged by the Seleucids thus became official policy.

Antiochus IV underestimated Jewish resistance to his reforms – many Jews were prepared to die rather than violate their traditions. Eventually a guerrilla band led by a priest Mattathias and his five sons engaged in armed revolt. After Mattathias's death, this movement was spearheaded by his son Judas (called 'Maccabi' meaning 'hammer'). Some Jews (the Hasideans) were opposed to armed struggle and retreated into the Judaean desert where they were slaughtered by the Seleucids when they refused to fight in battle on the Sabbath. The event drew other Jews to the side of the rebels, and after a series of military engagements the oppressive policies of the Seleucids were reversed. Jewish law was reinstituted, and the Temple was restored and rededicated on 14 December 164 BC, an event subsequently commemorated by the festival of lights (Hanukkah). This victory enabled Judas's clan (the Hasmoneans) to establish themselves as the ruling family in Judaea.

Following his campaign against the Seleucids, Judas made a treaty with the Roman Republic, but in 160 BC he fell in battle and was succeeded by his brother Jonathan. On the death of the High Priest, Jonathan was appointed supreme pontiff even though he lacked hereditary qualification. He was later formally recognized as governor of Judaea. The last surviving brother Simon, who succeeded Jonathan, asserted formal independence from the Seleucid empire. He expelled the Seleucid garrison from the Jerusalem citadel in 142–141 BC, captured the fortress of Gazara and compelled the Seleucid monarth to acquiesce. The Maccabean rebellion thus finally triumphed, and Simon took on the hereditary title of ethnarch, a designation which signified the ruler of an *ethnos* (nation). Many scholars believe that the Book of Daniel was written during this period of rebellion as a message of encouragement against the Seleucids, although it ostensibly deals with events belonging to the reign of Jehoiakim in the sixth century BC.

In 135 BC Simon was murdered in a palace intrigue, and his son, John Hyrcanus I (134–104 BC), became high priest and ethnarch. During the early part of his reign, the Seleucids beseiged Jerusalem and John Hyrcanus I was forced to give up some territory and join the Seleucid king in an unsuccesful campaign against the Parthians. Subsequently John Hyrcanus I conquered large areas in Transjordan and Samaria where he razed the Samaritan temple on Mt Gerizim. He also conquered Idumea and compelled the inhabitants to convert to Judaism. One of his sons, Aristobulus I (104–103 BC) completed the conquest of Galilee, and his second son Alexander Janneus (102–76 BC) annexed nearly all the Hellenized cities of the coastal region and northern Transjordan.

Judaism under Hellenism and Roman rule

Although all Jews professed allegiance to the Torah, the Jewish community in Judaea at this time was divided into various sects. According to the first-century-AD Jewish historian, Josephus, the three most important groups were the Sadducees, the Pharisees and the Essenes. The Sadducees consisted of a small group of influential individuals including the hereditary priests who controlled Temple worship. Possibly their name derives from King David's priest Zadok. For these Jews there was no reason to interpret and expand the written law, and they rejected any speculation about a future life. The second group consisted of the Pharisees – their name seems to derive from a Hebrew term *parush* (meaning 'separated'). Some scholars suggest that this name was applied to them because they separated themselves from the masses for the sake of holiness; others surmise that it was given by opponents who charged that they had separated themselves from the Sadducean interpretation of Scripture. Their rise appears to date from the Hasideans who broke from the Hasmonean regime in the second century because of its irreligious character. Initially they were not political activists; instead they advocated submission to God's will. Unlike the Sadducees, the Pharisees believed in the resurrection of the body and the world to come. Moreover, they were anxious to make Biblical law applicable to contemporary circumstances by offering oral expositions of the text. This procedure, they believed, had been commanded by God to Moses on Mt Sinai when he received the written commandments. For example, the fourth commandment forbade work on the Sabbath; the Pharisees devised thirty-nine categories of labour so that everyone was clear what it was that had to be avoided. In contrast to the Sadducees who were involved in the Temple cult, the Pharisees centred their activities on the synagogue. It was from this sector of society that the scribes emerged as an important force in Jewish life. Although there appear to have been scribes from the time of Jeremiah (such as the prophet's secretary, Baruch), they came to form a recognizable class who copied the law and decided how its prescriptions could be put into effect. Both the Pharisees and the Sadducees were involved in the Great Sanhedrin, the central religious and legislative body of the Judaean community.

The third principal sect were the Essenes who may also have been an offshoot of the Hasideans. Their name possibly derives from the Aramaic word '*hasa*' (pious). According to the Essenes, the Hellenizers and worldly Sadducees were violators of God's law. The most important characteristic which differentiates this group from Pharisees and Sadducees concerned their lifestyle: rejecting the corruption of town life, they congregated in semi-monastic communities. Most scholars believe it was this sect who produced the Dead Sea Scrolls. This literature was the work of a devoted community based near the Dead Sea who wrote about an ideal Teacher of Righteousness as their leader. The Essenes believed that they alone were members of the new Covenant prophesied by Jeremiah. In their community rule (the Manual of Discipline) and war rule, a cataclysmic end of the world is described, to be preceded by a struggle between good and evil in which Israel would emerge victorious.

During the reign of Alexander Jannaeus a number of Pharisees revolted against his Hellenizing influence. It appears that they seized Jerusalem and the royal mint, issuing coins of their own in the name of the Council of Elders. But this rebellion failed, resulting in the loss of many lives. After the death of Alexander Jannaeus, his widow Salome Alexandra (76–67 BC) succeeded him and reversed his religious policies, treating the Pharisees with favour. On her death, her two sons John Hyrcanus II and Aristobulus II struggled for power. A chieftain from Idumea Antipater attempted to assist John Hyrcanus II's cause by inviting his allies the Nabateans to march on Jerusalem. But it was left to the Roman leader Pompey, who had recently annexed Syria, to decide the matter of the Hasmonean succession. Pompey marched into Jerusalem, killed many of its inhabitants, and stepped inside the Holy of Holies in the Temple – an act of blasphemy in the eyes of the Jewish populace. Judaea became a client state of Rome, and John Hyrcanus II was appointed high priest and ethnarch of Judaea and Galilee (territory in the north). In addition he was given the right to intervene in matters relating to the Jewish communities abroad (the Jewish diaspora). After five years, however, he was deprived of his position as ethnarch, and the country was divided into five districts, each under a court of local dignitaries drawn largely from the Sadducees. Antipater was put in charge of Idumea but retained special powers in Jerusalem such as tax-collecting.

After Pompey's death in 48 BC, John Hyrcanus II and Antipater gave assistance to Julius Caesar in his battle against Egyptian forces. As a reward Caesar enlarged John Hyrcanus II's former state and recognized Antipater as chief minister. Caesar also introduced a number of measures to safeguard the security of Jewish communities outside Judaea: they were allowed liberty of religious observance, freedom to send gifts to the Jerusalem Temple, exemption from military duty and the right to their own jurisdiction. Antipater's son Phasael was made governor of Jerusalem, and his other son Herod became governor of Galilee. When Herod successfully crushed a Galilean revolt, he was censured by the Great Sanhedrin for his brutal behaviour towards those he conquered and was forced to leave Judaea. Nevertheless the new governor of Syria entrusted him with an important military command, as did Cassius when Caesar was assassinated. After Mark Antony and Octavian had avenged Caesar's death, they confirmed the appointments of Phasael and Herod as tetrarchs (subordinate rulers) of Judaea despite Jewish resistance. Yet it was not long before the Parthians invaded Roman Asia Minor, Syria and Judaea. John Hyrcanus II was dethroned in favour of his nephew Antigonus; Phasael was killed; and Herod was forced to escape.

The kingship of Herod

After the Parthian victory, Herod set off for Rome to meet Mark Antony who had secured the eastern provinces from Octavian in the division of the empire. Through Mark Antony's influence the Roman government made a treaty with Herod establishing him as king of Judaea. By this means the Romans hoped to depose Antigonus, the nominee of the Parthians. With a Roman army Herod conquered Judaea; after a five-month seige Jerusalem fell in 37 BC. Herod unified the country by incorporating Samaria, and replaced the council of elders by an advisory body similar to the privy councils of Hellenistic monarchs. Remembering that the Great Sanhedrin had previously censured him and had also supported the cause of Antigonus against his own, Herod executed forty-five of its seventy-one members, including many Sadducees who supported the Hasmonean dynasty. He did, however, spare the two leaders of the Great Sanhedrin – the Pharisees Hillel and Shammai – who continued to exert a profound influence through their schools on the direction of Pharisaic thought.

Since Herod was from an Iduamite family (descendants of the Edomites who were converted to Judaism by the Hasmoneans), he was ineligible for the high priesthood and bestowed this office upon

Hananel, a Babylonian Jew who claimed descent from the Zadokite house. According to Herod, Hananel's claims were better than had ever been offered by any Hasmonean ruler. Herod however had married a Hasmonean princess, Mariamne, and her mother Alexandra (daughter of John Hyrcanus II) complained to the Egyptian Queen Cleopatra about this nomination. As a result Herod was forced to appoint Alexandra's younger son Aristobulus instead; but he soon died, and Hananel was reinstated.

When Antony and Cleopatra were defeated by Octavian's admiral Marcus Agrippa at the battle of Actium in 31 BC, Herod pledged his loyalty to Octavian (later known as Augustus). His declaration was accepted and he received back most of the territory Pompey had taken from Judaea in 63 BC as well as two Greek cities across the Jordan – Hippos and Gadara. Alexandra and her daughter, Herod's wife Mariamne, were put to death along with Costobarus (governor of Idumaea) for plotting against Herod. For the next twenty-seven years Herod acted as Augustus's agent: he initiated games in honour of the victory at Actium, constructed a Greek theatre and amphitheatre in Jerusalem, transformed Samaria into a Graeco-Samaritan city and built the port Caesarea. In addition he created citadels and palaces at such strategic sites as Jericho, Herodium near Jerusalem and Masada on the Dead Sea. The great achievement of his reign was the rebuilding of the Jerusalem Temple on a magnificent scale. All that remains of this Temple are the foundations of the western wall which led in to the court of the gentiles. This was open to everyone and served as a meeting place, a market centre and a platform for preachers. Inside the court of the gentiles was another gateway through which only Jews could enter. This opened into the court of women, and beyond this was the court of priests where the Sadducees conducted the sacrifices witnessed by Jewish men over the age of thirteen. The most sacred place in the Temple was the Holy of Holies which was only entered by the High Priest on the Day of Atonement (Yom Kippur).

In the years that followed, Herod managed to obtain two large regions of southern Syria from Augustus. He also intervened with the Romans to stop Greek cities from withholding the privileges to which Jews in the diaspora were entitled. Yet despite such successes, Herod evoked Augustus's displeasure by his executions of those he suspected of intrigue as well as by his attack on his foes, the Nabataeans. To pacify the emperor, Herod ordered (in 7 or 6 BC) that all Jews in Judaea must swear an oath of loyalty to the Roman ruler and to himself. Such a practice was common in Roman client-monarchies, but a number of Pharisees feared it might involve worship of the emperor's statues and refused to comply. Increasingly these objectors began to indulge in messianic speculation. Previously such eschatological expectation had not been favoured in Pharisaic circles, but these Pharisees were persuaded that the period of messianic redemption was at hand. A few even succeeded in persuading Bagoas (a royal court official) that he was to be the father of the messianic king. Herod regarded such talk as high treason, and he executed Bagoas and others in 5 BC. In the following year a number of Pharisaic scholars instigated demonstrations against the erection of an eagle, a forbidden image, over the main gate of the Temple. The rioters pulled it down, and were put to death for this insurrection. After these final years of bloodthirsty upheavals, Herod himself died in 4 BC.

5
Rebellion and Dispersion

The period following Herod's death was a time of intense anti-Roman feeling among the Jewish population in Judaea as well as in the diaspora. Eventually such hostility led to war only to be followed by defeat and the destruction, once again, of the Jerusalem Temple. In AD 70, thousands of Jews were deported. Such devastation, however, did not quell the Jewish hope of ridding the Holy Land of its oppressors. In the second century a messianic rebellion led by Simon Bar Kosiba was crushed by Roman forces, who killed multitudes of Jews and decimated Judaea. Yet despite this defeat, the Pharisees carried on the Jewish tradition through teaching and study. Initially, the rabbinic academy at Javneh (Jamnia) near Jerusalem was the focus of Jewish learning. In time this centre of rabbinic scholarship was replaced by the great Babylonian academies of Sura, Nehardea and Pumpeditha. In these schools sages and scholars expounded the Mishnah, and there in the fifth century AD they codified the Babylonian Talmud which was to become the central religious text of Jewish life for all time. It was at Javneh that the rabbis continued to interpret the law and there in the second century Judah Ha-Nasi compiled their discussions in the Mishnah.

Rebellion against Rome

After Herod's death, Augustus divided Judaea between three of Herod's sons: Archelaus as ethnarch (4 BC to AD 6) was to rule the central region of Judaea including Samaria; Herod Antipas as tetrarch (4 BC to AD 39) was given Galilee and Peraea; Philip also as tetrarch (4 BC to AD 34) was to reign over the newly acquired lands in southern Syria. Archelaus' rule lasted only ten years; he was deposed and exiled by Augustus after he received complaints from Jews and Samaritans about his high-handedness. Judaea thereby became a small-scale Roman province administered by governors with the title of prefect (later called procurator). When the Romans instituted a census of the population, they provoked Jewish resentment since census-taking was contrary to Jewish law. Under the leadership of Judas the Galilean, a resistance movement (the Zealots) became active. At the same time there appeared a number of messianic aspirants who were regarded with suspicion by the authorities. The Sadducees however collaborated with the Romans who continued to appoint high priests from their ranks. Under the prefects, the Sanhedrin was resuscitated (in place of Herod's advisory body) and played an important role in the administration of the country.

Following his accession in AD 14, the emperor Tiberius relied more and more on the advice of Sejanus (the commander of his bodyguard). Sejanus appears to have been ill-disposed to the Jewish population since two Jews – Hasinai and Hanilai – had set up an autonomous community at Nehardea in Parthian Babylonia; Sejanus feared that such aspirations might spread to Judaea. The fourth prefect of Judaea, Pontius Pilate (AD 25–36) experienced a number of difficulties with the Jewish community. They regarded his military standards bearing medallions of the emperor as idolatrous. Following demonstrations in Jerusalem, protesters encamped in front of Pilate's official residence at Caesarea Maritima and then in the stadium. Pilate also caused considerable consternation when he used a Jewish religious fund to pay for an aquaduct, and again when he set up gilded shields inscribed with both his and the emperor's names in the former palace of Herod.

Under Tiberius' nephew and successor Caligula (AD 37–41), the Jews of Alexandria became embroiled in a conflict with the Roman authorities. These Jews had put forward a claim for full citizenship rights, thereby evoking a violent reaction from the gentile Greek community. Mobs broke into synagogues and set up statues of the emperor. The Roman governor of Egypt, Aulus Avillius Flaccus, ordered thirty-eight members of the Jewish council to be flogged in the theatre while Jewish women were forced to eat pork. To calm the situation Agrippa I (the grandson of Herod who had been appointed king after the death of Philip and the disgrace of Herod Antipas) secured the recall of Avillius Flaccus.

In AD 40 both the Greek and Jewish communities sent delegations to Rome to plead their cases before Caligula. According to an account written by the leader of the Jewish group, the neo-Platonic philosopher Philo from Alexandria, Caligula regarded the Jews' failure to recognize his divinity as lunacy. Meanwhile, at Jamnia on the coast of Judaea, the Greek community erected an altar in honour of Caligula. The Jewish community of Jamnia regarded this act as a deliberate provocation, and destroyed it. As a consequence, the emperor and his advisers decided to revive the policy of Antiochus IV Epiphanes: the Temple and all synagogues were to be transformed into shrines of the imperial cult. Orders were given to the governor of Syria, Publius Petronius, to construct a large statue of Caligula in the guise of Jupiter to be set up in Jerusalem. The governor decided he would need two legions to perform this task, but Agrippa I persuaded him not to carry out his plans on the condition that the Jews would cease trying to stop gentiles from engaging in imperial worship. A short time later Caligula was murdered, and the Jews celebrated this day as a joyful feast.

Claudius (AD 41–54) who succeeded Caligula immediately had to deal with renewed conflict between Jews and Greeks in Alexandria. In his surviving letter to both groups, he urged them to be tolerant of one another; specifically he urged the Jews not to behave with contempt towards the gods of other peoples. In Judaea itself Claudius abolished direct Roman rule and allowed the country the status of a self-governing client kingdom. Agrippa I was permitted to add the Roman province of Judaea to the territories he had already been given where he reigned as king.

But Agrippa I's death in AD 44 ended this period of relative tranquillity as Judaea reverted to the status of a Roman province. Under the governors that followed various problems became apparent: tensions developed between the rich and the poor; rebels, self-styled prophets and holy men roamed the country; and insurrections occurred in many localities. The procurator Tiberius Julius Alexander (AD 46–8) had to deal with an extensive famine; Ventidius Cumanus (AD 48–52) witnessed riots, a massacre at the Temple and conflict between Samaritans and Galileans; and Antonius Felix (AD 52–60) was confronted by bands of freedom fighters and miracle workers who preached a message of nationalism and messianic expectation.

The rise of Christianity

From the gospels of the New Testament as well as information from Jewish, Greek and Roman sources, it appears that a Jewish sect of

Christians emerged during the years of unrest following Herod's death in 4 BC. In consonance with messianic expectations of this period, these believers expected their messiah to bring about the fulfilment of human history. According to the Christian scriptures, Jesus of Nazareth spent most of his life in Galilee where he acted as a healer, exorcist and itinerant preacher who proclaimed the imminent arrival of the Kingdom of God. After a brief association with John the Baptist, he attracted disciples from among the most marginalized sectors of society but soon aroused suspicion and hostility and was put to death during the reign of Pontius Pilate in about AD 30. Afterwards his followers believed he had risen from the dead, appeared to them, and promised to return to usher in the period of messianic rule.

There has been considerable scholarly debate about Jesus's relationships with such groups as Sadducees, Pharisees, Essenes, scribes, priests and Roman officials. It is unclear, for example, if Jesus intended to violate Jewish law, whether the titles he used (such as 'Son of God' and 'Son of Man') simply reflect his own messianic consciousness or point to an acknowledgement of his divine nature. Further, scholars are undecided about who was responsible for his trial and crucifixion. Nevertheless, there is no doubt that Jesus inspired a considerable number of Jewish followers. According to the Acts of the Apostles, Jews who accepted Jesus as their Saviour in the 30s and 40s continued to pray at the Temple, observed Jewish laws, and considered themselves members of the Jewish people.

In the spreading of the gospel, Paul – a diaspora Jew from Tarsus in Asia Minor – played a pivotal role. His letters to scattered Christian communities provide first-hand evidence of the growth of this new religion. In his epistles to the Galatians, Paul describes himself as a Pharisee who had persecuted Christians until he had a revelation from God in which he was transformed into an apostle:

> For you have heard of my former life in Judaism, how I persecuted the church of God violently and tried to destroy it; and I advanced in Judaism beyond many of my own age among my people, so extremely zealous was I for the traditions of my fathers. But when he who had set me apart before I was born, and had called me through his grace, was pleased to reveal his Son to me, in order that I might preach him among the gentiles
>
> (Galatians 1:13–16).

Subsequently Paul travelled around Asia Minor and Greece as a Christian missionary.

For some time scholars have debated Paul's relationship with the Jewish faith, but it is likely that Paul's thought is largely a fusion of elements of Pharisaic and Hellenistic Judaism. According to Paul, the new era was at hand, but he distinguished between the period before the coming of Christ and the time afterwards in terms of two states of being. The first, fleshly state is the realm of death, bondage and the rule of sin; the second, the spiritual state, is a condition of eternal life, freedom and the right relationship to God. The crucifixion and resurrection represent the inbreaking of the eschaton, and even though the day of final judgement has not yet arrived, those who accept Christ are redeemed from the burden of evil, death and sin. Jesus was sent to conquer death, and as God's son, he humbled himself so that all could come to the Father. Central to this theology is the distinction between 'works' and 'faith'. Faith, Paul believed, is a gift – a sign of divine grace. Salvation cannot be earned by observing the law but 'he who through faith is righteous shall live' (Galatians 3:11).

In his epistles, Paul differentiates the new life in Christ from licentiousness as well as from the belief that all things are permitted to those who believe. On the basis of this belief, Paul stresses the importance of love – just as God's act in Christ was motivated by love, so love is the supreme spiritual gift. A second theme in Paul's letters is his rejection of the demands of the Mosaic law: it is unnecessary, he argued, for Christians to be circumcised and to follow Jewish food regulations. Underlying these attitudes was Paul's conception of an apocalyptic history of salvation. Through Adam's transgression, sin and death entered the world. Abraham's trust in God illustrates that faith is more important than law. Mosaic legislation was binding only for a limited period – it cannot by itself bestow justification. The more one attempts to observe legal prescriptions, the greater one is conscious of sin. Thus God made Christ available to overcome man's evil propensity. In this context Paul interprets Abraham's two sons – Ishmael and Isaac – allegorically: Ishmael symbolizes the old Covenant; Isaac represents the new dispensation. Now that Christ has come, it is not simply the Jews who are Israel; instead all those whom God has called through Christ are the true Israel.

The next stage in the development of Christianity took place in the decades following Paul's death. As time passed traditions about Jesus circulated and eventually formed the basis of the synoptic gospels and Acts which were written down in approximately the last quarter of the first century AD. Each gospel was composed with different religious intentions and concerns. Mark appears to be the earliest of the gospels and portrays Jesus as a divinely appointed figure whose task was to bring about God's kingdom on earth. In the Gospel of Matthew Jesus is presented as a lawgiver instructing the people in the principles of moral living. The Gospel of Luke and the Acts of the Apostles depict Jesus as the fulfilment of the Old Testament and portray the subsequent transference of the Church to the gentiles of the Graeco-Roman world. In the Gospel of John (in all likelihood later than the synoptic gospels) Jesus is described as the divine Logos who is 'the way, the truth, and the life'. Not surprisingly the message of the New Testament was firmly rejected by mainstream Judaism, and the Jewish community responded to the challenge of Christianity by anathematizing its followers.

Roman Jewish war and aftermath

Two decades of procurators after the death of Agrippa I marked a period of constant friction between Roman rulers and the Jewish population. Under the procurator Florus (AD 64–66) fighting took place between Greeks and Jews in Caesarea Maritima. The procurator adopted an anti-Jewish stance and allowed his troops to riot in Jerusalem and execute a number of eminent Jews. After Florus returned to Caesarea, pro-Roman Jews as well as the small Roman legion in Judaea were killed by Jewish rebels and sacrifices on behalf of the Roman people and the emperor were stopped. To quell this revolt, the governor of Syria and an army marched to Jerusalem. He began a siege of the Temple, but was met with resistance and retreated to the sea coast. This success drove out the Roman military presence in Judaea and in its place a provisional government was established. To pacify the country the general Vespasian, acting under the emperor Nero's orders, assembled an army in the north in AD 67. Sepphoris in Galilee refused to join in the revolt, and the Jewish rebels were unable to stand against the Roman legions. Though the fortress of Jotapata held out for forty-seven days, it eventually fell and the Romans slaughtered most of the population. During the winter of AD 67–8 the Zealots overthrew the moderate government in Jerusalem. Those suspected of aiding the Romans were arrested or killed, and anti-Roman groups occupied the city. But in March 67, Vespasian marched against the Jewish population; he subjugated Transjordan, western Judaea, Idumea, Sameria and Jericho. The only parts of the country remaining in Jewish hands were Jerusalem and several

Herodian fortresses in other parts of the country. When Nero committed suicide in June 68 the Roman military effort ceased.

During the next year Roman armies in different parts of the empire elevated three generals to the throne; in July 69 the eastern provinces proclaimed Vespasian. Before long Vespasian put his son Titus in charge of the Judaean campaign. Just before Passover in April 70 Titus encamped outside the walls of Jerusalem. In late May the Romans occupied the newer part of Jerusalem, north of the Temple; by the end of July they took the citadel adjacent to the Temple; on 6 August the sacrifices were suspended. A week later the porticos surrounding the Temple courtyards were burned, and on 28 August the Temple went up in flames during the fighting. After another month the Romans captured the upper city west of the Temple, and thus the entire city was taken, although with considerable effort. All resistance ceased, and Titus ordered that Jerusalem be devastated except for the towers of Herod's palace. For the rest of the year Titus held celebrations in various cities of the Near East during which Jewish prisoners were thrown to wild animals or were forced to fight with gladiators. In 71 Titus and Vespasian held a triumphal procession in which ritual objects and rebel leaders were exhibited; the surviving Arch of Titus in Rome depicts the menorah and other objects that were taken from the Temple. Over the next few years the Romans captured the remaining fortresses including Masada which fell in April 74 when its defenders committed suicide rather than surrender to the Romans. The historian Josephus describes the end of the rebels in vivid detail, and the tale has been an inspiration to Jews struggling against oppression ever since. Archaelogists have excavated the site and have learned a great deal both about King Herod's original fortress and the day-to-day existence of the revolutionaries.

The Roman conquest of Judaea brought about enormous destruction and the enslavement of thousands of Jews. Nevertheless, reconstruction began immediately and the Jews continued as the largest population in the country. Though the Romans heavily taxed the Jewish community, they recognized Judaism as a lawful religion, and exempted Jews from emperor worship and other religious duties. During this period it appears that the Sadducees and Essenes disappeared; in their place the Pharisees became the dominant religious group led by Rabban Johanan ben Zaccai, who escaped from Jerusalem during the siege. In the town of Jamnia near the Judaean sea coast he assembled a group of distinguished Pharisaic scholars (known as Tannaim). There these sages engaged in the development of the legal tradition. Under Johanan ben Zaccai and later in the century under Rabban Gamaliel II, the rabbinic assembly (Sanhedrin) summarized the teachings of the earlier schools of Hillel and Shammai. In addition they determined the canon of Scripture, organized the daily prayers, and transferred to the synagogue some of the observances of the Temple such as the rituals associated with the pilgrim festivals, the Passover seder and the blowing of the ram's horn at the New Year. They also instituted a procedure of rabbinical ordination (*semikhah*).

Though this body was presided over by a head (nasi), the rabbis collectively reached decisions which were binding on the populace. Its members were drawn from all sectors of society and they attracted numerous students to hear their oral teachings. The first generation of sages (including such figures as R. Eliezer ben Hyrcanus, R. Elazar ben Azaria and R. Joshua ben Haninah) was followed by a second generation of eminent scholars such as R. ben Taradion, R. Tarphon and R. Ishmael ben Elisha. The most prominent scholar of the first decades of the second century was R. Akiva ben Joseph (AD 50–135) who was an exegete, mystic and legal systematizer as well as a pioneer of a method of scriptural interpretation based on the view that no word in Scripture is redundant.

Jews in the Roman Empire

Despite the devastating victory of the Romans, Jewish revolts continued into the second century. When the emperor Trajan (AD 98–117) invaded the east up to the Persian coast, uprisings among Babylonian Jews took place. Moreover, riots occurred in many parts of the Roman diaspora; according to the fourth-century writer Eusebius, Jews were massacred in these rebellions:

> In Alexandria and the rest of the east, and in Cyrene as well . . . [the Jews] rushed into a faction fight against their Greek fellow citizens . . . against them the emperor sent Marcius Turbo with land and sea forces, including a contingency of cavalry. He pursued the war against them relentlessly in a long series of battles, destroying many thousands of Jews.

Between 114 and 117 Jewish centres in Alexandria, Cyrenaica, Egypt and Cyprus were decimated. After Trajan's death his successor Hadrian (117–138) abandoned the effort to extend the empire eastwards, leaving the Jewish diaspora in Babylonia free from Roman domination.

In Judaea a messianic revolt was led in AD 132 by Simon bar Kosiba (also called Bar Kochba) which appears to have been aided by Rabbi Akiva and other scholars from Jamnia and touched off by Hadrian's programme of Hellenization. This Jewish revolt was inspired by the conviction that God would empower the Jews to regain control of their country and rebuild the Temple. Yet despite valiant efforts on the part of the rebels, the Romans crushed this uprising. In addition to archaeological evidence – including coins issued by Bar Kochba's government as well as letters sent to him by deputies – the third-century historian Dio Cassius provides information about this period. According to his account, hundreds of thousands of Jews were killed and Judaea was almost completely devastated. In AD 135 the rebellion came to an end with the fall of Bethar, south-west of Jerusalem. According to tradition this event occurred on the 9th of Av (in the summer), the same day as the destruction of the first and second Temples, later commemorated by Tishah B'Av (Fast of Av). During the course of the campaign Bar Kochba was killed in battle, and Rabbi Akiva was eventually flayed alive.

Following the Bar Kochba war, Hadrian outlawed Judaism throughout the land, but after his death in 138 prohibitions against the religion were rescinded. As far as the Jews were concerned, their defeat under Bar Kochba initiated a conciliatory policy towards the Roman authorities resulting in the flourishing of rabbinic learning. The centre of Jewish life was transferred to Galilee, and under the disciples of Rabbi Akiva, the Sanhedrin reassembled at Usha. The outstanding scholars of this period included Rabban Simeon ben Gamaliel II (who served as nasi), R. Elazar ben Shammua, R. Jose ben Halafta, R. Judah bar Illai, R. Simeon bar Yohai and R. Meir. Under these sages, the Sanhedrin emerged as the decisive force in Jewish life; through its deliberations the legal decisions of previous generations were systematized and disseminated.

By the third century economic conditions in Galilee improved and the Jewish population attained a harmonious relationship with the Roman administration. The Severan dynasty of Roman emperors entrusted the nasi with the authority to appoint judges for Jewish courts, collect taxes and send messengers to diaspora communities. The most important nasi of this epoch was Judah ha-Nasi (the son of Simeon ben Gamaliel II), whose main achievement was the redaction of the Mishnah. This volume consisted of the discussions and rulings of scholars whose teachings had been transmitted orally. According to the rabbis, the law recorded in the Mishnah was given orally to

Moses along with the written law: 'Moses received the Torah from Sinai, and handed it down to Joshua, and Joshua to the Elders, and Elders to the Prophets and Prophets to the men of the Great Assembly' (Avot 1:1). This view implies that there was an infallible chain of transmission from Moses to the leaders of the nation and eventually to the Pharisees.

The Mishnah itself is almost entirely halachic in content, consisting of six sections (or orders) comprising a series of chapters (known as tractates) on specific subjects. The first order (Seeds) begins with a discussion of benedictions and required prayers and continues with the other tractates dealing with various matters (such as the tithes of the harvest to be given to priests, Levites and the poor). The second order (Set Feasts) contains twelve tractates dealing with the Sabbath, Passover, the Day of Atonement and other festivals as well as shekel dues and the proclamation of the New Year. In the third section (Women) seven tractates consider matters affecting women (such as betrothal, marriage contracts and divorce). The fourth section (Damages) contains ten tractates concerning civil law: property rights, legal procedures, compensation for damage, ownership of lost objects, treatment of employees, sale and purchase of land, Jewish courts, punishments, criminal proceedings, etc. In addition a tractate of rabbinic moral maxims (sayings of the fathers) is included in this order. In the fifth section (Holy Things) there are eleven tractates on sacrificial offerings and other temple matters. The final section (Purifications) treats in twelve tractates the various types of ritual uncleanliness and methods of purification. According to some scholars this comprehensive collection of Jewish law based on Scriptural precedent was indirectly influenced by a similar codification of Roman law undertaken by Latin jurists in the reign of Hadrian.

The Sanhedrin which had been so fundamental in the compilation of this work met in several cities in Galilee, but later settled in the Roman district of Tiberius. The nasi remained the head of the Sanhedrin but other scholars established their own schools in other parts of the country where they applied the Mishnah to everyday life together with old rabbinic teachings (beraitot) which had not been incorporated in the Mishnah.

By the 230s, the Roman empire was encountering numerous difficulties including inflation, population decline and a lack of technological development to support the army. In the next few decades rival generals struggled against one another for power and the government became increasingly inefficient. During this time of upheaval, the Jewish community underwent a parallel decline as a result of famine, epidemics and plunder.

At the end of the third century the emperor Diocletian (AD 284–305) inaugurated reforms that strengthened the empire. Under his reign the republican veneer of Roman rule was replaced by an absolutist structure. An elaborate system of prices, offices and occupations was introduced to halt economic decline. In addition Diocletian introduced measures to repress the spread of Christianity which had become a serious challenge to the official religion of the empire. Diocletian's successor Constantine the Great (AD 306–37) reversed his predecessor's hostile stance and extended official toleration to Christians in 313. By this stage Christianity had succeeded in gaining a substantial number of adherents among the urban population; eventually Constantine became more involved in Church affairs, and just before his death he himself was baptized. The Christianization of the empire continued throughout the century and by the early 400s, Christianity was fully established as the state religion. This merger of the Roman government and the Church did not affect the legal rights of the Jews, but it did provide an important channel for anti-Jewish hostility.

By the first half of the fourth century Jewish scholars in Israel had collected together the teachings of generations of rabbis in the academies of Tiberius, Caesarea and Sepphoris. These extended discussions of the Mishnah became the Palestinian Talmud. The text of this multi-volume work covered four sections of the Mishnah (Seeds, Set Feasts, Women and Damages) but here and there various tractates were missing. No doubt the discussions in these academies included matters in these missing tractates, but it is not known how far the recording, editing and arrangement of these sections had progressed before they were lost. The views of these Palestinian teachers (known as Amoraim) had an important influence on scholars in Babylonia, though this work never attained the same prominence as that of the Babylonian Talmud.

Although Jewish scholarship prospered during this time, the Jews were facing new legal handicaps. When Christianity became the dominant religion of the Roman Empire, Judaism was relegated to a position of legal inferiority. Imperial laws of the middle of the fourth century prohibited conversion to Judaism as well as intermarriage between Jews and Christians. At the beginning of the fifth century Jews were formally barred from government positions, and this attitude continued throughout the rest of the century and was reinforced by the emperor Justinian's (AD 525–65) decrees. The official stance of the Church was to attempt to bring Jews to the true faith. Judaism was allowed to continue because the existence of the Jewish people was seen as a testimony to the truth of Scripture. In the eyes of the Church, the Jews would eventually recognize Jesus's messiahship and sovereignty.

Jews in Babylonia

From the sixth century BC when Nebuchadnezzar deported Jews from their native land, Babylonia had become an important centre of Jewish life. By the second century AD the Persian king who had become overlord of Mesopotamia recognized an exilarch (in Aramaic *resh galuta* meaning 'head of the exiles') as leader of the Jewish community in Babylonia. This figure (who claimed descent from kings of Judah taken in captivity by Nebuchadnezzar) collected taxes, appointed judges, supervised the judiciary and represented the Jewish population in the Persian royal court. By the middle of this century rabbinic Judaism spread eastwards and some Palestinian scholars temporarily settled in Babylonia during the Bar Kochba revolt and Hadrian's persecutions. Subsequently a number of Babylonian Jews went to the centres of learning in Galilee to study under the leading sages in the Holy Land; the codification of the Mishnah further intensified such interchange. In this context the exilarch encouraged the emergence of a Babylonian class of scholars from whom he appointed administrators and judges. While post-Mishnaic scholars in Israel engaged in learned debate about the application of Jewish law, the same development was taking place in Babylonia. The great third-century teacher Rav (Abba bar Aivu, a student of Judah ha-Nasi) founded an academy at Sura in central Mesopotamia; his contemporary Samuel was simultaneously head of another Babylonian academy at Nehardea. After Nehardea was destroyed in an invasion in AD 259, the school at Pumbeditha also became a dominant Babylonian academy of Jewish learning. Some years previously (in AD 226) the Arsacid dynasty in Parthia was overthrown by the Sassanians who developed a more centralized administration in the Persian empire and authorized greater government supervision. In addition they promised a revised form of Zoroastrianism as the established religion of the empire with a hierarchical priestly structure. This priestly class attempted to pressurize Jews and others to adopt their religion during the reign of Ardashir (AD 226–40), the first Sassanian monarch. After his death, his successor Shapur I (AD

240–71) permitted religious freedom for non-Zoroastrians and officially recognized the Jewish exilarchate in Babylonia. Jewish leaders were compelled to accept the authority of Persian state law. Such an arrangement was enshrined in the Jewish sage Samuel's formula: *Dina de-malkhuta dina* ('The law of the government is the law'). In Israel there had never been an equivalent recognition of Roman law, but Samuel's formula provided a basis for allowing Jewish law to be superseded by non-Jewish civil law as long as it did not touch on Jewish religious rituals and ceremonies.

The Babylonian Jews under the Sassanian dynasty encountered a number of new religious sects (such as the Manichaeans), but they remained faithful to the religion of their fathers. Their religious leaders were revered for their mastery of the tradition, and the academies they founded became major centres of Jewish learning. The Babylonian sages carried on and developed the Galilean tradition of disputation, and the fourth century produced two of the most distinguished scholars of the Amoratic period: Abbaye (AD 278–338) and Rava (AD 229–352), who both taught at Pumbeditha. With the decline of Jewish institutions in Israel, Babylonia became the most important centre of Jewish scholarship.

When Christianity became the official religion of the Roman Empire, Christians rather than Jews were subject to persecution by the Sassanian dynasty, since Rome was perceived as its main military enemy. In the fourth and fifth centuries clergy, monks and lay Christians were attacked and martyred. Only during a short period in the fifth century (445–75) did repression flare up against the Jewish population: the exilarchate was suspended, synagogues and academies were closed and the Torah was banned. But by the sixth century a new period of prosperity had begun, and Babylonian scholars completed the redaction of the Talmud – an editorial task begun by Rav Ashi (335–427) at Sura.

This massive work parallels the Palestinian Talmud and is largely a summary of the Amoraic discussions that took place in the Babylonian academies. Both Talmuds are essentially elaborations of the Mishnah though neither commentary contains material on every Mishnah passage. The Palestinian Talmud treats thirty-nine Mishnaic tractates whereas the Babylonian deals with slightly fewer (thirty-seven), but the Babylonian Talmud is 2,500,000 words, nearly four times the size of the Palestinian Talmud (approximately 750,000 words). The text itself consists largely of summaries of rabbinic discussion: a phrase of Mishnah is interpreted, discrepancies are resolved and redundancies are explained. In this compilation conflicting opinions of the earlier Tannaim are contrasted, unusual words are explained and anonymous opinions are identified. Frequently individual teachers cite specific cases to support their views and hypothetical eventualities are examined to reach a solution on the discussion. Debates between outstanding scholars in one generation are often cited, as are differences of opinion between contemporary members of an academy or a teacher and his students. The range of Talmudic exploration is much broader than that of the Mishnah itself and includes a wide range of rabbinic teachings about such subjects as theology, philosophy and ethics; this aggadic (non-legal) material is usually presented as digressions and comprises about one-third of the Babylonian Talmud (only one-sixth of the Palestinian Talmud).

6
Rabbinic Judaism

During the Tannaitic period (between the first century BC and the second century AD) and Amoraic period (between the second and sixth centuries AD), scholars – referred to as Tannaim and Amoraim respectively – actively engaged in the interpretation of Scripture. According to Pharisaic tradition both the written Torah and its interpretation (oral Torah) were given by God to Moses on Mt Sinai. This belief implies that God is the direct source of all laws recorded in the Pentateuch and is also indirectly responsible for the authoritative legal judgements of the rabbis, and served as the justification for the rabbinic exposition of Scriptural ordinances. Alongside this exegesis of the Jewish law (*halachah*), scholars also produced interpretations of Scripture in which new meanings of the text were expounded (*aggadah*) in rabbinic commentaries (*midrashim*) and in the Talmud. Within the aggadic texts is found a wealth of theological speculation about such topics as the nature of God, divine justice, the coming of the Messiah and the hereafter. In addition, ethical considerations were of considerable importance in the discussions of these teachers of the faith. Also in these sources and in short treatises the rabbis recounted their mystical reflections about God and his creation. Early rabbinic Judaism thus covered a wide variety of areas all embraced by the holy word revealed on Mt Sinai, and this literature served as the foundation of later Judaism as it developed through the centuries.

Rabbinic Scriptural interpretation

The exegesis found in rabbinic literature of the Tannaitic and Amoraic periods is largely of two types: direct and explicit exegesis where the Biblical text is commented upon or accompanied by a remark, and indirect exegesis where a Scriptural text is cited to support an assertion. As an example of the first type, it was common practice among the rabbis to clear up a possible confusion about the meaning of a Biblical verse. In a *midrash* on Psalms, for example, R. Simlai (third century AD) explained that the fact that Psalm 50 begins with the words 'The Mighty One, God the Lord speaks' does not signify that God has a trinitarian nature. Rather 'all three appellations are only one name, even as one man can be called workman, builder, architect. The psalmist mentions these three names to teach you that God created the world with three names, corresponding with the three good attributes by which the world was created.'

The rabbis frequently reinforced their exhortations by a Biblical sentence which expressed their sentiments. Such a homiletical use of Scripture was illustrated in the first century BC by Simeon ben Shetach, who declared in a *midrash* on Deuteronomy:

> When you are judging, and there come before you two men, of whom one is rich and the other poor, do not say, 'The poor man's words are to be believed, but not the rich man's.' But just as you listen to the words of the poor man, so listen to the words of the rich man, for it is said, 'Ye shall not be partial in judgement.'
>
> (Deuteronomy 1:17)

It was also a usual custom in rabbinic circles to cite a text and then draw out its meaning. For example in a *midrash* on Deuteronomy the verse 'Thou shalt open wide your hand to your brother' (Deuteronomy 15:11) is explained as meaning that one should give according to particular needs: 'To him for whom bread is suitable, give bread; to him who needs dough, give dough; to him for whom money is required, give money; to him for whom it is fitting to put food in his mouth, put it in.'

It was also a principle in rabbinic hermeneutics that a word should be understood in its strictest sense. For example, in the Talmud R. Meir (second century AD) said: 'Where is the resurrection derived from the Torah? As it is said, "Then will Moses and then will the children of Israel sing this song unto the Lord." (Exodus 15:1); it is not said "sang", but "will sing".' Hence, he argued, the resurrection is deducible from the Torah. In the same passage R. Joshua b. Levi (third century AD) asked the same question, and quoting Psalm 84 pointed out that it is not stated, 'They will have praised Thee', but 'will be praising Thee'. Thus, he believed, the doctrine of resurrection is grounded in the Torah.

Occasionally the rabbis employed typological exegesis to explain the meaning of Scripture. An example found in the Talmud of this type of interpretation concerns Isaiah 43:9 ('Let all the nations gather together') where the kingdom of Edom is understood as prefiguring Rome. The kingdom of Edom, we read, shall enter first. Why do we know they are so important? Because it is written, 'And it shall devour the whole earth and trample it down and break it in pieces.' (Daniel 7:23). According to R. Johanan (third century AD) 'this refers to Rome, whose power is known to the whole world'. Related to this type of explanation, one also encounters allegorical exegesis in rabbinic sources. For example, in a *midrash* of Genesis, Bar Kappara (second century AD) interpreted Jacob's dream (Genesis 28:12) in an allegorical manner: ' "A ladder set up on the earth", that is the Temple: "the top of it reached to heaven", that is the pillar of smoke from the sacrifices; "the angels of God were ascending and descending on it", these are the priests who mount and descend the steps leading to the altar.'

Turning to the method of indirect exegesis, it was a frequent practice in rabbinic literature to draw deductions from Scriptural texts by means of a number of formal hermeneutical rules. Hillel the elder who flourished about a century before the destruction of the second temple, is reported to have been the first to lay down these principles. Hillel's seven rules were expanded in the second century AD by R. Ishmael ben Elisha into thirteen by sub-dividing some of them, omitting one, and adding a new one of his own. The first rule (the inference from minor and major) states that if a certain restriction applies to a matter of minor importance, we may infer that the same restriction is applicable to a matter of major importance. Conversely, if a certain allowance is applicable to a thing of major importance, we may infer that the same allowance pertains to that which is of comparatively minor importance. In the Mishnah, for example, we read that the Sabbath is in some respects regarded as being of more importance than a common holiday. If therefore a certain kind of work is permitted on the Sabbath, we may infer that such work is more permissible on a common holiday; conversely, if a certain work is forbidden on a common holiday, it must be all the more forbidden on the Sabbath.

Another rule of indirect exegesis (rule six) was intended to solve a problem by means of a comparison with another passage in Scripture. For example, in the Talmud the question why Moses had to hold up his hands during the battle with Amalek (Exodus 17:11) is answered by referring to Numbers 21:8. There the text states that in order to be cured from snakebite the Israelites were to look at the fiery serpent raised up in the wilderness. The hands of Moses could no more bring victory than could the brass serpent cure those who had been bitten. But the point is that, just as in the case of the fiery serpent, it was necessary for the Israelites to lift up their hearts to God in order to be saved.

A final example of indirect exegesis concerns the reconciliation of conflicting passages. Rabbi Ishmael's thirteenth rule states that if two passages contradict one another they are to be reconciled by a third if possible. Thus Exodus 13:6 ('Seven days you shall eat unleavened bread'), and Deuteronomy 16:8 ('For six days you shall eat unleavened bread') are an example of contradictory passages. But in a *midrash* on Exodus this conflict is resolved by referring to Leviticus 23:14 where the law enjoins that no use whatsoever was allowed to be made of the new corn until the offering of the first produce of the barley harvest had taken place on the morning after the first day of Pesach. Hence unleavened bread prepared of the new corn was to be eaten only during the six remaining days of that festival. Referring to this circumstance the passage in Deuteronomy 16:8 speaks of six days while the passage in Exodus 13:6 refers to the unleavened bread prepared of the produce of the former year's harvest which might be eaten during seven days.

These various methods of exegesis were based on the conviction that the Bible is sacred, that it is susceptible of interpretation and that, properly understood, it guides the life of the worthy. By means of this process of explanation of God's revelation, the rabbinic authorities were able to infuse the tradition with new meaning and renewed relevance. The literary outpouring of the first few centuries of Pharisaic Judaism bears witness to the fervent conviction that God's eternal word can have a living message for each generation of Jewry.

Rabbinic theology

Unlike the Mishnah which consists of legislation presented without explicit reference to a Scriptural source, rabbinic *aggadah* focuses on the contemporary relevance of specific Biblical texts. The early halachic *midrashim* consists of Tannaitic commentaries on the legal verses of the Bible such as the Mekhilta on Leviticus and the Sifrei on Numbers and Deuteronomy. Narrative *midrashim*, on the other hand, derive from sermons given by the Amoraim in synagogues and academies and include such texts as Midrash Rabbah (a series of commentaries on the Pentateuch and the Hagiographa – the Song of Songs, Ruth, Lamentations, Ecclesiastes and Esther). Though the rabbis were not speculative philosophers, they nevertheless expressed their theological views in these works and attempted to apply this teaching to daily life. This midrashic literature along with the aggadic sections of the Talmud serves as the basis for reconstructing the theology of early rabbinic Judaism.

Within these texts the rabbis expressed their theological views by means of stories, legends, parables and maxims based on Scripture. According to the sages of the *midrashim* and the Talmud, God's unity was of paramount importance; repeatedly they pointed out that though God has many different Hebrew names in the Bible, He is always the same. Thus in the third century R. Abba ben Nemel declared in a *midrash* on Exodus: 'God said to Moses, "Thou desirest to know my name. I am called according to my deeds. When I judge my creatures, I am called Elohim; when I wage war against the wicked, I am called Sabbaoth; when I suspend judgement for a man's sins, I am called El Shaddai; but when I have compassion upon my world, I am called Yahweh." ' The rabbis also stressed that God alone is the source of the universe and directs it according to a preordained plan. To illustrate this notion, scholars utilized such parables as a ship and its captain: just as it is impossible for a ship to reach its destination without a captain, so the government of the cosmos is inconceivable without a directing force.

In the light of this belief, aggadic literature condemns idolatry even more vigorously than the Bible. Thus a *midrash* on Numbers proclaims: 'He who commits idolatry denies the Ten Commandments, and all that was commanded to Moses, to the Prophets and to the Patriarchs . . . He who renounces idolatry is as if he professed the whole Law.' For the rabbis God is a transcendent creator, yet He is imminent as well. As the Talmud explains, He is near to all who call upon Him: 'God is far and yet He is near . . . For a man enters a synagogue and stands behind a pillar, and prays in a whisper, and God hears his prayer, and so it is with all His creatures. Can there be a nearer God than this? He is as near to His creatures as the ear to the mouth.'

The view of Tannanitic and Amoraic scholars regarding God's omniscience and man's free will was summarized in a statement by Rabbi Akiva in the second century AD: 'All is foreseen but freedom of choice is given; and the world is judged with goodness, and all is in accordance with Thy works.' Here it is asserted that although God knows all things, human beings have nevertheless been accorded free will and as a consequence they will be judged on the basis of their actions. But such judgement is tempered by mercy as a *midrash* on Leviticus records: 'In the hour when the Israelites take up their ram's horns, and blow them before God, He gets up from the throne of judgement and sits down upon the throne of mercy and He is filled with compassion for them, and He turns the attribute of Judgement into the attribute of Mercy.'

For the rabbis God is concerned with all mankind but the Jewish people play a special role in the divine plan. Israel's love of God is reciprocated by God's tender loving concern. In the words of R. Simeon bar Yohai (second century AD): 'Like a king who entrusted his son to a tutor, and kept asking him, "Does my son eat, does he drink, has he gone to school, has he come back from school?" So God yearns to make mention of the Israelites at every hour.' It is out of this love that God has entrusted his chosen people with the Torah; the purpose of Israel's election is to sanctify God's name and be a holy people dedicated to His service. As one *midrash* explains: 'It says in Leviticus 11:45, "For I am the Lord who brought you up out of the land of Egypt, to be your God: you shall therefore be holy, for I am holy." That means, I brought you out of Egypt on the condition that you should receive the yoke of the commandments.' In some rabbinic sources the Torah is described as pre-existent; it is the instrument with which the world was created. Thus a *midrash* on Genesis proclaims: 'God created the world by the Torah: the Torah was His handmaid and His tool by the aid of which He set bounds to the deep, assigned the functions to sun and moon, and formed all nature.' As the word of God, every letter is sacrosanct and the study and doing of Torah is the Jew's most sacred task. As Ben Bag Bag recommends: 'Turn it and turn it over again, for everything is in it, and contemplate it, and wax grey and old over it, and stir not from it, for thou can have no better rule than this.' Beneath the literal meaning of the text, the rabbis asserted, it is possible to discover layers of deeper meaning in which the divine mysteries are revealed.

The Torah also played a central role in the rabbinic depiction of the afterlife. This conception was a significant development from Biblical Judaism in which there was no explicit doctrine of eternal salvation. According to rabbinic sources, the world to come is divided into several stages. First there is the period of messianic redemption which is to take place on earth after a period of decline and calamity and will result in the complete fulfilment of every human aspiration. Peace will reign throughout nature; Jerusalem will be rebuilt, and at the close of this era the dead will be resurrected and rejoined with their

souls and the final judgement will come upon all mankind. Those
Jews who have fulfilled the precepts of the law and are thereby judged
righteous will enter into Heaven (*Gan Eden*) as well as gentiles who
have lived in accord with the Noahcide laws (the laws which Noah
and his descendents took upon themselves).

In rabbinic sources the heavenly realm is depicted in various ways;
in one *midrash* for example the inner chamber is built of precious
stones, gold and silver and surrounded by myrrh and aloes. In front of
the chamber runs the river Gihon on whose banks are planted flowers
giving off perfume and aromatic incense. There are couches of gold
and silver and fine drapery. There are also extensive descriptions of
Hell (*Gehinnom*) in rabbinic literature. Confinement to Hell is a
result of disobeying God's Torah as is illustrated by a *midrash* which
describes Moses' visit there:

> When Moses and the Angel of Hell entered Hell together they saw men
> being tortured by the Angels of Destruction. Some sinners were
> suspended by their eyelids, some by their ears, and some by their
> hands, and some by their tongues. In addition, women were suspended
> by their hair and their breasts by chains of fire. Such punishments were
> inflicted on the basis of the sins that were committed.

These central themes within rabbinic theology do not exhaust the
scope of rabbinic speculation. In addition early rabbinic authorities
discussed a wide variety of religious issues including martyrdom,
prayer, charity, atonement, forgiveness, repentance and peace.
Within aggadic sources, the rabbis expressed their profound reflections on human life and God's nature and activity in the world.
Unlike the legal precepts of the Torah and the rabbinic expansion of
these Scriptural ordinances, these theological opinions were not
binding on the Jewish community. They were formulated instead to
educate, inspire and edify those to whom they were addressed. Study
of the Torah was a labour of love which had no end, a task whose
goal was to serve the will of God.

Rabbinic ethics

Moral precepts are grounded in the will of God. In this light the
Torah serves as the blueprint for moral action, and it is through the
admonitions of the rabbis in midrashic and Talmudic sources that the
Jewish people are encouraged to put the teachings of the law into
effect in their everyday lives. In the hierarchy of values, the rabbis

declared that justice is of fundamental importance. R. Simeon ben Gamaliel in the second century AD, for example, remarked: 'Do not sneer at justice, for it is one of the three feet of the world, for the sages taught that the world stands on three things: justice, truth and peace.' According to R. Elazar (second century AD): 'The whole Torah depends upon justice. Therefore God gave enactments about justice (Exodus 21:1) immediately after the Ten Commandments, because God punishes them, and He teaches the inhabitants of the world. Sodom was not overthrown till the men of Sodom neglected justice and the men of Jerusalem were not banished till they disregarded justice' (Ezekiel 16:49; Isaiah 1:23). Similarly, Simon ben Shetach said in the first century BC: 'When you are judging, and there come before you two men, of whom one is rich and the other poor, do not say, "the poor man's words are to be believed, but not the rich man's". But just as you listen to the words of the poor man, listen to the words of the rich man, for it is said, "Ye shall not be partial in judgement" ' (Deuteronomy 1:17).

Like justice, charity was viewed as an essential virtue. The Talmud declared: 'He who gives alms in secret is greater than Moses.' In another Talmudic passage R. Elazar stated: 'Almsgiving is greater than all sacrifice for it says, "To do righteousness and justice is more acceptable to the Lord than sacrifice" (Proverbs 21:3). But loving deeds are greater than almsgiving, as it says, "Sow for yourself righteousness, reap the fruit of steadfast love" (Hosea 10:12).' 'Of his sowing, a man may ear or no; of his reaping, he will eat assuredly.' He also said: 'Almsgiving becomes increasingly perfect according to the amount of love that is shown in it.' According to the *midrash* on the psalms, the gates of the Lord are open to one who cares for others:

> In the future world, man will be asked, 'What was your occupation?' If he replies, 'I fed the hungry', then they reply 'This is the gate of the Lord; the righteous shall enter through it.' (Psalm 118:20). So with giving drink to the thirsty, clothing to the naked, with those who look after orphans, and with those, generally, who do deeds of loving kindness. All these are gates of the Lord, and those who do such deeds shall enter within them.

Hospitality was also considered a cardinal virtue. In a commentary on Exodus we read:

> God said to Moses, 'I will send thee to Pharaoh'. Moses answered, 'Lord of the world, I cannot; for Jethro has received me, and opened his house door to me, so that I am as a son with him. If a man opens his

house to his fellow, his guest owes his life to him. Jethro has received me, and has honourably entertained me; can I depart without his leave?' Hence it says, 'Moses went and returned to Jethro his father-in-law'.

Hospitality is a great virtue, the rabbi decreed, 'greater even than early attendance at the House of Study or than the reception of the Shekhinah [God's presence]'.

These few examples indicate that the Kingdom of God is inconsistent with injustice and social misery; the effort to bring about the perfection of the world so that God will reign in majesty is a human responsibility. Jewish ethics as enshrined in rabbinic literature were inextricably related to the coming of God's kingdom. In this context a number of distinctive characteristics of Jewish morality are expressed in the Jewish tradition. First rabbinic ethics require that each person be treated equally. Rabbinic sources show a constant concern to eliminate arbitrary distinctions between individuals so as to establish a proper balance between competing claims. On the basis of the Biblical view that everyone is created in the image of God, the rabbis declared that false and irrelevant distinctions must not be introduced to disqualify human beings from the right to justice. Since all humanity is created in the image of God, the rabbis maintain that there is no fundamental difference between Jew and non-Jew: God's ethical demands apply to all. In a *midrash* we read: 'This is the gate of the Lord into which the righteous shall enter: not priest, Levites, or Israelites, but the righteous, though they be non-Jews.'

A second characteristic of Jewish morality is its emphasis on human motivation. The Jewish faith is not solely concerned with actions and their consequences; it also demands right intention. The rabbis explained: 'The Merciful One requires the heart'. It is true that Judaism emphasizes the importance of moral action, but the rabbis also focus attention on rightmindedness: inner experiences – motives, feelings, dispositions and attitudes – are of supreme moral significance. For this reason the rabbis identified a group of negative commandments in the Torah involving thought. The following are representative examples: 'Thou shalt not take vengeance, or bear any grudge against the sons of your own people' (Leviticus 19:18). 'There are six things which the Lord hates . . . a heart that devises wicked plans' (Proverbs 6:16,18). 'Take heed lest there be a base thought in your heart' (Deuteronomy 15:9). In the Mishnah the rabbis elaborated on this concern for the human heart: in the second century Rabbi Eliezer said 'be not easily moved to anger', and Rabbi Joshua said 'The evil eye, the evil inclination, and hatred of his fellow creatures drives a man out of the world.' Rabbi Levitas of Yavneh said 'Be exceedingly lowly of spirit'.

Thirdly, connected with right thought is the Jewish emphasis on right speech. Rabbinic sources insist that individuals are morally responsible for the words they utter. Evil words spoken about one person by another could arouse hatred and enmity and destroy human relations. The rabbis considered slander to be a particular evil: 'Whoever speaks slander is as though he denied the fundamental principle [existence of God]. The Holy One, blessed be He, says of such a person who speaks slander, "I and he cannot dwell together in the world".' There was also a positive aspect to this emphasis on human speech. Just as the rabbis condemned false utterance, they urged their disciples to offer cheerful greetings. Anger could be soothed with gentle words and reconciliation could be brought about.

A fourth dimension of Jewish morality concerns the traditional attitude toward animals. According to the rabbis, human beings are morally obliged to refrain from inflicting pain on animals. We read, for example, of the second-century Rabbi Judah ha–Nasi: Rabbi Judah was sitting and studying the Torah in front of the Babylonian synagogue in Sepphoris, when a calf passed before him on its way to the slaughter and began to cry out as though pleading, 'Save me!' Said he to it, 'What can I do for you? For this you were created.' As a punishment for his heartlessness, he suffered toothache for thirteen years. One day, a weasel ran past his daughter, who was about to kill it, when he said to her, 'My daughter, let it be, for it is written, "and His tender mercies are over all His works".' Because the Rabbi prevented an act of cruelty, he was once again restored to health.

A final aspect of Jewish ethics is its concern for human dignity; the rabbis put a strong emphasis on the respect due to all individuals. The Torah's concern for human dignity even includes thieves. Rabbi Jochanan ben Zaccai pointed out in the first century AD that, according to the law, whoever stole a sheep should pay a fine of four times the value of the sheep; whoever stole an ox must pay five times its value. Those who stole sheep had to undergo the embarrassment of carrying the sheep off in their arms and the Torah compensated them for this indignity, but those who stole oxen were spared such embarrassment because they could simply lead the ox by its tether.

These specific qualities of Jewish ethics illustrate their humane orientation to all of God's creatures. Throughout rabbinic literature, Jews were encouraged to strive for the highest conception of life, in which the rule of truth, righteousness and holiness would be established among humankind. Such a desire is the eternal hope of

God's people – a longing for God's kingdom. The coming of God's rule requires a struggle for the reign of justice and righteousness on earth. The kingdom is not an internalized, spiritualized, other-worldly concept, rather it involves human activity in a historical context.

Early rabbinic mysticism

Within aggadic sources the rabbis also engaged in mystical speculation based on the Biblical text. These doctrines were frequently of a secret nature; in a *midrash* on Genesis it is reported that these mystical traditions were repeated in a whisper so they would not be overheard by those for whom they were not intended. Thus in the third century R. Simeon ben Jehozedek asked R. Samuel Nahman: 'Seeing that I have heard you are adept at aggadah, tell me how light was created.' He replied in a whisper, upon which the other sage retorted, 'Why do you tell this in a whisper, seeing that it is taught clearly in a Scriptural verse?' The first sage responded: 'Just as I have myself had it whispered to me, even so I have whispered it to you.' Such knowledge was restricted to a select group of scholars. In the same century, R. Judah, for example, said in the name of Rab that God's secret name could only be entrusted to one who is 'modest and meek, in the midway of life, not easily provoked to anger, temperate, and free from vengeful feelings'.

In their mystical reflections, the first chapter of Ezekiel played an important role in early rabbinic mysticism. In this Biblical text the divine chariot (*Merkavah*) is described in detail, and this Scriptural source served as the basis for rabbinic speculation about the nature of the Deity. It was the aim of the mystic to be a 'Merkavah rider' so that he would be able to penetrate the heavenly mysteries. Within this contemplative system, the rabbis believed that the pious could free themselves from the fetters of bodily existence and enter paradise. A further dimension of this theory is that certain pious individuals can temporarily ascend into the unseen realm and having learnt the deepest secrets may return to earth. These mystics were able to attain a state of ecstasy, to behold visions and hear voices. As students of the Merkavah they were the ones able to attain the highest degree of spiritual insight. A description of the experiences of these Merkavah mystics is contained in *hekhalot* (heavenly hall) literature from the later Gaonic period (from the seventh to the eleventh centuries AD). In order to make their heavenly ascent, these mystics followed strict ascetic disciplines, including fasting, ablution and the invocation of God's name. After reaching a state of ecstasy, the mystic was able to enter the seven heavenly halls and attain a vision of the divine chariot.

Closely associated with this form of speculation were mystical theories about creation (*Maaseh Bereshit*). Within aggadic sources the rabbis discussed the hidden meanings of the Genesis narrative. The most important early treatise, possibly from the second century AD, which describes the process of creation is *The Book of Creation* (*Sefer Yetsirah*). According to this cosmological text God created the universe by thirty-two mysterious paths consisting of twenty-two letters of the Hebrew alphabet together with ten spheres (*sefirot*). Of these twenty-two letters we read: 'He hewed them, combined them, weighed them, interchanged them, and through them produced the whole creation and everything that is destined to come into being.'

These letters are of three types: mothers, doubles and singles. The mothers (*shin, mem, aleph*) symbolize the three primordial elements of all existing things: water (the first letter of which is *mem* in Hebrew) is symbolized by *mem*; fire (of which *shin* is the most prominent sound) is represented by *shin*; air (the first letter of which in Hebrew is *aleph*) is designated by *aleph*. These three mothers represent in the microcosm (the human form), 'the head, the belly and the chest – the head from fire; the belly from water, and the chest from the air that lies in between'.

In addition to these three mother letters, there are seven double letters (*beth, gimel, daleth, caph, peh, resh, tau*) which signify the contraries in the universe (forces which serve two mutually opposed ends). These letters were 'formed, designed, created and combined into the stars of the universe, the days of the week, and the orifices of perception in man . . . two eyes, two ears, two nostrils and a mouth through which he perceives by his senses'. Finally there are twelve simple letters (*he, vav, zayin, chet, tet, yod, lamed, nun, samek, ayin, tsade, kof*) which correspond to man's chief activities – sight, hearing, smell, speech, desire for food, the sexual appetite, movement, anger, mirth, thought, sleep and work. The letters are also emblematic of the twelve signs of the zodiac in the heavenly sphere, the twelve months, and the chief limbs of the body. Thus man, world and time are linked to one another through the process of creation by means of the Hebrew alphabet.

These recondite doctrines are supplemented by a theory of divine emanation through the ten heavenly spheres (*sefirot*). The first of the *sefirot* is the spirit of the living God; air is the second of the spheres and is derived from the first – on it are hewn the twenty-two letters.

The third sphere is the water that comes from the air: 'It is in the water that He has dug the darkness and the chaos, that He has formed the earth and the clay, which was spread out afterwards in the form of a carpet, hewn out like a wall and covered as though by a roof.' The fourth of the spheres is the fire which comes from water through which God made the heavenly wheels, the seraphim and the ministering angels. The remaining six *sefirot* are the six dimensions of space – north, south, east, west, height and depth.

These ten spheres are the moulds into which all created things were originally cast. They constitute form rather than matter. The twenty-two letters, on the other hand, are the prime cause of matter: everything that exists is due to the creative force of the Hebrew letters, but they receive their form from the *sefirot*. According to this cosmological doctrine, God transcends the universe; nothing exists outside of Him. The visible world is the result of the emanation of the divine: God is the cause of the form and matter of the cosmos. By combining emanation and creation in this manner, the *Sefer Yetsirah* attempts to harmonize the concept of divine immanence and transcendence. God is immanent in that the *sefirot* are an outpouring of His spirit, and He is transcendent in that the matter which was shaped into the forms is the product of His creative action. Such speculation served as the basis for later mystical reflection of the medieval period.

7

The Emergence of Medieval Jewry

By the sixth century the Jews had become largely a diaspora people. Despite the loss of a homeland, they were unified by a common heritage: law, liturgy and shared traditions bound together the scattered communities stretching from Spain to Persia and Poland to Africa. Though subcultures did form during the Middle Ages which could have divided the Jewish world, Jews remained united in their hope for messianic redemption, the restoration of the Holy Land, and an ingathering of the exiles. Living amongst Christians and Muslims, the Jews were reduced to a minority group and their marginal status resulted in repeated persecution. Though there were times of tolerance and creative activity, the threats of exile and death were always present in the Jewish consciousness during this period.

Jews under early Islamic rule

The Arabs of the Arabian peninsula in the sixth and seventh centuries were polytheists living in nomadic tribes or settled in urban centres. At the beginning of the seventh century Muhammad, a caravan merchant from Mecca, denounced such paganism as a perversion of God's will. Claiming to have received a revelation from the One True God, he proclaimed a doctrine of divine reward and punishment. In the first phase of his preaching he stressed that Biblical figures such as Abraham and Moses had been sent by God to warn humankind to abandon idolatry. Those who rejected this message were destroyed except for Jews and Christians who had transmitted the revelations given them in the Torah and the Gospels. According to Muhammad, these earlier revelations were superseded by a new revelation from God which was transmitted to them through his prophecy.

Initially Muhammad hoped to convert Jews to this new faith, but the Jewish community refused to recognize him as a true prophet. This rejection led Muhammad to denounce the Jewish nation: 'Now that a Book confirming their Scriptures has been revealed to them by Allah, they deny it, although they know it to be the truth and have long prayed for help against the unbelievers. May Allah's curse be upon the infidels!' According to Muhammad, the Jews distorted Allah's message, and their Scripture contains falsehoods; a number of Biblical stories for example diverge from the Koran (the record of God's communication to Muhammad). Muhammad's view was that the Koran confirms and corrects the Torah. Islam is thus superior to Judaism, and Muhammad is the last and decisive apostle of God. Judaism is therefore a legitimate but incomplete religious system.

By 626 – only six years before Muhammad's death – two Jewish tribes had been expelled from Medina and a third had been exterminated, except for women and children who were enslaved. In 628 Muslims conquered the Jewish oasis of Khaybar to the north; there Jews were subsequently permitted to remain if they gave half their produce as a tribute to the Muslims. By 644 Syria, Israel, Egypt, Iraq and Persia were occupied by Muslim soldiers. The eastern frontier of the Byzantine empire was pushed back to Asia Minor, and the Persian state was destroyed. In the next sixteen years the Ummayad dynasty of caliphs had consolidated their control of the Islamic empire, and Muslim armies continued their campaign. At the beginning of the eighth century a mixed army of Arabs and Muslim Berbers crossed the straits of Gibraltar to conquer the Iberian peninsula, thereby bringing Islam to continental Europe. The Arab empire in this first century of its existence was plagued by unrest over the right of leadership, and in 750 the Ummayads were overthrown and replaced by the Abbasid dynasty of caliphs who moved the capital from Damascus to Baghdad.

During the following century the Abbasid caliphate was at its height – the Islamic post-Scriptural oral tradition was formed, and Muslim jurisprudence, philosophy, theology and science flourished. At first widespread conversion to Islam was not encouraged; Jews along with Christians were recognized as Peoples of the Book and were guaranteed religious toleration, judicial autonomy and exemption from the military. In turn they were required to accept the supremacy of the Islamic state. Such an arrangement was formally codified by the Pact of Omar dating from about 800. According to this treaty, Jews were restricted in a number of spheres: they were not allowed to build new houses of worship, make converts, carry weapons or ride horses. In addition, they were required to wear distinctive clothing and pay a yearly poll tax. Jewish farmers were also obligated to pay a land tax consisting of a portion of their produce. Under these conditions, Jewish life nevertheless prospered. In various urban centres many Jews were employed in crafts such as tanning, dyeing, weaving, silk manufacture and metal work; other Jews participated in interregional trade and established networks of agents and representatives.

This political and economic framework enabled Jews to migrate from Babylonia which was held by the Arabs to other parts of the diaspora. Some Jews created new centres of Jewish life and even went outside the Islamic empire to conduct trade. It was just such merchants who during this period converted to Judaism the kings of a Turkish people on the Volga, the Khazars. Jews in the former Byzantine provinces welcomed the Muslim regime. Instead of enduring oppression at the hands of the Christian community, they had a defined legal standing as protected subjects of the state. The political status of Jews under Islam resembled the position of Jews of Sassanian Persia in the third century AD when rabbis adapted Jewish law to the diaspora environment.

During the first two centuries of Islamic rule under the Ummayad and Abbasid caliphates, Muslim leaders confirmed the authority of traditional Babylonian Jewish institutions. When the Arabs conquered Babylonia, they officially recognized the position of the exilarch who for centuries had been the ruler of Babylonian Jewry. The exilarch represented Jews in the caliphal court, collected the poll tax, and supervised Jewish juridical and charitable institutions. By the Abbasid period, the exilarch shared his power with the heads of the rabbinical academies, which in Babylonia had for centuries been the major centres of rabbinic learning, with their rulings based on the interpretation of Talmudic precedent widely accepted. The head of each academy was known as the *gaon* (excellency) who delivered lectures as well as learned opinions (*responsa*) on halachic inquiries. These religious leaders were largely drawn from a small number of families who dominated Jewish life in Babylonia. In the eighth century the exilarch was supreme over the academies and appointed their heads, but soon the *gaonim* became more independent and claimed the right to appoint the exilarch. Gradually the influence of the exilarch declined in relation to the *gaonim*, and by the tenth century the academies moved from Sura and Pumpbeditha to Baghdad. By the eleventh century the exilarch's position became honorific and the academy of Pumpbeditha–Baghdad gained pre-eminence over the Sura–Baghdad academy, thereby reversing their relationship in the earlier Muslim period.

Karaism

During the eighth century messianic movements appeared in the Persian Jewish community which led to armed uprisings against Muslim authorities. Such revolts were quickly crushed, but an even more serious threat to traditional Jewish life was posed later in the century by the emergence of an anti-rabbinic sect, the Karaites. This group was founded in Babylonia in the 760s by Anan Ben David, who had earlier been passed over as exilarch, and traced its origin to the time of Jeroboam in the eighth century BC. According to some scholars, Anan's movement absorbed elements of an extra-Talmudic tradition and took over doctrines from Islam. The guiding interpretative principle formulated by Anan, 'Search thoroughly in Scripture and do not rely on my opinion', was intended to point to Scripture itself as the sole source of law. Jewish observances, the Karaites insisted, must conform to Biblical legislation rather than rabbinic ordinances. Anan however was not lenient concerning legal matters. He did not for example recognize the minimum quantities of forbidden foods fixed by the rabbis; in addition, he introduced more complicated regulations for circumcision, added to the number of fast days, interpreted the prohibition of work on the sabbath in stricter terms than the rabbis, and extended the prohibited degrees of marriage. In short he made the yoke of the law more burdensome.

After the death of the founder, new parties within the Karaite movement soon emerged. The adherents of Anan were referred to as the 'Ananites' and remained few in number. In the first half of the ninth century the Ukarite sect was established by Ishmael of Ukbara (near Baghdad); some years later another sect was formed in the same town by Mishawayh Al-Ukbari. Another group was formed by a contemporary of Mishawayh, Abu Imram Al-Tiflisi. In Israel, yet another sect was established by Malik Al-Ramli. By the end of the ninth century Karaism had become a conglomerate of groups advocating different anti-rabbinic positions, but these sects were short-lived and in time the Karaites consolidated into a uniform movement. The central representative of mainstream Karaism was Benjamin ben Moses Nahavendi (of Nahavendi in Persia) who advocated a policy of free and independent study of Scripture which became the dominant ideology of later Karaism. By the tenth century a number of Karaite communities were established in Israel, Iraq and Persia. These groups rejected rabbinic law and devised their own legislation, which led eventually to the foundation of a Karaite rabbinical academy in Jerusalem; the Karaite community there produced some of the most distinguished scholars of the period who composed legal handbooks, wrote Biblical commentaries, expounded on Hebrew philology and engaged in philosophical and theological reflection.

The growth of Karaism provoked the rabbis to attack it as a heretical movement. The first prominent authority to engage in anti-Karaite debate was Saadiah Gaon who in the first half of the ninth century wrote a book attacking Anan; this polemic was followed by other anti-Karaite tracts by eminent rabbinic authorities. After the Jerusalem Jewish community was decimated by the First Crusade, Karaite scholarly activity shifted to the Byzantine empire, and from there Jews founded communities in the Crimea, Poland and Lithuania. In Egypt the Karaite community continued to flourish, but after the eleventh century the movement diminished in influence, and in the centuries that followed down to the present day Karaism survived only as a tiny minority within Jewry.

Jews in Muslim Spain and other Islamic lands

As early as the eighth century the Muslim empire began to undergo a process of disintegration. When Abbasid caliphs conquered the Ummayads in 750, Spain remained independent under a Ummayad ruler. As the century progressed, the Abbasids began to lose control of the outlying territories. After 850 Turkish troops managed to gain control over the Abbasids and the caliph became essentially a figurehead behind which Turkish generals exerted power. In 909 Shi'ite Muslims (followers of Ali, Muhammad's son-in-law), the Fatimids, took control over North Africa; in 969 they conquered Egypt and Israel. By the end of the tenth century the Islamic world was divided into a number of separate states pitted against one another.

The disappearance of the political unity of the Islamic empire was accompanied by a decentralization of rabbinic Judaism. The rabbinic academies of Babylonia began to lose their hold on the Jewish scholarly world; in many places rabbinic schools (*yeshivot*) were established in which rabbinic sources were studied. The growth of these local centres of learning enabled individual teachers to exert their influence on Jewish learning independent of the academies of Sura and Pumpbeditha. The locality in which the local rabbinate asserted itself was the Holy Land. Tiberius was the location of the rabbinical academy there as well as the centre of the Masoretic scholars such as the families of Ben Asher and Ben Naphtali who produced the standard tradition (*masorah*) of the Bible by adding vowels and punctuation to the Hebrew text. By the ninth century the rabbinic academy moved to Ramleh and then to Jerusalem; this institution was supported by the Jewish communities of Egypt, Yemen and Syria, but due to Turkish and Christian invasions its influence waned in the eleventh century.

Egyptian Jewry also underwent a transformation during this period. Under the Fatimids Jewish life prospered in Egypt, and by the end of the tenth century a *yeshiva* had been established in Cairo. Kairouan had also become a centre of scholarship: at this time academies were established by distinguished Talmudists and affluent Jewish families who supported Jewish scientists and philosophers. The city of Fez also reached a degree of eminence, producing one of the most important rabbinic scholars of the period, Isaac Alfasi (1013–1103) who compiled an influential code of Jewish law. But it was in Spain that the Jewish community attained the greatest level of achievement. In the tenth-century Spanish royal court the Ummayad caliphs Abd Al-Rahman III (912–61) and Hakam II (961–72) employed the Jewish statesman Hisdai Ibn Shaprut (915–70) as court physician, administrator and diplomat. In addition he acted as head of the Jewish community and patron of Jewish scholarship. Cordova, the capital of the Ummayad caliphate, became a vibrant centre of Jewish civilization, attracting poets, grammarians and *yeshiva* students from throughout the diaspora.

As the Ummayad caliphate began to disintegrate in the eleventh century, small Muslim principalities were often at odds with one another. Several of the rulers of these states used Jewish courtiers, such as Samuel Ibn Nagrela of Granada (Samuel ha-Nagid: 993–1056), in their administrations. This figure was knowledgeable about mathematics and philosophy, wrote in Hebrew and Arabic, and served as vizier of Granada for thirty years. In commemoration of his own military victories, he composed Hebrew poetry, and he also wrote an introduction to the Talmud. Other scholars of the period lived in Seville, Saragossa, Toledo, Calatayud and Lucena, which became renowned for its Jewish academy.

In 1086 the life of Spanish Jewry was shaken when the Almoravides from North Africa were invited to Spain to lead an attack on Christian communities in the north and persecuted the Jewish population as well. Soon however Jews were restored to their former secure position and the next generation saw outstanding poets, philosophers, Biblical commentators, theologians and rabbinic authorities. But in the middle of the twelfth century the golden age of Spanish Jewry came to an end. Fearing Christian conquest, the Almohades – a Berber dynasty from Morocco – came to defend the country and simultaneously persecuted the Jewish community. Jews were forced to convert to Islam, and academies and synagogues were closed. Some Jews practised Judaism in secret; others escaped to the Middle East or migrated to Christian Spain. At the beginning of the thirteenth century the dominance of the Almohades came to an end when Christian kingdoms managed to seize control of most of the former Muslim territories in Spain.

In other parts of the Muslim empire, Jews faced changing circumstances during these centuries. In the mid-twelfth century, during the Almohade persecution, some Spanish Jews migrated to Egypt, including the Jewish philosopher Moses Maimonides. In Israel a small Jewish community survived during the Crusades and was augmented by Jewish pilgrims who went to the Holy Land. Babylonian Jewry continued after the death of the last important *gaon*, Hai bar Sherira, in 1038, but the Mongol invasions in the middle of the thirteenth century had devastating consequences for the region. In western North Africa Jewish communities were able to practise their faith as before when the Almohades were removed and many Jews prospered. Some North African Jewish merchants participated in the Saharan gold trade, maintaining links with the kingdom of Aragon in Spain.

Jewry in Christian Europe in the Middle Ages

The Muslims did not manage to conquer all of Europe in their campaigns in the seventh century – many countries remained under Christian rule as did much of the Byzantine empire. The early Jewish communities in western Europe (Ashkenazic Jewry) lived in small, self-contained communities and engaged in local trades. The Jews in each town constituted a separate unit since there was no equivalent of an exilarch (as in Muslim lands) to serve as the official leader of the Jewish population. Each community (*kahal*) established its own rules (*takkanot*) and administered local courts, in a form of self-government which was the Ashkenazic adaptation to the feudal structure of medieval Christian Europe. In this environment Jewish study took place in a number of important centres such as Mainz and Worms in the Rhineland and Troyes and Sens in northern France and produced such leading scholars as the legal expert Rabbenu Gershom of Mainz (960–1040) and the greatest commentator of the medieval period, Solomon ben Isaac of Troyes (known as Rashi: 1040–1105). In subsequent generations, the study of the Talmud reached great heights: in Germany and northern France scholars known as the tosafists (which included some of Rashi's family) utilized new methods of Talmudic interpretation. In addition, Ashkenazic Jews of this period composed religious poetry modelled on the liturgical compositions (*piyyutim*) of fifth- and sixth-century Israel.

Despite this efflorescence of Jewish learning, Jews in Christian countries were subject to frequent outbursts of anti-Jewish sentiment. In 1095 Pope Urban II proclaimed the First Crusade – an act which stimulated mobs in the Rhineland in 1096 to attack Jews in towns such as Worms and Mainz. Jews in these communities willingly martyred themselves as an act of sanctification rather than convert to the Christian faith. These massacres at the end of the century were not officially authorized by the state, and Jews who had converted under duress were subsequently allowed to return to the Jewish tradition.

In the following two centuries the Jewish community of Christian Europe became increasingly more involved in moneylending as the Christian guilds forced Jews out of trade. The practice of usury intensified anti-Semitism especially by those who were unable to pay back loans. Added to this economic motive, Christians in the Middle Ages persecuted the Jews on religious grounds: the Jew was stereotyped as a demonic Christ-killer and murderer. As early as 1144 in Norwich, England, the Jewish community was accused of killing Christian children at Passover to use their blood in the preparation of unleavened bread. Later the same accusation was made in Blois, France, in 1171 and in Lincoln, England, in 1255. Another frequent charge against the Jews was that they defamed the host in order to torture Jesus's body. Further, Jews were also regarded with enmity since they obtained Church property through defaulted loans. Such factors led the Fourth Lateran Council in 1215 to strengthen the Church's restrictions regarding the Jewish people: 'It is decreed that henceforth Jews of both sexes will be distinguished from other peoples by their garments, as moreover has been prescribed to them by Moses. They will not show themselves in public during Holy Week, for some among them on these days wear their finest garments and mock the Christians clad in mourning. Trespassers will be duly punished by the secular powers, in order that they no longer dare flout Christ in the presence of Christians.'

In the same century Dominican priests were active against the Jewish community. In 1240 they participated in a disputation about the Talmud in Paris with leading Jewish scholars. Among the points raised were the following queries: 'Was it true that in the first century after the fall of Jerusalem Rabbi Simeon bar Yochai proclaimed: "Seize the best of the goyim and kill them"? Does the Talmud claim that Jesus was an illegitimate child? Is it the Talmud's view that Jesus will suffer the torment of boiling mud in Hell?' In reply the Jewish authorities stressed that many commandments prescribe an equal charity toward Jews and non-Jews. Yet as a result of the debate, the Talmud was condemned and all copies were burned.

Expulsion of the Jews from countries in which they lived also became a dominant policy of Christian Europe. In 1182 the king of France, Philip Augustus, expelled all Jews from the royal domains near Paris, cancelled nearly all Christian debts to Jewish moneylenders, and confiscated Jewish property. Though the Jews were recalled in 1198, they were burdened with an additional royal tax and in the next century they increasingly became the property of the king. In thirteenth-century England the Jews were continuously taxed and the entire Jewish population was expelled in 1290, as was that in France by Philip IV some years later. At the end of the thirteenth century in Germany, the Jewish community suffered violent attack. In 1286 the most eminent scholar of the period, R. Meir of Rothenberg (1220–93), was taken prisoner and died in custody; twelve years later mobs rampaged the country destroying about 140 Jewish communities. In the next century Jews were blamed for bringing about the Black Death by poisoning the wells of Europe, and from 1348 to 1349 Jews in France, Switzerland, Germany and Belgium suffered at the hands of their Christian neighbours. In the following two centuries, Jewish massacre and expulsion became a frequent occurrence.

The Jews in Christian Spain

After the Christians had conquered most of the Iberian peninsula in the thirteenth century, Sephardic Jews in Spain combined many features of their life in Muslim lands with aspects of Jewish existence in Christian feudal countries. The Jewish population was employed in a wide range of occupations, including shopkeeping, artisan crafts, medicine and moneylending. The community was stratified into a broad range of social classes: many Jews were poor but a small minority participated in the administration of the country as royal councillors and financial experts.

Legally there were important similarities between the communities of Spanish Jews and their counterparts in northern Europe. Each corporate body (*aljama*) was granted a charter guaranteeing the economic rights of its members as well as their freedom to live according to the Jewish tradition. As a consequence each community was able to regulate its own social services, bureaucratic institutions and judicial system. As under Islamic rule, a number of Spanish Jews studied humanistic and scientific subjects and made notable contributions to a variety of disciplines; the thirteenth century witnessed a flowering of Jewish scholarly activity in the fields of mysticism, theology and halachic studies. Throughout this century Jews were generally secure relative to the plight of their co-religionists in other European lands.

At the end of the fourteenth century, however, political instability led to the massacre of many Jewish communities in Castile and Aragon. Fearing for their lives, thousands of Jews converted to Christianity in 1391. Two decades later, in 1412, Spanish rulers introduced the Castilian laws which attempted to segregate Jews from their Christian neighbours. In the following year a public disputation was held in Tortosa about the doctrine of the Messiah; as a result increased pressure was applied to the Jewish population to convert. Those who became Christian apostates (*conversos*) found life much easier and some reached high positions in the government and the Church. But as the *conversos* were achieving social acceptance and recognition, those who had remained loyal to their faith attempted to rebuild Jewish life: *aljamas* were reconstituted and new communities were established in towns in northern Castile.

By the fifteenth century anti-Jewish sentiment had again become a serious problem; initially hatred was directed against *conversos* who had become tax-collectors. These attacks were justified on the grounds that these former Jews had not acted in good faith, and the term '*marrano*' was applied to those who were suspected of practising Judaism in secret. In 1480 King Ferdinand and Queen Isabella established the Inquisition to determine if such charges were valid: thousands of Jewish converts were subsequently convicted and punished, and those who refused to repent were burned at the stake. In the late 1480s inquisitors used torture to extract confessions regarding a blood libel case (alleging that *marranos* crucified a Christian boy to use his heart for performing witchcraft), and in 1492 the entire Jewish community was expelled from Spain.

8
Medieval Jewish Philosophy and Theology

In the Hellenistic period the Jewish philosopher Philo attempted to integrate Greek philosophy and Jewish teaching into a unified whole. By applying an allegorical method of interpretation to Scripture, he explained the God of Judaism in Greek philosophical categories and reshaped Jewish notions about God, man and the world. Philo was the precursor of medieval Jewish philosophy which also attempted to combine alternative philosophical systems with the received Biblical tradition. The beginnings of this philosophical development took place in ninth-century Babylonia during the height of the Abbasid caliphate when rabbinic Judaism was challenged by Karaite scholars who criticized the anthropomorphic views of God in midrashic and Talmudic sources. Added to this internal threat was the Islamic contention that Muhammad's revelation in the Koran superseded the Jewish faith. In addition Zoroastrians and Manichaeans attacked monotheism as a viable religious system. Finally some gentile philosophers argued that the Greek scientific and philosophical world view could account for the origin of the cosmos without reference to an external Deity. In combating these challenges, Jewish writers were influenced by the teachings of Muslim schools (*kalam*) of the eighth to the eleventh centuries; in particular the contributions of one school of Muslim thought, (the Mutazilite *kalam*) had a profound effect on the development of Jewish thought. These Islamic scholars maintained that rational argument was vital in matters of religious belief and that Greek philosophy could serve as the handmaiden of religious faith. In their attempt to defend Judaism from internal and external assault, rabbinic authorities frequently adapted the Mutazilite *kalam* as an important line of defence and as time passed also employed other aspects of Graeco-Arabic thought in their expositions of the Jewish faith.

Saadiah Gaon

The earliest philosopher of the medieval period, Saadiah ben Joseph al-Fayyumi (882–942), was Egyptian by origin and became a central spokesman against the Karaite movement. As Gaon of one of the Babylonian academies, he wrote treatises on a wide range of subjects – Hebrew philology, Jewish liturgy and *halachah* – and produced the first major Jewish theological treatise of the Middle Ages: *The Book of Beliefs and Opinions*. In this study Saadiah attempted to refute the religious claims of Christians, Muslims and Zoroastrians. Basing his approach on the teachings of the *kalam*, he argued that there are four sources of knowledge: sense experience, intuition of self-evident truths, logical inference and reliable tradition. This fourth category, derived from the first three, is the mainstay of civilization; it was given by God to man to provide guidance and protection against uncertainty since the vast majority of humanity is incapable of engaging in philosophical speculation.

Adapting the teaching of the Mutazilites, Saadiah argued that religious faith and reason are fully compatible. On this basis he attempted to demonstrate that God exists since the universe must have had a starting point. Time, he believed, is only rational if it has a beginning because it is impossible to pass from an infinite past to the present. The Divine Creator, he believed, is a single, incorporeal Being who created the universe out of nothing. In connection with God's unity, Saadiah, like the Mutazalite philosophers, assumed that if God has a plurality of attributes this implies He must be composite in nature. Thus, he argued, such terms as 'life', 'omnipotence' and 'omniscience' should be understood as implications of the concept of God as Creator rather than attributes of the Deity. The reason we are forced to describe God by means of these descriptions is because of the limitations of language, but they do not in any way involve plurality in God. In this light Saadiah argued that the anthropomorphic expressions in the Bible must not be taken literally since this would imply that God is a plurality. Hence when we read in the Bible that God has a head, eye, ear, mouth, face or hand, these terms should be understood figuratively. Similarly when human activity is attributed to God or when He appears in a theophany such depictions should not be interpreted in a literal way.

Turning to the nature of man, Saadiah contended that human beings possess souls which are substances created by God at the time when bodies are brought into being. The soul is not pre-existent nor does it enter the body from the outside; rather it uses the body as an instrument for its functions. When it is connected to a corporeal frame the soul has three central faculties (reason, spirit and desire), yet it is incapable of activity if it is divorced from the body. As for the sufferings which the soul undergoes because of its bodily connection, some are due to its negligence whereas others are inflicted for the soul's own good so it may later be rewarded.

In order to lead a fulfilled life, humans have been given commandments and prohibitions by God. These consist of two types: the first embraces such acts as reason recognizes as good or bad through a feeling of approval or disapproval which has been implanted in humans. We perceive for example that murder is wrong because it would lead to the destruction of humanity and would also frustrate God's purpose in creating the world. The second group of ordinances refers to acts which are intrinsically neither right nor wrong but are made so by God's decree. Such traditional laws are imposed on human beings essentially so that we may be rewarded for obeying them. Nevertheless these laws are not arbitrary; they have beneficial consequences as well. For instance laws of ceremonial purity teach humility and make prayer more precious for those who have been prevented from praying because of their ritual uncleanliness.

Since these traditional laws are not inherently rational in character, divine revelation is necessary to supplement man's rational capacity. In addition, divine legislation is needed to clarify the moral principles known by reason. According to Saadiah, the corpus of Jewish law cannot be abrogated; it is valid for all time. Though God rewards in an afterlife those who keep His commands and punishes those who violate his law, people have free will. Thus the Bible declares: 'I have set before you life and death . . . therefore choose life' (Deuteronomy 30:19). Similarly the rabbis proclaimed: 'Everything is in the hands of God except the fear of God.' God's foreknowledge is not the cause of a man's action – it is rather that God knows beforehand the outcome of a person's free deliberation. In propounding these theological views, Saadiah laid the groundwork for the development of Jewish philosophy in the centuries that followed.

Jewish philosophy in Muslim Spain

After the eleventh century the Mutazilite *kalam* ceased to play a central role in Jewish philosophical thought. In Islam the Mutazilites were replaced by the more orthodox Asharyites who attempted to provide a rational basis for unquestioning traditionalism. These Muslim scholars argued, for example, that everything happens because it is God's will. Further they maintained that all existing things are composed of elements of time and space directly created by God. Such doctrines were less attractive to Jewish theologians than the systems of neo-Platonism and Aristotelianism as advocated by a number of Muslim philosophers.

The first Spanish Jewish philosopher to produce a work in the neo-Platonic tradition was Solomon ben Joseph ibn Gabirol (1020–57) from Malaga. In the *Fountain of Life* ibn Gabirol argued that God and matter are not opposed as two ultimate principles – instead matter is identified with God. It emanates from the essence of the Creator forming the basis of all subsequent emanations. For ibn Gabirol the universe consists of cosmic existences flowing out of the superabundant light and goodness of the Creator; it is a reflection of God though God remains in Himself and does not enter His creation with His essence. In a religious poem 'Kingly Crown', ibn Gabirol uses neo-Platonic images to describe God's activity: 'Thou art wise and from Thy wisdom didst cause to emanate a ready will, an agent and artist as it were, to draw existence out of non-existence, as light proceeds from the eye.'

Another important Spanish writer of this period, Bahya ben Joseph ibn Pakuda (1050–1120) from Saragossa, drew on neo-Platonic ideas in the composition of his ethical work, *Duties of the Heart*. The aim of this study was to correct what he saw as the overemphasis on ritualism within rabbinic Judaism. According to ibn Pakuda, human obligations are of two types. First there are duties involving action such as ritual and ethical observances commanded by the Torah. The second category consists of responsibilities related to the inner life. Like works of Islamic mysticism, this treatise attempts to lead Jews through various ascending stages of man's inner life toward spiritual perfection and communion with God. In accordance with neo-Platonism, ibn Pakuda maintained that man's soul is celestial in origin and is placed in the body by God. But with the aid of reason and revealed law the soul can triumph over the evil inclination. The ten chapters of this book deal with various aspects of this spiritual quest including divine worship, trust in God, sincerity of purpose, humility, repentance, self-examination and asceticism.

Another important philosopher of this period was Abraham ben David Halevi ibn Daud (1110–80) from Cordova. In his major philosophical writing, *The Exalted Faith*, ibn Daud utilized Aristotelian categories in attempting to harmonize the Bible with rational thought. Following Islamic Aristotelians, ibn Daud deduced God's absolute unity from His necessary existence. For ibn Daud this concept of divine oneness precludes the possibility of any positive attributes of God. Regarding the afterlife, ibn Daud believed that the human soul is able to continue after death without the body because the activities of the intellect are not dependent on bodily existence. The most radical feature of this treatise concerns ibn Daud's view of free will and divine omniscience. Unlike other Jewish philosophers, he argued that since man has free will God does not know beforehand the undecided outcome of man's decision.

In opposition to such rationalistic formulations of Jewish belief, the contemporary Spanish theologian Judah Halevi (1075–1141) composed a treatise, *The Book of the Khazars*, to demonstrate that Judaism cannot be understood by the intellect alone. This work consists of a dialogue between a king of the Khazars and a Jewish sage who defends the Jewish faith against Aristotelian philosophy, Christianity and Islam. Though Halevi counters Christianity and the Karaites, his criticisms are directed primarily at Aristotelian philosophy which he considered the greatest threat to Judaism. For Halevi Biblical revelation rather than philosophy offers the true guide to the spiritual life. Despite its claims Aristotelianism is not scientific; its conclusions are ultimately inadequate. The God of the philosophers is unconcerned with human affairs – He is not attentive to prayer, nor does he guide history. The Torah however is based on divine encounter, and the God of the Jewish faith is concerned with human existence and is near to those who call upon Him.

Aristotelian philosophers maintain that the highest human attainment is knowledge of the most elevated type, but according to Halevi the Torah proclaims that man's highest ideal is the experience of God in prophecy. For Halevi, prophetic activity is not an actualization of the intellect, but rather a gift from God. Such prophetic inspiration is given to a few individuals and can only take place in the land of Israel. Since most Jews live in exile, no prophets have appeared since the Biblical period. Only when the messianic redemption takes place will prophetic activity again be actualized. Regarding Biblical law, Halevi stressed suprarational features. Reason can attain a conception of morality, but ritual ordinances transcend rational explanation.

Despite these criticisms of a rational understanding of God, prophecy and ritual, Halevi believed that science originated among Jews. The Jewish faith, he argued, does not conflict with the study of the natural world, nor does the Torah disagree with the conclusions of reason. Yet faith is not explained by the intellect. Thus the king of the Khazars concluded after listening to the arguments of the Jewish sage: 'I see how the God of Abraham is different from that of Aristotle.' In propounding this position, Halevi offered a serious challenge to the rationalism of medieval Jewish philosophy that preceded him and was to flourish in subsequent centuries.

The philosophy of Maimonides

Moses Maimonides (1135–1204), the greatest Jewish philosopher of the twelfth century, was born in Cordova but when the Almohades came to power he and his family were forced to emigrate. After travelling through Spain and North Africa, Maimonides eventually settled in Cairo where he wrote numerous studies ranging from *halachah* to philosophy. In his major philosophical treatise, *The Guide for the Perplexed*, he relied on the great Muslim expositors of Aristotle such as Avicenna and al-Farabi. For Maimonides reason and faith are harmoniously interrelated, and in this study he criticized various aspects of Mutazilite and Asharyite philosophy and attempted to reconcile the Torah with a number of central tenets of Aristotelianism.

The Guide for the Perplexed was deliberately written for the intellectual elite. In the introduction Maimonides explained that his book was intended only for those whose study of logic, mathematics, natural science and metaphysics had led them to a state of perplexity about seeming contradictions between the Torah and human reason. The first part of this work begins with a discussion of the anthropomorphic terms in the Bible. A literal reading of these passages implies that God is a corporeal being but according to Maimonides this is a mistake: such depictions must be understood figuratively. In this connection he argued, as did ibn Daud, that no positive attributes can be predicated of God since the Divine is an absolute unity. Thus when God is described positively in the Bible, such ascriptions must refer to his activity. The only true attributes, he contended, are negative ones; they lead to a knowledge of God because in negation no plurality is involved. Each negative attribute excludes from God's essence some imperfection. Thus when one says God is incorporeal, this means He has no body. Such negation, Maimonides believed, brings one nearer to the knowledge of the Godhead.

Turning from God's nature to prophecy, Maimonides pointed out that most people believe that God chooses any person He desires and inspires him with the prophetic spirit. Such a view is opposed by the philosophers who contend that prophecy is a human gift requiring ability and study. Rejecting both these positions, Maimonides stated that prophecy is an inspiration from God which passes through the mediation of the active intellect and then to the faculty of imagination. It requires perfection in theoretical wisdom, morality and development of the imagination. On the basis of this conception, Maimonides asserted that human beings can be divided into three classes according to the development of their reasoning capabilities. First there are those whose rational faculties are highly developed and receive influences from the active intellect but whose imagination is defective. These are wise men and philosophers. The second group consists of those where the imagination alone is in good condition, but the intellect is defective – these are statesmen, lawgivers and politicians. Thirdly there are the prophets – those whose imagination is constitutionally perfect and whose active intellect is well developed.

Maimonides insisted that God withholds prophetic inspiration from certain individuals but those whom he has selected teach speculative truth and adherence to the Torah. Unlike the other prophets who only intermittently received prophecy, Moses prophesied continuously and was the only one to give legislation. The purpose of the body of Mosaic law is to regulate society and provide for spiritual well-being and perfection. As far as ceremonial law is concerned, Maimonides argued that the purpose of a number of ritual commandments was to prevent Israel from participating in pagan cultic practices which could lead to idolatry. Sacrifice, he suggested, was a concession to the popular mentality of the ancient Israelites since the nation could not conceive of worship without sacrificial offerings.

The problem of evil is also a central theological issue in the *Guide*. Maimonides contended that evil does not exist as an independent entity; rather it is a privation of good. What appears evil, such as man's immorality to man, is frequently man's fault and can be corrected through good government. Similarly personal suffering is often the result of vice. Physical calamities – earthquakes, floods and disease – are not the result of human failing but are part of the natural order. To complain that there is more evil than good in the world results from an anthropomorphic conception of man's place in the universe – God's final purpose cannot be known. Unlike Aristotelian philosophers, Maimonides conceived of God's providence as concerned with each person. For him such providential care is proportionate to the degree that an individual has activated his intellect. In this regard, Maimonides argued that the ideal of human perfection involves reason and ethical action. To illustrate his view, he used a parable about a king's palace: those who are outside the walls have no doctrinal belief; those within the city but with their backs to the palace hold incorrect positions; others wishing to enter the palace not knowing how to do so are traditionalists who lack philosophical sophistication. But those who have entered the palace have speculated about the fundamental principles of religion. Only the person who has achieved the highest level of intellectual attainment can be near the throne of God.

Such philosophical attainment however is not in itself sufficient; to be perfect a person must go beyond communion with God to a higher state. Quoting Jeremiah 9:23–4 Maimonides proclaimed:

> Let not the wise man glory in his wisdom, let not the mighty man glory in his might, let not the rich man glory in his riches; but let him who glories glory in this, that he understands and knows me, that I am the Lord who practice steadfast love, justice, and righteousness in the earth; for in these things I delight, says the Lord.

Just as God is merciful, just and righteous, so the perfected individual should emulate God's actions in his daily life. Here then is a synthesis of the Aristotelian emphasis on intellectualism and Jewish insistence on the moral life. Such a philosophical exposition of the Jewish faith not only influenced later Jewish writers, but also had an impact on medieval Christian scholars such as Albertas Magnus and St Thomas Aquinas.

Jewish philosophy after Maimonides

By the thirteenth century most of the important philosophical texts had been translated into Hebrew by Jews living in southern France. Judah ibn Tibbon (1120–90) who emigrated from Muslim Spain to Provence translated such works as ibn Pakudah's *Duties of the Heart*, Halevi's *The Book of the Khazars*, and Saadiah Gaon's *Book of Beliefs and Opinions*; his son Samuel (1150–1230) translated Maimonides' *Guide for the Perplexed*. Furthermore, the writings of

Plato and Aristotle as well as commentaries on Aristotle by such Islamic scholars as Averroes were translated into Hebrew as well. As a consequence of this scholarly activity, Jews in Spain, Provence and Italy produced philosophical and scientific writings including commentaries on Maimonides' *Guide*. Though Maimonides was admired as a halachic authority, some Jewish scholars were troubled by his views. In particular they were dismayed that he appeared not to believe in resurrection; that he viewed prophecy, providence and immortality as dependent on intellectual attainment; that he regarded the doctrine of divine incorporality as a fundamental tenet of the Jewish faith; and that he felt that knowledge of God should be based on Aristotelian principles. For these sages Maimonides' theology was seen as a threat to Judaism and to rabbinic learning. In 1230 some of those opposed to the Maimonidean philosophical system attempted to prevent the study of the *Guide* as well as the philosophical sections of Maimonides' legal code, the *Mishnah Torah*. The bitter antagonism between Maimonideans and anti-Maimonideans came quickly to an end when Dominican inquisitors in France burned copies of Maimonides' writings – both sides were appalled by such an action. Yet opposition to Maimonides continued throughout the century. In 1300 anti-Maimonideans issued a ban against studying Greek philosophy before the age of twenty-five, but the conflict subsided when many Jews were expelled from France in 1306.

The most prominent Jewish philosopher after Maimonides who was attracted to Aristotelianism was Levi ben Gerson, known as Gersonides (1288–1344). Originally from Provence, he wrote works on a wide range of topics including mathematics, astronomy, law and philosophy. In his philosophical treatise, *The Wars of the Lord*, he discussed a variety of theological issues. Like medieval Christian thinkers he first surveyed the main Aristotelian authorities on each subject and then offered his own views. As opposed to Maimonides, Gersonides maintained that God only knows human events if they are determined by heavenly bodies; He does not know them insofar as they are dependent upon individual choice. This limitation to divine knowledge, Gersonides believed, is entirely consonant with Scripture and it is also coherent with the concept of the freedom of the will. Regarding providence, Gersonides' view was similar to that of Maimonides: the nearer a person is to the active intellect the more he receives God's care. When a person's intellectual faculties are activated, God gives him knowledge through dreams, divination or prophecy.

Another important topic in Gersonides' study is God's nature and attributes. Here again Gersonides took issue with Maimonides; it is not necessary, he argued, to confine knowledge of God to negative attributes. Positive attributes are legitimate since there is a resemblance between the qualities ascribed to God and the same attributes in human beings. According to Gersonides, if divine knowledge bears no relation to human knowledge, such attribution would make no sense. How could we be certain that knowledge is found in God if knowledge means a totally different thing for God from what it means for us? Indeed if we have no idea what the term means when applied to God, what reason could one have for preferring knowledge as a divine attribute rather than ignorance? To overcome this dilemma, Gersonides asserted that God's knowledge and human knowledge differ only in degree.

Despite this affinity between the human and the divine, God was understood by Gersonides as remote from the world. Pure intelligences, he believed, control the heavenly spheres, and the lowest sphere – the active intelligence – has dominion over earthly life. In this light miracles were seen as part of the natural order rather than as divine intrusions into the universe. As far as creation is concerned Gersonides suggested that the Biblical concept of creation should be seen not as creation *ex nihilo* but as the imposition of forms of being on eternal matter. Such theological ideas were grounded in Aristotelianism but soon this philosophical approach lost its hold on most Jewish thinkers. Jewish persecution in France, pogroms at the end of the century and conversions of Jews in Spain eclipsed such a concern to explain the Jewish faith in concepts borrowed from Greek philosophy.

The last major philosopher of Spanish Jewry was Hasdai Crescas (1340–1412) from Barcelona. After the Barcelona riots of 1391 Crescas settled in Saragossa, where he composed his philosophical treatise, *The Light of the Lord*. The purpose of this study was to offer an alternative account of the basic principles of the Jewish faith in opposition to Maimonides's thirteen principles. According to Crescas, there are several categories of belief in relation to the Torah. First there are the logical presuppositions of the law – the belief in the existence and nature of God. Added to these are the fundamental principles of the Torah, concerning providence, omniscience, prophecy, omnipotence, free will, the purpose of the law and human life. The third category consists of the logical consequences of belief in the Torah – creation, immortality, resurrection, the eternity of the Torah, the superiority of Moses and the coming of the Messiah.

In this work Crescas attempted to refute Aristotelianism by criticizing a number of doctrines found in the writings of Aristotle and Maimonides. In opposition to these thinkers Crescas argued that there is an infinite void outside the universe – hence there may be many worlds. By positing the existence of the infinite, Crescas also called into question the Aristotelian concept of an unmoved mover which was based upon the impossibility of a regress to infinity. Similarly Crescas argued that Maimonides' proofs of the existence, unity and incorporeality of God are invalid because they are based on the concept of finitude. In addition Crescas disagreed with Maimonides' opinion that no positive attributes can be applied to God. According to Crescas we cannot avoid making a comparison with human beings when we apply the terms 'cause' and 'attribute of action' to God. Maimonides was simply mistaken in thinking that such ascriptions did not imply a relationship between God and man.

Regarding divine providence, Crescas held that God acts either directly or through intermediate agents such as angels and prophets. Providence itself is essentially of two types: general providence governs the order of nature whereas special providence is concerned with the Jewish nation as well as the lives of individuals. In this respect Crescas rejected the intellectualism of Jewish philosophers such as Maimonides. Intellectual perfection, he insisted, was not the criterion of divine providence nor the basis for reward and punishment. In his discussion of prophecy, Crescas also adopted an anti-intellectual position. Unlike Maimonides Crescas accepted the traditional understanding of the prophet as a man chosen by God because of his moral virtues rather than intellectual attainment. In advocating such views Crescas was anxious to present a rational defence of the Jewish faith on non-Aristotelian grounds. Throughout his treatment of the central beliefs of the Jewish tradition, Crescas presented a view of Judaism based on the spiritual and emotional sides of man's nature rather than his intellectual and speculative capacities. In this respect he shared the same view as Judah Halevi who was equally critical of a rational presentation of the faith.

After Crescas the philosophical approach to religion lost its appeal for most Jewish thinkers in Spain. Though some thinkers were still attracted to the Maimonidean system, Aristotelianism ceased to be the dominant philosophy in the Jewish world. Instead of philosophizing about Judaism a number of subsequent Jewish writers directed their attention to defining the basic doctrines of the Jewish faith. Such Spanish thinkers as Simon ben Zemah Duran (1361–1444), Joseph Albo (1380–1445) and Isaac Arama (1420–94) devoted their writings to critiques of Maimonides' formulation of the thirteen principles of the Jewish religion.

Another Spanish Jewish philosopher, Isaac Abarbanel (1437–1508), on the other hand attempted to defend Maimonides against his critics and offered an examination of the concept of the principles of faith. Yet paradoxically Abarbanel argued that since every part of the Torah is of equal value, it is not possible to formulate an underlying list of central beliefs. According to Abarbanel, the impetus to isolate the principles of the Jewish faith is based on an analogy between religion and science. Such an approach is misguided since science requires first principles, but this is not the case for Judaism. It is a mistake, he believed, to think that one part of the Torah is superior to any other part. 'Therefore', he wrote, 'I am convinced that it is improper to postulate principles or foundations with regard to God's Torah.' By the end of the fifteenth century the impulse to rationalize the Jewish tradition in the light of Greek philosophy had come to an end, and succeeding generations of Jews turned to the mystical tradition as a basis for speculation about God's nature and His creation.

9
Medieval Jewish Mysticism

Contemporaneous with the development of Jewish philosophy and theology, Jewish thinkers during the Middle Ages elaborated a complex system of mystical thought. Drawing on the traditions of early rabbinic Judaism, these thinkers expanded and elaborated many of the mystical doctrines found in midrashic and Talmudic literature as well as in mystical tracts such as the *Sefer Yetsirah*. In their writings these mystics saw themselves as the transmitters of a secret tradition (Kabbalah) which describes a supernatural world to which all human beings are linked. One strand of this heritage focused on the nature of the spiritual world and its relationship with the terrestrial plane; the other more practical side attempted to utilize energies from the spiritual world to bring about miracle-working effects. According to these kabbalists, all of creation is in a struggle for redemption and liberation from evil, and their goal was to restore world harmony so that universal salvation would be attained through the coming of the Messiah and the establishment of the Kingdom of God.

The Hasidei Ashkenaz

The mystical texts of early rabbinic Judaism were studied by Jewish settlers in the Rhineland from approximately the ninth century. During the twelfth and thirteenth centuries these authorities – the Hasidei Ashkenaz – delved into *hekhalot* literature, the *Sefer Yetsirah*, as well as the philosophical works of such scholars as Saadiah Gaon and various Spanish and Italian Jewish neo-Platonists. Among the greatest figures of this period were the twelfth-century

Samuel ben Kalonymus of Speyer, his son Judah ben Samuel of Regensburg (1150–1217) who wrote *The Book of the Pious*, and Eleazar ben Judah of Worms (1165–1230), who composed the treatise *The Secret of Secrets*. Though the writings of these and other mystics were not systematic in character, their works do display a number of common characteristics.

In their writings these mystics were preoccupied with the mystery of divine unity. God Himself, they believed, cannot be known by human reason – thus all anthropomorphic depictions of God in Scripture should be understood as referring to God's glory which was formed out of divine fire. This divine glory – *kavod* – was revealed by God to the prophets and is made manifest to mystics in different ways through the ages. The aim of German mysticism was to attain a vision of God's glory through the cultivation of the life of pietism (*chasiduth*) which embraced devotion, saintliness and contemplation. *Chasiduth* made the highest demands on the devotee in terms of humility and altruism. The ultimate sacrifice for these Hasidim was martyrdom (*kiddush hashem*), and during this period there were ample opportunities for Jews to die in this way in the face of Christian persecution. Allied to such a manifestation of selfless love of God was the Hasidic emphasis on a profound sense of God's presence in the world; for these sages God's glory permeates all things.

Within this theological framework the concept of the Hasid (the pious one) was of paramount importance. To be a Hasid was a religious ideal which transcended all intellectual accomplishments. The Hasid was remarkable, not because of any scholarly qualities, but through his spiritual attainments. According to these scholars, the Hasid must reject and overcome every temptation of ordinary life; insults and shame must be endured. In addition, he should renounce worldly goods, mortify the flesh and make penance for any sins. Such an ascetic way of life against all obstacles would lead the devotee to the heights of true fear and love of God. In its most sublime form, such fear was conceived as identical with love and devotion, enabling joy to enter the soul. In the earlier Merkavah tradition the mystic was the keeper of holy mysteries, but for these German sages humility and self-abnegation were the hallmarks of the authentic religious life. Allied with these personal characteristics, the Hasid was perceived as capable of mastering magical powers. In the writings of Eleazar of Worms, for example, are found tracts on magic and the effectiveness of God's secret names as well as recipes for creating the *golem* (an artificial man) through letter manipulation.

Another feature of this movement concerned prayer mysticism. In the literature of the Pietists attention was given to techniques of mystical speculation based on the calculation of the words in prayers, benedictions and hymns. The number of words in a prayer as well as the numerical value were linked to Biblical passages of equal numerical value as well as with designations of God and angels. Here prominence was given to the techniques of *gematria* (the calculation of the numerical value of Hebrew words and the search for connections with other words of equal value) and *notarikon* (the interpretation of the letters of a word as abbreviations of whole sentences). According to these German Hasidim, prayer is like Jacob's ladder extended from earth to Heaven; it is a process of mystical ascent. It was in this milieu that the famous Hymn of Glory was composed – a prayer which subsequently gained a central place in the Ashkenazi liturgy. Here the unknowability of God is suffused with a longing for intimacy with the Divine:

> Sweet hymns and songs will I recite
> To sing to Thee by day and night
> Of Thee who art my soul's delight
>
> How doth my soul within me yearn
> Beneath Thy shadow to return,
> The secret mysteries to learn.
>
> Thy glory shall my discourse be,
> In images I picture Thee,
> Although myself I cannot see.
>
> In mystic utterances alone,
> By prophet and by seer made known,
> Hast Thou Thy radiant glory shown.
>
> My meditation day and night,
> May it be pleasant in Thy sight,
> For Thou art my soul's delight.

For the Hasidei Ashkenaz, such prayers as well as mystical practices and beliefs provided a means of consolation and escape from the miseries that beset the Rhineland communities during the twelfth and thirteenth centuries.

The emergence of Kabbalah

Parallel with these developments in Germany, Jewish mystics in southern France engaged in mystical speculation about the nature of

God, the soul, the existence of evil and the religious life. In twelfth-century Provence the earliest kabbalistic text, the *Bahir*, reinterpreted the concept of the *sefirot* as depicted in the *Sefer Yetsirah*. According to the *Bahir*, the *sefirot* are conceived as vessels, crowns or words that constitute the structure of the divine realm. Basing themselves on this anonymous work, various Jewish sages of Provence engaged in similar mystical reflection. Isaac the Blind (1160–1235), the son of Abraham ben David of Posquières, for example, conceived of the *sefirot* as emanations of a hidden dimension of the Godhead. Utilizing neo-Platonic ideas, he argued that out of the infinite (*Ayn Sof*) emanated the first supernal essence, the Divine Thought, from which came the remaining *sefirot*. Beings in the world beneath, he believed, are materializations of the *sefirot* at lower degrees of reality. The purpose of mystical activity is to ascend the ladder of emanations to unite with Divine Thought.

In Gerona the traditions from Isaac the Blind were broadly disseminated. One of the most important of these Geronese kabbalists was Azriel ben Menahem who replaced the Divine Thought with the Divine Will as the first emanation of the *Ayn Sof*. The most famous figure of this circle was Moses ben Nahman (1194–1270), known as Nahmanides, who helped this mystical school gain general acceptance. His involvement in kabbalistic speculation combined with his halachic authority persuaded many Jews that mystical teachings were compatible with rabbinic Judaism. In his commentary on the Torah he frequently referred to kabbalistic notions to explain the true meaning of the text. In his discussion of sacrifice, for instance, Nahmanides stated: 'By means of the sacrifices blessing emanates to the higher powers.' Here sacrifice is conceived as providing emanation to the *sefirot*; it raises human desire in order to draw it near and unite it with the desire of the higher powers and then draws the higher desire and lower desire into one desire.

During the time that these Geronese mystics were propounding their kabbalistic theories, different mystical schools of thought developed in other parts of Spain. Influenced by the Hasidei Ashkenaz and the Sufi traditions of Islam, Abraham ben Samuel Abulafia (1240–71) wrote meditative texts concerning the technique of combining the letters of the alphabet as a means of realizing human aspirations toward prophecy. As an admirer of Maimonides, he believed his system was a continuation and elaboration of the teaching of *The Guide for the Perplexed*. Another Spanish kabbalist, Isaac ibn Latif, also attempted to elaborate ideas found in Maimonides' *Guide*. For ibn Latif, the Primeval Will is the source of all emanation.

Adopting neo-Platonic conceptions, he argued that from the first created thing emanated all the other stages, referred to symbolically as light, fire, ether and water. Each of these, he believed, is the subject of a branch of wisdom: mysticism, metaphysics, astronomy and physics. According to ibn Latif, Kabbalah is superior to philosophy – the highest intellectual understanding reaches only the 'back' of the Divine whereas the 'face' is disclosed only in supra-intellectual ecstasy. True prayer leads to communion with the active intellect, and then to union of the active intellect with the first created thing. Beyond this union is the union through thought which is intended to reach the Prime Will and ultimately to stand before God Himself.

Other Spanish kabbalists were more attracted to Gnostic ideas. Isaac ha-Kohen, for example, elaborated the theory of a demonic emanation whose ten spheres are counterparts of the holy *sefirot*. The mingling of such Gnostic teaching with the Kabbalah of Gerona resulted in the publication of the major mystical work of Spanish Jewry, the *Zohar*, composed by Moses ben Shem Tov de Leon (1250– 1305) in Guadalajara. Although the author places the work in a second-century-AD setting, focusing on Rabbi Simeon bar Yochai and his disciples after the bar Kokhba uprising, the doctrines of the *Zohar* are of a much later origin. Written in Aramaic, the text is largely a *midrash* in which the Torah is given a mystical or ethical interpretation.

God and Creation

According to these various kabbalistic systems God in Himself lies beyond any speculative comprehension. To express the unknowable aspect of the Divine, early kabbalists of Provence and Spain referred to the Divine Infinite as *Ayn Sof* – the absolute perfection in which there is no distinction or plurality. The *Ayn Sof* does not reveal itself; it is beyond all thought and at times is identified with the Aristotelian First Cause. In kabbalistic teaching, creation is bound up with the manifestation of the hidden God and His outward movement. According to the *Zohar*, the *sefirot* emanate out of the hidden depths of the Godhead like a flame:

> Within the most hidden recess a dark flame issued from the mystery of the Ayn Sof, the Infinite, like a fog forming in the unformed–enclosed in a ring of that sphere, neither white nor black, neither red nor green, of no colour whatever. Only after this flame began to assume size and

dimension, did it produce radiant colours. From the innermost center of the flame sprang forth a well out of which colours issued and spread upon everything beneath, hidden in the mysterious hiddenness of Ayn Sof.

These *sefirot* emanate successively from above to below, each one revealing a stage in the process. The common order of the *sefirot* and the names most generally used are: (1) supreme crown; (2) wisdom; (3) intelligence; (4) greatness; (5) power (or judgement); (6) beauty (or compassion); (7) endurance; (8) majesty; (9) foundation (or righteous one); (10) kingdom. These ten *sefirot* are formally arranged in threes. The first triad consists of the first three *sefirot* and constitutes the intellectual realm of the inner structure of the Divine. The second triad is composed of the next three *sefirot* from the psychic or moral level of the Godhead. Finally *sefirot* 7, 8 and 9 represent the archetypes of certain forces in nature. The remaining *sefirah*, kingdom, constitutes the channel between the higher and the lower worlds. The ten *sefirot* together demonstrate how an infinite, undivided and unknowable God is the cause of all the modes of existence in the finite plane.

In their totality these *sefirot* are frequently represented as a cosmic tree of emanation. It grows from its root – the first *sefirah* – and spreads downwards in the direction of the lower worlds to those *sefirot* which constitute its trunk and its main branches. According to the *Bahir*: 'All the divine powers of the Holy One, Blessed be He, rest one upon the other and are like a tree.' Another depiction of the *sefirot* is in the form of a man: the first *sefirah* represents the head; the next three *sefirot* the cavities of the brain, the fourth and fifth *sefirot* the arms; the sixth the torso; the seventh and eighth the legs; the ninth the sexual organ; and the tenth the all-embracing totality of this image. In kabbalistic literature this heavenly man is also divided into two parts – the left column is made up of the female *sefirot* and the right column of the male. Another arrangement presents the *sefirot* as ten concentric circles, a depiction related to medieval cosmology in which the universe is understood as made up of ten spheres.

For the kabbalists the *sefirot* are dynamically structured; through them divine energy flows from its source and separates into individual channels, reuniting in the lowest *sefirah*. These *sefirot* were also understood as divine substances as well as containers of His essence; often they are portrayed as flames of fire. Yet despite their individuality, they are unified with the *Ayn Sof* in the moment of creation. According to the *Zohar*, all existences are emanations from the Deity – He is revealed in all things because He is immanent in them: 'He is separated from all things, and is at the same time not separated from all things. For all things are united in Him, and He unites Himself with all things. There is nothing which is not in Him. . . . In assuming a shape, He has given existence to all things. He has made ten lights spring from His midst.' To reconcile this process of emanation with the doctrine of creation *ex nihilo*, some kabbalists argued that the *Ayn Sof* should be seen as *Ayin* (nothingness); thus the manifestation of the Divine through the *sefirot* is a self-creation out of divine nothingness. Other kabbalists however maintained that creation does not occur within the Godhead. It takes place at a lower level where created beings are formed independent of God's essence.

The problem of evil

For the kabbalists the existence of evil was a central issue. According to one tradition evil has no objective reality. Human beings are unable to receive all of the influx from the *sefirot*, and it is this inability which is the origin of evil. Created beings are therefore estranged from the source of emanation and this results in the illusion that evil exists. Another view, as propounded in the *Bahir*, depicts the *sefirah* of power as 'an attribute whose name is evil'. On the basis of such a teaching Isaac the Blind concluded that there must be a positive root of evil and death. During the process of differentiation of forces below the *sefirot* evil became concretized. This interpretation led to the doctrine that the source of evil was the supra-abundant growth of the power of judgement – this was due to the separation and substitution of the attribute of judgement from its union with compassion. Pure judgement produced from within itself 'the other side' (*Sitra Ahra*) just as a vessel which is filled to overflowing spills its contents on the ground. The *Sitra Ahra* consists of the domain of emanations and demonic powers. Though it originated from one of God's attributes, it is not part of the Divine realm.

In the *Zohar* there is a detailed hierarchical structure of this emanation in which the *Sitra Ahra* is depicted as having ten *sefirot* of its own. The evil in the universe, the *Zohar* explains, has its origins in the leftovers of worlds that were destroyed. Another view in the *Zohar* is that the Tree of Life and the Tree of Knowledge were harmoniously bound together until Adam separated them, thereby bringing about evil into the world. This event is referred to as the cutting of the shoots and is the prototype of sins in the Bible. Evil thus originated through human action. Both these views concerning the origin of evil were reconciled in another passage where it is asserted that the disposition towards evil derives from the cosmic evil which is in the realm of the *Sitra Ahra*.

According to the *Zohar*, evil is like the bark of a tree of emanation; it is a husk or shell in which lower dimensions of existing things are encased. As the *Zohar* explains: 'When King Solomon went into the nut garden, he took a nut-shell and drew an analogy from its layers to these spirits which inspire sensual desires in human beings, as it is written, "and the delights of the sons of men are from male and female demons" ' (Ecclesiastes 2:8). This verse also indicates that the pleasures in which men indulge in the time of sleep give birth to multitudes of demons. 'The Holy One, blessed be He, found it necessary to create all things in the world to ensure its permanance, so that there should be, as it were, a brain with many membranes encircling it.' In this context evil is understood as a waste product of an organic process – it is compared to bad blood, foul water, dross after gold has been refined and the dregs of wine. Yet despite this depiction, the *Zohar* asserts that there is holiness even in the *Sitra Ahra* regardless of whether it is conceived as a result of the emanation of the last *sefirah* or as a consequence of man's sin. The domains of good and evil are intermingled and it is man's duty to separate them.

In explaining this picture of the Divine Creation, kabbalists adopted a neo-Platonic conception of a ladder of spiritual reality composed of four worlds in descending order. First is the domain of *Atzilut* (Emanation) consisting of the ten *sefirot* which form Adam Kadmon (primordial man). The second world based on *hekhalot* literature, is the realm of *Beriyah* (Creation) which is made up of the throne of glory and the seven heavenly palaces. In the third world *Yetsirah* (Formation) most of the angels dwell presided over by the angel Metatron. This is the scene of the seven heavenly halls guarded by angels to which Merkavah mystics attempt to gain admission. In the fourth world of *Asiyah* (Making) are the lower order of angels – the *ophanim* who combat evil and receive prayers. This is the spiritual archetype of the material cosmos, Heaven and the earthly world. *Asiyah* is both the last link in the divine chain of being and the domain where the *Sitra Ahra* is manifest; in this realm the forces of good struggle with the demons.

The soul

For the mystics the doctrine of a hidden God who brings about creation had important implications for the kabbalistic view of man. The Biblical idea that human beings were created in the image of God implies that man was modelled on the *sefirot*; he is a microcosm reflecting the nature of the cosmos. Since the *sefirot* are reflected in man, he is able to act as a perfecting agent through his own life and deeds. As far as souls are concerned, they are stored in one of the palaces in the sphere of *Beriyah* where they are taught divine secrets. But when they enter the world of *Asiyah*, such knowledge disappears. According to some kabbalists, the body which houses the soul is the work of the *Sitra Ahra*; others contend that corporeality is neither intrinsically good nor bad. On the other hand, there were those who saw bodily processes as reflecting heavenly processes – in such a context the sexual union was regarded as metaphysically significant.

The soul itself consists of three faculties. The lowest is the *nefesh*, the gross side of the soul – it is the vital element which is the source of animation. From the *nefesh* springs all movement, instincts and physical desires. The next faculty is the *ruah* which constitutes the moral element. Finally *neshamah* is the rational component – it functions in the study of Torah and facilitates the apprehension of the Divine. These three dimensions of the soul derive from three *sefirot*: *neshamah* which is the soul in its most perfected state emanates from the *sefirah* of wisdom; *ruah* comes from the *sefirah* of beauty; *nefesh* originates from the *sefirah* of foundation – it is the aspect of divinity which comes most into contact with the material universe. These three dimensions of the soul enable humans to fit into God's plan of creation and empower them with various duties to the cosmos which is seen as a reflection of the heavenly realm. As the *Zohar* states:

> In these three [*neshamah*, *ruah*, and *nefesh*] we find an exact image of what is above in the celestial world. For all three form only one soul, one being, where all is one ... above the nefesh is the ruah which dominates the nefesh, imposes laws upon it and enlightens it as much as its nature requires. And then high above the ruah is the neshamah which in turn rules the ruah and sheds upon it the light of life.

After death the soul leaves the body for its ascent to the higher realms. It is only after death that the soul becomes conscious of the *neshamah*. For the kabbalists the *neshamah* must become pure and perfected in order to return to the Infinite from which it emanated. In this light the doctrine of transmigration of the soul became an important element of the kabbalist system. According to the *Zohar*: 'All souls must undergo transmigration; and men do not understand the ways of the Holy One. They know not that they are brought before the tribunal both before they enter into this world and after they leave it. They know not the many transmigrations and hidden trials which they have to undergo.' Such transmigration is required because the soul must reach the highest state of its evolution before it can return to its source. Related to this view is the Zoharic theory of the pre-existence of the body: 'At the moment when the earthly union takes place, the Holy One sends to earth a form resembling a man and bearing upon itself the divine seal.'

Although the soul in its most exalted state can experience love in the union with the Infinite, it is possible to realize ecstatic love while the soul is in the body. One way to attain such realization is through serving God. The service of the Divine through love leads the soul to union with its place of origin and gives a foretaste of what will occur at death. As the *Zohar* explains: 'Whosoever serves God out of love comes into union with the holiness of the world which is to be.' Though such self-perfection of the soul is a major goal of earthly existence, the soul also has a central role in the cosmic drama of repair (*tikkun*) of disharmony in the world which was due to Adam's sin. Through the cutting off of the *sefirah* Kingdom from other *sefirot*, the *Sitra Ahra* attained dominance. Yet human beings can bring about *tikkun* since their souls can ascend higher than the angels. As the *Zohar* explains, human action has a profound effect on the higher worlds: 'It is from below that the movement starts, and there after is all perfected. If the community of Israel failed to initiate the impulse, the One above also would not move to go to her, and it is thus the yearning from below which brings about the completion above.'

The mystic way

For the mystic, deeds of *tikkun* sustain the world, activate nature to praise God, and bring about the coupling of the tenth and the six *sefirot*. Such repair is accomplished by keeping the commandments which were conceived as vessels for establishing contact with the Godhead and for ensuring divine mercy. Such a religious life provided the kabbalist with a means of integrating into the divine hierarchy of creation – the Kabbalah was able to guide the soul back to its Infinite source.

The supreme rank attainable by the soul at the end of its sojourn is the mystical cleaving to God (*devekut*). The early kabbalists of Provence defined *devekut* as the goal of the mystic way. According to Isaac the Blind: 'The principal task of the mystics and of they who contemplate on His name is, "And you shall cleave to Him" [Deuteronomy 13:4] and this is a central principle of the Torah and of prayer, and of blessings, to harmonize one's thought above, to conjoin God in His letters and to link the ten sefirot to Him.' For Nahmanides *devekut* is a state of mind in which one constantly remembers God and His love 'to the point that when [a person] speaks with someone else, his heart is not with them at all but is still before God . . . whoever cleaves in this way to his Creator becomes eligible to receive the Holy Spirit.' According to Nahmanides, the true Hasid is able to attain such a spiritual state. *Devekut* does not completely eliminate the distance between God and man – it denotes instead a state of beatitude and intimate union between the soul and its source.

In ascending the higher worlds, the path of prayer paralleled the observance of God's commandments. Yet unlike the *mitzvot*, prayer is independent of action and can become a process of meditation. Mystical prayer, accompanied by meditative *kavvanot* (intention) focusing on each prayer's kabbalistic content, was a feature of the various systems of Kabbalah. For the kabbalists prayer was seen as the ascent of man into the higher realms where the soul could integrate with the higher spheres. By using the traditional liturgy in a symbolic fashion, prayer repeats the hidden processes of the cosmos. At the time of prayer, the hierarchy of the upper realms is revealed as one of the names of God. Such disclosure is what constitutes the mystical activity of the individual in prayer as the kabbalist concentrates on the name that belongs to the domain through which his prayer is passing. The *kavvanah* involved in mystic prayer was seen as a necessary element in the mystery of heavenly unification which brought the divine down to the lowest realm and tied the *sefirot* to each other and the *Ayn Sof*. As the *Zohar* explains: 'Both upper and lower worlds are blessed through the man who performs his prayer in a union of action and word, and thus affects a unification.'

In addition to mystical meditation, the kabbalists made use of the letters of the alphabet and of the names of God for the purposes of meditative training. By engaging in the combination of letters and names, the mystic was able to empty his mind so as to concentrate on divine matters. Through such experiences the kabbalists believed they could attempt to conduct the soul to a state of the highest rapture in which divine reality was disclosed.

10
Judaism in the Early Modern Period

In the centuries following the medieval period the majority of Jews lived in Eastern Europe and in the lands of the Ottoman empire. Throughout this period most Jewish centres continued as autonomous communities regulated by traditional law. In the sphere of *halachah* the development of legal codes standardized religious observance and kabbalistic study enriched Jewish theological speculation. Yet despite these developments the Jewish population endured pogroms and massacres. Such suffering engendered messianic longing which culminated in the appearance of a messianic pretender, Shabbatai Zevi, who eventually converted to Islam to the dismay of most of his followers. This early modern period of Jewish life bridged the gap between the world of medieval Jewry and the later modern age when traditional Judaism underwent a major transformation in the light of emancipation, secularism and scientific advance.

Jews in the Ottoman empire

By the fifteenth century the Ottoman Turks had become a major world power and many Ashkenazic Jews settled in Ottoman lands. In the next century the population was supplemented by large numbers of Jewish *marranos* fleeing from the Spanish and Portuguese inquisitions. The Jewish population was further increased when many Spanish Jews sought refuge after the expulsion of Jews from Spain in 1492. In various parts of the empire – such as the Balkans, Greece, Cairo, Damascus and Istanbul – Jewish communities flourished into the sixteenth century. Some of these Sephardic immigrants prospered and became part of the Ottoman court, such as Dona Gracia (1510–69) who resided in Istanbul and served as leader as well as patron of the Jewish community. Her nephew Joseph Nasi (1524–79) was also an important figure in the Ottoman court and sponsored the establishment of a Jewish settlement of textile workers in Tiberias. This project was partly inspired by messianic longing and laid the foundations for later spiritual and social activity in Israel. This influx of Jews into the Ottoman empire revitalized Jewish religious life as well, and rabbinical academies were founded in several important centres such as Cairo, Istanbul and Salonika.

Prominent among the rabbinic scholars of this period was Joseph ben Ephraim Caro (1488–1575) who emigrated from Spain to the Balkans. In the 1520s Caro commenced a vast study of Jewish law, *The House of Joseph*, based on a number of previous codes by such scholars as Maimonides, Isaac ben Jacob Alfasi of Lucena (1013–1103), Asher ben Yecheil (1250–1327), and Jacob ben Asher (1270–1340). Caro's study was a detailed commentary to Jacob ben Asher's code, *The Sefer Ha-Turim*.

Relying on previous legal codes, Caro asserted as binding the majority decisions of the earlier scholars he regarded as most authoritative: Alfasi, Maimonides and Asher ben Yechiel. Though *The House of Joseph* was regarded as a monumental contribution to halachic learning, Caro compiled a shorter work the *Shulchan Arukh*, which listed only the binding rulings of the *halachah*. This collection, which appeared in 1564, became the authoritative code of law in the Jewish world.

Following the pattern of Asher's code, the *Shulchan Arukh* begins with laws concerning Jewish behaviour in the home and synagogue. Regarding dressing and deportment, for example, Caro's code states:

> In the Talmud it is said that a Jew is not allowed to resemble the idolater even in shoe laces; if they tie them in one way and the Israelites in another way, or if it is their custom to have red shoe laces and Israelites have black ones. An Israelite is not allowed to change the knot or the colour in order to imitate them.

In the next part, objects which are forbidden and permitted are elaborated and discussed in detail. Concerning dietary laws, for example, the *Shulchan Arukh* decrees that meat and dairy products must be separated: 'Meat and dairy products must not be eaten or cooked together . . . two Jewish acquaintances may not eat at one table, if one eats meat and the other dairy products, even though they are at odds, unless they make a noticeable mark between them.'

In the following part of the *Schulchan Arukh* marriage and family matters are explained, such as the laws regarding taking of a wife:

> It is the duty of every man to take a wife to himself, in order to fulfill the precept of propagation. The precept becomes obligatory on a man as soon as he reaches the age of eighteen. At any rate, no man should pass his twentieth year without taking a wife. Only in the event when one is deeply engrossed in the study of Torah, and he is afraid that marriage might interfere with his studies, may he delay marrying, providing he is not lustful.

The final part of Caro's compendium deals with various aspects of civil law. Regarding theft, for instance, Caro's code contends that: 'It is forbidden to derive even the slightest benefit from the property stolen or robbed which is in the criminal's possession. Even if the benefit is so trivial that the owner would not mind it, it is forbidden.' These few examples illustrate the range and complexity of this massive compendium of halachic decisions reached over centuries of rabbinic debate.

While working on the *Schulchan Arukh* Caro emigrated to Safed in Israel which had become a major centre of Jewish religious life. In the sixteenth century this small community had become a centre for the manufacture of cloth and had grown in size to a population of over 10,000 Jews. Here Talmudic academies were established and small groups engaged in the study of kabbalistic literature as they piously awaited the coming of the Messiah. Heightened by the expulsion of Jews from Spain and Portugal, such messianic expectation became a prevalent theme of religious poetry written in Safed during this period. The hymn composed by Solomon ha-Levy Alkabetz, 'Come, My Beloved', for instance, speaks of the Holy City as an abode for the Sabbath bride and the Davidic King: 'Come, my beloved, to meet the bride . . . O Sanctuary of our King, O city, arise, go forth from thy overthrow; long enough hast Thou dwelt in the valley of weeping . . . shake thyself from the dust; arise, put on the garments of Thy glory O My people.' In this town mystics also participated in various ascetic practices such as fasting, public confessions of sins, wearing sackcloth and ashes, and praying at the graves of venerable sages. Such self-mortification was carried to an extreme by Abraham ha-Levi Beruchim who wandered through the streets of Safed calling on people to repent; he then led those he attracted to the synagogue, climbed into a sack, and ordered these individuals to throw stones at him.

Lurianic Kabbalah

In this centre of kabbalistic activity one of the greatest mystics of Safed, Moses Cordovero (1522–70), collected, organized and interpreted the teachings of earlier mystical authors. His work constitutes a systematic summary of the Kabbalah up to his time, and in his most important treatise, *Pardes*, he outlined the Zoharic concepts of the Godhead, the *sefirot*, the celestial powers and the earthly processes. In this study he described the *sefirot* as vessels in which the light of the *Ayn Sof* is contained and through which it is reflected in different forms. For Cordovero the Godhead is in this way manifest in every part of the finite world. In another important work, *The Palm Tree of Deborah*, he expressed the notion that in order to achieve the highest degree of the religious life, one should not only observe the commandments but also imitate divine processes and patterns.

Later in the sixteenth century kabbalistic speculation was transformed by the greatest mystic of Safed, Isaac Luria (1534–72). Originally brought up in Egypt where he studied the Talmud and engaged in business, Luria withdrew to an island on the Nile where he meditated on the *Zohar* for seven years. In 1569 he arrived in Safed and died two years later after having passed on his teaching to a small group of disciples. Of primary importance in the Lurianic system is the mystery of creation. In the literature of early kabbalists creation was understood as a positive act: the will to create was awakened within the Godhead and this resulted in a long process of emanation. For Luria however creation was a negative event: the *Ayn Sof* had to bring into being an empty space in which creation could occur since divine light was everywhere leaving no room for creation to take place. This was accomplished by the process of *tzimtzum* – the contraction of the Godhead into itself. Thus the first act was not positive, but rather one that demanded withdrawal. God had to go into exile from the empty space (*tehiru*) so that the process of creation could be initiated. *Tzimtzum* therefore postulates divine exile at the first step of creation.

After this act of withdrawal, a line of light flowed from the Godhead into the *tehiru* and took on the shape of the *sefirot* in the form of Adam Kadmon. In this process divine lights created the vessels – the external shapes of the *sefirot* – which gave specific characteristics to each divine emanation. Yet these vessels were not strong enough to contain such pure light and they shattered. This breaking of the vessels (*shevirat ha-kelim*) brought disaster and upheaval to the emerging emanations: the lower vessels broke down and fell; the three highest emanations were damaged; and the empty space was divided into two parts. The first part consisted of the broken vessels with many divine sparks clinging to them; the second part was the upper realm where the pure light of God escaped to preserve its purity.

In explaining the purpose of the *tzimtzum*, Luria pointed out that the *Ayn Sof* before creation was not completely unified – there were elements in it that were potentially different from the rest of the Godhead. The *tzimtzum* separated these different elements from one another. After this contraction occurred a residue was left behind (*reshimu*) like water clinging to a bucket after it was emptied. This residue included different elements that were part of the Godhead, and after the withdrawal, they were emptied into the empty space. Thus the separation of different elements from the Godhead was accomplished. The reason for the emanation of the divine powers and the formation of primordial man was the attempt to integrate these now separate elements into the scheme of creation and thereby transform them into co-operative forces. Their task was to create the vessels of the *sefirot* into which the divine lights would flow. But the breaking of the vessels was a rebellion of these diferent elements, a refusal to participate in the process of creation. And by this rebellious act they were able to attain a realm of their own in the lower part of the *tehiru*; after the breaking of the vessels, these elements expressed themselves as the powers of evil.

Following the shattering of the vessels the cosmos was divided into two parts – the kingdom of evil in the lower part and the realm of divine light in the upper part. For Luria evil was seen as opposed to existence; therefore it was not able to exist by its own power. Instead it had to derive spiritual force from the divine light. This was accomplished by keeping captive the sparks of the divine light that fell with them when the vessels were broken and subsequently gave sustenance to the satanic domain. Divine attempts to bring unity to all existence now had to focus on the struggle to overcome the evil forces. This was achieved by a continuing process of divine emanation which at first created the *sefirot*, the sky, the earth, the Garden of Eden and human beings. Man was intended to serve as the battleground for this conflict between good and evil. In this regard Adam reflected symbolically the dualism in the cosmos – he possessed a sacred soul while his body represented the evil forces. God's intention was that Adam defeat the evil within himself and bring about Satan's downfall. But when Adam failed, a catastrophe occurred parallel to the breaking of the vessels; instead of divine sparks being saved and uplifted, many new divine lights fell and evil became stronger.

Rather than relying on the action of one person, God then chose the people of Israel to vanquish evil and raise up the captive sparks. The Torah was given to symbolize the Jews' acceptance of this allotted task. When the ancient Israelites undertook to keep the law, redemption seemed imminent. Yet the people of Israel then created the golden calf, a sin parallel to Adam's disobedience. Again divine sparks fell and the forces of evil were renewed. For Luria, history is a record of attempts by the powers of good to rescue these sparks and unite the divine and earthly spheres. Luria and his disciples believed they were living in the final stages of this last attempt to overcome evil in which the coming of the Messiah would signify the end of the struggle.

Related to the contraction of God, the breaking of the vessels and the exiled sparks, was Luria's conception of *tikkun*. For Lurianic mystics, this concept refers to the mending of what was broken during the *shevirah*. After the catastrophe in the divine realm, the process of restoration began and every disaster was seen as a setback in this process. In this battle, keeping God's commandments was understood as contributing to repair – the divine sparks which fell down can be redeemed by ethical and religious deeds. According to Luria, a spark is attached to all prayers and moral acts; if the Jew keeps the ethical and religious law these sparks are redeemed and lifted up. When the process is complete, evil will disappear. But every time a Jew sins a spark is captured and plunges into the satanic abyss. Every deed or misdeed thus has cosmic significance in the system of Lurianic Kabbalah.

The Shabbatean movement

By the beginning of the seventeenth century Lurianic mysticism had made a major impact on Sephardic Jewry, and messianic expectations had also become a central feature of Jewish life. In this milieu the arrival of a self-proclaimed messianic King, Shabbatai Zevi (1626–76) brought about a transformation of Jewish life and thought. Born in Smyrna into a wealthy family, Shabbatai had received a traditional Jewish education and later engaged in study of the *Zohar*. After leaving Smyrna in the 1650s he spent ten years in various cities in Greece as well as in Istanbul and Jerusalem. Eventually he became part of a kabbalistic group in Cairo and travelled to Gaza where he encountered Nathan Benjamin Levi (1644–80) who believed Shabbatai was the Messiah. In 1665 his Messiahship was proclaimed, and Nathan sent letters to Jews in the diaspora asking them to repent and recognize Shabbatai Zevi as their redeemer. Shabbatai, he announced, would take the Sultan's crown, bring back the lost tribes, and inaugurate the period of messianic redemption.

After a brief sojourn in Jerusalem, Shabbatai went to Smyrna where he encountered strong opposition on the part of some local rabbis. In response he denounced the disbelievers and declared that he was the Anointed of the God of Jacob. This action evoked a hysterical response – a number of Jews fell into trances and had visions of him on a royal throne crowned as King of Israel. In 1666 he journeyed to Istanbul, but on the order of the grand vizier he was arrested and put into prison. Within a short time the prison quarters became a messianic court; pilgrims from all over the world made their way to Istanbul to join in messianic rituals and in ascetic activities. In addition hymns were written in his honour and new festivals were introduced. According to Nathan, who remained in Gaza, the alteration in Shabbatai's moods from illumination to withdrawal symbolized his soul's struggle with demonic powers: at times he was imprisoned by the powers of evil (*kelippot*) but at other moments he prevailed against them.

This same year Shabbatai spent three days with the Polish kabbalist, Nehemiah ha-Kohen, who later denounced him to the Turkish authorities. Shabbatai was brought to court and given the choice between conversion and death. In the face of this alternative, he converted to Islam and took on the name Mehemet Effendi. Such an act of apostasy scandalized most of his followers, but he defended himself by asserting that he had become a Muslim in obeisance to God's commands. Many of his followers accepted this explanation and refused to give up their belief. Some thought it was not Shabbatai who had become a Muslim, but rather a phantom who had taken on his appearance; the Messiah himself had ascended to Heaven. Others cited Biblical and rabbinic sources to justify Shabbatai's action. Nathan explained that the messianic task involved taking on the humiliation of being portrayed as a traitor to his people. Furthermore, he argued on the basis of Lurianic Kabbalah that there were two kinds of divine light – a creative light and another light opposed to the existence of anything other than the *Ayn Sof*. While creative light formed structures of creation in the empty space, the other light became after the *tzimtzum* the power of evil. According to Nathan, the soul of the Messiah had been struggling against the power of evil from the beginning; his purpose was to allow divine light to penetrate this domain and bring about repair (*tikkun*). In order to do this, the soul of the Messiah was not obliged to keep the law, but was free to descend into the abyss to liberate sparks and thereby conquer evil. In this light Shabbatai's conversion to Islam was explicable.

After Shabbatai's act of apostasy, Nathan visited him in the Balkans and then travelled to Rome where he performed secret rites to bring about the end of the Papacy. Shabbatai remained in Adrianople and Istanbul where he lived as both Muslim and Jew. In 1672 he was deported to Albania where he disclosed his own kabbalistic teaching to his supporters. After he died in 1676, Nathan declared that Shabbatai had ascended to the supernal world. Eventually a number of groups continued in their belief that Shabbatai was the Messiah including a sect, the Dissidents (Doenmeh), which professed Islam publicly but nevertheless adhered to their own traditions. Marrying among themselves, they eventually evolved into antinomian sub-groups which violated Jewish sexual laws and asserted the divinity of Shabbatai and their leader, Baruchiah Russo. In Italy several Shabbatean groups also emerged and propagated their views.

In the eighteenth century the most important Shabbatean sect was led by Jacob Frank (1726–91) who was influenced by the Doenmeh in Turkey. Believing himself to be the incarnation of Shabbatai, Frank announced that he was the second person of the Trinity and gathered together a circle of disciples who indulged in licentious orgies. In the 1750s disputations took place between traditional Jews and Frankists; subsequently Frank expressed his willingness to become a Christian but he wished to maintain his own group. This request was refused by Church leaders, yet Frank and his disciples were baptized. The clergy however became aware that Frank's trinitarian beliefs were not consonant with Christian doctrine, and he was imprisoned in 1760 for thirteen years; Frank then settled in Germany where he continued to subscribe to a variant of the Shabbatean kabbalistic tradition.

Jewry in eastern Europe

During the medieval period Ashkenazic Jewry in Poland was increased by migration from the Crimea, the Russian steppes, the Middle East and Spain. In 1264 the Prince of Kalisz issued a charter to the Jews granting them legal protection; this was followed in the next century by a series of decrees by King Casimir III which expanded their charter to include the entire Polish kingdom. In 1388 the Grand Duke of Lithuania granted similar rights to the Jews which were renewed in the middle of the fifteenth century by Casimir IV Jagiello. By these decrees Polish and Lithuanian rulers provided a relatively secure basis for Jewish communal existence. In this environment Polish Jews became fiscal agents, tax collectors and managers of nobelemen's estates; in addition some Jews leased lands and supervised various agricultural activities such as farming, harvesting, manufacture and export. Yet despite such prosperity, the Polish Jewish community was subject to various forms of discrimination: Jews were forced to wear garments different from other members of society; they were the victims of outbursts of anti-Jewish persecution; and occasionally Jews were accused of desecrating the host and using the blood of Christians for ritual purposes.

By the beginning of the fifteenth century the Polish Jewish community numbered 10–15,000 Jews, and in the next century the population grew to over 150,000. In the sixteenth and seventeenth centuries the Polish nobility who owned large tracts of land in the Ukraine employed Jews on their estates; there they collected taxes, fees, tolls and produce from the serfs. Noblemen also established private cities in which they welcomed Jews as employees in their houses, where they undertook business activities. Within this milieu Polish Jewry was regulated along the lines of communal self-government. Each local community (*kehillah*) engaged a Board of Trustees that collected taxes for the government and provided educational and other necessary facilities for Jewish life. In the larger cities, the *kehillot* were supervised by paid officials including rabbis who were usually employed for three-year periods to serve as authorities in matters of Jewish law as well as heads of Talmudic academies.

As a result of this efflorescence of Jewish life, Poland became a great centre of scholarship. In the rabbinical academies the method of *hilluk* (the differentiation and reconciliation of rabbinical opinions) generated considerable activity in the study of Talmudic law. Moreover, a number of scholars collected together the legal interpretations of previous halachists, and commentaries were written on the *Schulchan Arukh*. To regulate Jewish life in the country at large, Polish Jews established regional federations that administered Jewish affairs from the mid-sixteenth to the mid-eighteenth centuries. Further, a Council of the Four Lands composed of the most eminent rabbinical and lay leaders met twice a year to allocate taxes to the synods of *kehillot*, select and finance Jewish representatives to the Polish court, and issue ordinances regarding a wide range of Jewish interests and activities.

In the midst of this general prosperity, the Polish Jewish community was subject to a series of massacres in the seventeenth century carried out by Cossacks of the Ukraine as well as Crimean Tartars and Ukrainian peasants who rebelled against the Polish nobility. In 1648 Bogdan Chmielnicki was elected hetman of the Cossacks and thereupon instigated an insurrection against the Polish gentry which had previously oppressed the Cossack population. As administrators of noblemen's estates, Jews were slaughtered in these revolts. Estates and manor houses were destroyed and victims were flayed, burned alive and mutilated. Infants were murdered and cast into wells; women were cut open and sewn up again with live cats thrust into their wounds. According to a contemporary Jewish account:

> These persons died cruel and bitter deaths. Some were skinned alive and their flesh was thrown to the dogs; some had their hands and limbs chopped off, and their bodies thrown on the highways only to be trampled by wagons and crushed by horses; some had wounds inflicted on them . . . some children were pierced by spears, roasted on the fire, and then brought to their mothers to be eaten.

In these massacres thousands of Jews died in towns east of the Dnieper and elsewhere.

As the Cossacks advanced, the Polish king died and was succeeded by John Casimir who attempted to negotiate with the Cossacks who demanded an independent Ukrainian state. After several more years of battle, Chmielnicki appealed to the Russian allies who invaded north-western Poland and the Ukraine. In 1655 the Swedes advanced into western Poland, but by the following year a Polish partisan movement drove back these foreign invaders. Finally in 1667 Russia and Poland signed the Treaty of Adrusovo which distributed the western Ukraine to Poland, and the eastern Ukraine and the Smolensk region to Russia. During these years of war the Jewish population was decimated by the various opposing forces: the Cossacks and Ukrainian peasants regarded Jews as representatives of the Polish aristocracy; the Russians who did not allow Jews to settle in the lands joined the Cossack hordes in this slaughter; and the Polish partisans saw Jews as allied with the Swedes. Approximately a quarter of the entire Jewish community died in this onslaught, and thousands were ransomed from the Tartars in the slave markets in Istanbul.

As the century progressed, Jewish life in Poland became more insecure due to political instability; nevertheless the Jewish community considerably increased in size during the eighteenth century. Approximately a third of Polish Jewry lived in the countryside in small groups where they were subject to repeated blood libel accusations. In the 1730s and 1740s Cossacks known as Haidemaks invaded the Ukraine robbing and murdering Jewish inhabitants, and finally butchering the Jewish community of Uman in 1768. Throughout this period the Polish *kehillot* were heavily taxed, and at times claims were made that the leaders of the Jewish community placed most of the tax burdens on the poor.

In Lithuania, on the other hand, Jewish life flourished, and Vilna became an important centre of rabbinic scholarship. Here Elijah ben Solomon Zalman (1720–97), referred to as the Vilna Gaon, lectured to disciples on a wide range of subjects and composed commentaries on the Bible, Mishnah, Talmud, *midrashim*, the *Sefer Yetsirah*, *Zohar* and the *Shulchan Arukh*. Unlike earlier eastern European sages, he rejected the method of *hilluk* and focused on the simple meaning of the text. In addition his interests extended to secular fields such as algebra, geometry, astronomy and geography. As a symbol of rabbinic learning, he stood out against the excesses of religious piety which began to make an impact on Polish Jewry in the later half of the eighteenth century.

Jewry in Italy, Germany and Holland

In the medieval period Spain and Provence played leading roles in the development of Jewish philosophy and mysticism. Yet by the fourteenth century these communities had lost their influence as a result of increased persecution, and many Jews were attracted to northern Italian states to act as moneylenders for the middle classes. In 1500 Jewish communities existed in such cities as Ferrara, Mantua, Venice, Padua, Florence and Rome. During the Renaissance, some Jews emulated the lifestyle of the Italian aristocracy and contacts were established with Italian humanists such as Pico della Mirandola. The *Zohar* in particular exerted a strong influence on these Italian thinkers and resulted in the outpouring of Christian kabbalistic writing. On the Jewish side, the study of classical sources in the Renaissance made a significant impression on Jewish scholars and preachers. In addition Italy became a major centre for Jewish printing; synagogue music was written in Italy in the Renaissance style, and a Jewish theatre was established by Leone de'Sommo (1527–92) for the production of Hebrew drama. Among Jewish scholars influenced by the Renaissance, Azariah dei Rossi (1511–78) applied the writings of classical antiquity to the understanding of rabbinic sources (although this modern approach evoked a hostile response among rabbis in Italy, central Europe and the Middle East).

Despite this positive contact between humanists and Jews, Christian persecution and expulsion occurred repeatedly. In the sixteenth century the Counter-Reformation Church attempted to isolate the Jewish community. The Talmud was burned in 1553, and two years later Pope Paul IV reinstated the segregationist edict of the Fourth Lateran Council forcing Jews to live in ghettos and barring them from most areas of economic life. In addition, *marranos* who took up the Jewish tradition were burned at the stake and Jews were expelled from most Church domains. As a result of these measures Italian Jewry retreated to the more secure world of traditional rabbinic study and kabbalistic speculation.

In Germany the growth of Protestantism frequently led to adverse conditions for the Jewish population. Though Martin Luther was initially well disposed to the Jews, he soon came to realize that the Jewish community was intent on remaining true to its faith. As a consequence he composed a virulent attack on the Jews: 'Their synagogues or churches', he declared,

> should be set on fire, and whatever does not burn up should be covered or spread over with dirt so that no one may ever be able to see a cinder or stone of it. And this ought to be done for the honour of God and of Christianity in order that God may see that we are Christians, and that we have not wittingly tolerated or approved of such public lying, cursing, and blaspheming of His Son and His Christians . . . their homes should likewise be broken down and destroyed. For they perpetrate the same things there that they do in their synagogues . . . they should be deprived of their prayerbooks and Talmuds in which such idolatry, lies, cursing and blasphemy are taught.

At the beginning of the early modern period German Jews lived primarily in villages where they were oppressed by discriminatory legislation, but by the middle of the sixteenth century they were freed from the restrictions against living in cities. As a result a new class of court Jews (*hofjuden*) offered their services to German princes. These Jews utilized their connections with co-religionists in North Atlantic countries, in Poland and Lithuania as well as in Mediterranean states to the commercial advantage of their employers. They were engaged in providing military equipment, arranging loans, managing mints, providing the court with clothes and jewellery and founding industries. In return these court Jews were released from many Jewish disabilities and were free to settle in restricted areas; a number of these favoured individuals were appointed by the rulers as chief elders of the Jewish community, and they acted as spokesmen and defenders of German Jewry.

In Holland some Jews had also attained an important influence on trade and finance. By the mid-seventeenth century both *marranos* and Ashkenazic Jews came to Amsterdam and established themselves in various areas of economic activity. By the end of the century there were nearly 10,000 Jews in Amsterdam; there the Jewish community was employed on the stock exchange, in the sugar, tobacco and diamond trades, and in insurance, manufacturing, printing and banking. In this milieu Jewish cultural activity flourished: Jewish writers published works of drama, theology and mystical lore. Though Jews in Holland were not granted full rights as citizens, they nevertheless enjoyed religious freedom, personal protection and the liberty of participating in a wide range of economic affairs.

11
From Hasidism to the Enlightenment

By the middle of the eighteenth century, the Jewish community had suffered numerous waves of persecution and was deeply dispirited by the conversion of Shabbatai Zevi. In this environment the Hasidic movement – grounded in Kabbalah – sought to revitalize Jewish life. Though Hasidism appealed to a large number of Jews, the spirit of humanism transformed Jewish existence. The French Revolution followed by the Napoleonic period radically changed the status of the Jewish masses, enabling them to enter into European life and culture. The spirit of emancipation unleashed by these events swept across Europe and freed Jews from their traditional lifestyle. These changes affected the structure of the *kehillah* and raised important questions about the nature of Jewish life and existence in modern society.

The rise of the Hasidic movement

Following the massacres of the previous century, many Polish Jews became disenchanted with rabbinic Judaism and through Hasidism sought individual salvation by means of religious pietism. The founder of this new movement was Israel ben Eleazer (1700–60) known as the Baal Shem Tov (or Besht). According to tradition, Israel ben Eleazar was born in southern Poland and in his twenties journeyed with his wife to the Carpathian mountains. In the 1730s he travelled to Mezibozh where he performed various miracles and instructed his disciples about kabbalistic lore. By the 1740s he had attracted a considerable number of disciples who passed on his teaching. After his death in 1760, Dov Baer (1710–72) became the leader of this sect and Hasidism spread to southern Poland, the Ukraine and Lithuania.

The growth of this movement engendered considerable hostility on the part of rabbinic authorities. In particular the rabbinic leadership of Vilna issued an edict of excommunication; the Hasidim were charged with permissiveness in their observance of the commandments, laxity in the study of the Torah, excess in prayer, and preference for the Lurianic rather than the Ashkenazic prayerbook. In subsequent years the Hasidim and their opponents (the *mitnagdim*) bitterly denounced one another. Relations deteriorated further when Jacob Joseph of Polonnoye published a book critical of the rabbiniate; his work was burned and in 1781 the *mitnagdim* ordered that all relations with the Hasidim cease. By the end of the century the Jewish religious establishment of Vilna denounced the Hasidim to the Russian government, an act which resulted in the imprisonment of several leaders. Despite such condemnation the Hasidic movement was eventually recognized by the Russian and Austrian governments; in the ensuing years the movement divided into a number of separate groups under different leaders who passed on positions of authority to their descendants.

Hasidism initiated a profound change in Jewish religious pietism. In the medieval period, the Hasidei Ashkenaz attempted to achieve perfection through various mystical activities. This tradition was carried on by Lurianic kabbalists who engaged in various forms of self-mortification. In opposition to such ascetic practices, the Besht and his followers emphasized the omnipresence of God rather than the shattering of the vessels and the imprisonment of divine sparks by the powers of evil. For Hasidic Judaism there is no place where God is absent; the doctrine of the *tzimtzum* was interpreted by Hasidic sages as only an apparent withdrawal of the divine presence. Divine light, they believed, is everywhere. As the Besht explained: in every one of man's troubles, physical and spiritual, even in that trouble God Himself is there.

For some Hasidim cleaving to God (*devekut*) in prayer was understood as the annihilation of selfhood and the ascent of the soul to divine light. In this context joy, humility, gratitude and spontaneity were seen as essential features of Hasidic worship. The central obstacles to concentration in prayer are distracting thoughts; according to Hasidism such sinful intentions contain a divine spark which can be released. In this regard the traditional kabbalistic stress on theological speculation was replaced by a preoccupation with mystical psychology in which inner bliss was conceived as the highest aim rather than repair (*tikkun*) of the cosmos. For the Beshtian Hasidim it was also possible to achieve *devekut* in daily activities including eating, drinking, business affairs and sex. Such ordinary acts become religious if in performing them one cleaves to God, and *devekut* is thus attainable by all Jews rather than a scholarly elite. Unlike the earlier mystical tradition, Hasidism provided a means by which ordinary Jews could reach a state of spiritual ecstasy. Hasidic worship embraced singing, dancing and joyful devotion in anticipation of the period of messianic redemption.

Another central feature of this new movement was the institution of the zaddik (or rebbe) which gave expression to a widespread disillusionment with rabbinic leadership. According to Hasidism, the zaddikim were spiritually superior individuals who have attained the highest level of *devekut*. The goal of the zaddik was to elevate the souls of his flock to the divine light; his tasks included pleading to God for his people, immersing himself in their everyday affairs, and counselling and strengthening them. As an authoritarian figure the zaddik was seen by his followers as possessing miraculous power to ascend to the divine realm. In this context *devekut* to God involved cleaving to the zaddik. Given this emphasis on the role of the rebbe, Hasidic literature included summaries of the spiritual and kabbalistic teachings of various famous zaddikim as well as stories about their miraculous deeds. Foremost among these leading figures was Zusya of Hanipol (eighteenth century), Shneur Zalman of Liady (1747–1812), Levi Yitzhak of Berdichev (1740–1810), and Nahman of Bratzlav (1772–1811). These various leaders developed their own customs, doctrines and music and gathered around themselves disciples who made pilgrimages to their courts in the Ukraine and in Polish Galicia. In central Poland Hasidism emphasized the centrality of faith and Talmudic study; Lubavich Hasidim in Lithuania, on the other hand, combined kabbalistic speculation and rabbinic scholarship.

The status of Jewry in central and western Europe

In many respects the medieval period extended into the eighteenth century for the Jewish community. Despite the numerous changes taking place in European society, monarchs continued to rule by divine right. In addition the aristocracy was exempt from taxation and enjoyed special privileges; the established Church retained control over religious matters; and merchants and artisans closed ranks against outsiders. At the other end of the social scale peasants continued to be burdened with obligations to feudal masters, and in eastern and central Europe serfs were enslaved and exploited. By 1770 nearly 2 million Jews lived in this environment in Christian Europe. In some countries such as England and Holland they were relatively free from economic and social restrictions. The English and Dutch governments, for example, did not interfere with the private affairs and religious life of the Jewish population. Central European Jewry however was subject to a wide range of oppressive legal restrictions, and Jews were confined to special areas of residence. Furthermore Jews were forced to sew signs on their cloaks or wear special hats to distinguish them from their non-Jewish neighbours.

By the 1770s and 1780s the treatment of Jews in central Europe greatly improved due to the influence of such polemicists as Wilhelm Christian Dohm (1751–1820). In an influential tract, *Concerning the Amelioration of the Civil Status of the Jews*, Dohm argued that Jews did not pose any threat and could become valuable and patriotic citizens. A wise and benevolent society, he stressed, should abolish restrictions which prevent the Jewish population from having close contact with Christians and acquiring secular knowledge. All occupations, he argued, should be open to Jews and educational opportunities should be provided. The Holy Roman Emperor Joseph II (1741–90) echoed such sentiments. In 1781 he abolished the Jewish badge as well as taxes imposed on Jewish travellers; in the following year he issued an edict of toleration which granted Jews of Vienna a freedom in trade and industry and the right of residence outside Jewish quarters. Moreover, regulations prohibiting Jews from leaving their homes before noon on Sunday and attending places of public amusement were abolished. Jews were also permitted to send their children to state schools or set up their own educational institutions. In 1784 Jewish judicial autonomy was abolished and three years later some Jews were inducted into the Hapsburg army.

As in Germany, reforms in France during the 1770s and 1780s ameliorated the situation of the Jewish population. Though Sephardic Jews in Paris and in the south and south-west lived in comfort and security, the Ashkenazic Jews of Alsace and Lorraine had a traditional Jewish lifestyle and were subject to a variety of disabilities. In 1789 the National Assembly issued a declaration proclaiming that all human beings are born and remain free and equal in rights and that no person should be persecuted for his opinions as long as they do not subvert civil law. In 1790 the Sephardim of south-west France and Jews from Papal Avignon were granted citizenship. This decree was followed in September 1791 by a resolution which granted citizenship rights to all Jews:

> The National Assembly, considering that the conditions requisite to be a French citizen, and to become an active citizen, are fixed by the constitution, and that every man who, being duly qualified, takes the civic oath, and engages to fulfil all the duties prescribed by the constitution, has a right to all the advantages it ensures – annuls all adjournments, restrictions and exceptions, contained in the preceding decrees, affecting individuals of the Jewish persuasion who shall take the civic oath.

This change in Jewish status occurred elsewhere in Europe as well – in 1796 the Dutch Jews of the Batavian republic were also granted full citizenship rights and in 1797 the ghettos of Padua and Rome were abolished.

In 1799 Napoleon became the First Consul of France and five years later he was proclaimed Emperor. Napoleon's Code of Civil Law propounded in 1804 established the right of all inhabitants to follow any trade and declared equality for all. After 1806 a number of German principalities were united in the French kingdom of Westphalia where Jews were granted the same rights. Despite these advances the situation of Jews did not undergo a complete transformation, and Napoleon still desired to regulate Jewish affairs. In July 1806 he convened an Assembly of Jewish Notables to consider a number of issues: do Jewish marriage and divorce procedures conflict with French civil law? Are Jews allowed to marry Christians? Do French Jews consider Frenchmen their compatriots and is France their country?

In reply the Assembly decreed that Jewish law is compatible with French civil law; Jewish divorce and marriage are not binding unless preceded by a civil act; mixed marriage is legal but cannot be sanctioned by the Jewish faith; France is the homeland of French Jews and Frenchmen should be seen as their kin. In the next year Napoleon summoned a Grand Sanhedrin consisting of rabbis and laymen to confirm the views of the Assembly. This body pledged its allegiance to the Emperor and nullified any features of the Jewish tradition that conflicted with the particular requirements of citizenship. In 1808 Napoleon issued two edicts regarding the Jewish community. In the first he set up a system of district boards of rabbis and laymen (consistories) to regulate Jewish affairs under the supervision of a central body in Paris. These consistories were responsible for maintaining synagogues and religious institutions, enforcing laws of conscription, overseeing changes in occupations ordered by the government and acting as a local police force. Napoleon's second decree postponed, reduced or abrogated all debts owed to Jews, regulated Jewish trade and residence rights and prohibited Jewish army conscripts from hiring substitutes.

After Napoleon's defeat and abdication, the map of Europe was redrawn by the Congress of Vienna between 1814 and 1815 and in addition the diplomats at the Congress issued a resolution that instructed the German confederation to ameliorate the status of the Jews. Yet despite this decree the German governments disowned the rights of equality that had previously been granted to Jews by the French and instead imposed restrictions on residence and occupation. In place of the spirit of emancipation unleashed by the French Revolution, Germany became increasingly patriotic and xenophobic. Various academics maintained that the Jews were 'Asiatic aliens' and insisted that they could not enter into German–Christian culture without converting to Christianity – in 1819 German Jewry was attacked in cities and the countryside (the Hep-Hep riots). After 1830 however a more liberal attitude prevailed and various writers advocated a more tolerant approach. The most important Jewish exponent of emancipation, Gabriel Riesser (1806–63), argued that the Jews were not a separate nation and were capable of loving Germany as their homeland. Jewish converts to Christianity such as Heinrich Heine (1797–1856) and Ludwig Buevne also defended the rights of Jews during this period.

The French revolution of 1848 which led to outbreaks in Prussia, Austria, Hungary, Italy and Bohemia forced rulers to grant constitutions which guaranteed freedom of speech, assembly and religion. In Germany a National Assembly was convened to draft a constitution which included a bill of rights designating civil political and religious liberty for all Germans. Although this constitution did not come into effect because the revolution was suppressed, the 1850s and 1860s witnessed economic and industrial expansion in Germany in which liberal politicians advocated a policy of civil equality. In 1869 the parliament of the North German Federation proclaimed Jewish emancipation for all its constituents, and in 1871, when all of Germany excluding Austria became the German Reich under the Hohenzollern dynasty, Jewish emancipation was complete. All restrictions concerning professions, marriage, real estate and the right to vote were eliminated.

The Jewish community of eastern Europe

Compared with the west the social and political conditions of eastern European Jewry were less conducive to emancipation. After the partitions of Poland in the later half of the eighteenth century and the decision of the Congress of Vienna to place the Duchy of Warsaw under Alexander I, most of Polish Jewry was under Russian rule. At the beginning of the nineteenth century Russia preserved its previous social order: social classes were legally segregated; the aristocracy maintained its privileges; the peasantry lived as serfs; and the Church was under state control. In many towns and villages during this period Jews were in the majority and engaged in a wide range of occupations. In the countryside they worked as leasers of estates, mills, forests, distilleries and inns, but increasingly many of these village Jews migrated to larger urban centres where they laboured as members of the working class. Despite this influx into the cities, the Jewish population retained its traditional religious and ethnic distinctiveness.

Initially Catherine the Great exhibited tolerance toward her Jewish subjects, but in 1791 Jewish merchants were prohibited from settling in central Russia. Only in the southern Ukraine were Jews allowed to establish a community; this exception was followed several years later by the granting of permission for Jews to live in other areas such as Kiev. In 1804 Alexander I (1801–25) specified territory in western Russia as an area in which Jews would be allowed to reside, and this was known as the Pale of Settlement. After several attempts to expel Jews from the countryside, the Tsar in 1817 initiated a new policy of integrating the Jewish community into the poulation by founding a society of Israelite Christians which extended legal and financial concessions to baptized Jews. In 1824 the deportation of Jews from villages began; in the same year Alexander I died and was succeeded by Nicholas I (1825–55) who adopted a severe attitude to the Jewish community. In 1827 he initiated a policy of inducting Jewish boys into the Russian army for a twenty-five-year period in order to increase the number of converts to Christianity. Nicholas I also deported Jews from villages in certain areas; in 1827 they were expelled from Kiev and three years later from the surrounding province. In 1835 the Russian government propagated a revised code of laws to regulate Jewish settlement in the western border. In order to reduce Jewish isolation the government set out to reform education in 1841; a young Jewish educator, Max Lilienthal (1815–82), was asked to establish a number of reformed Jewish schools in the Pale of Settlement which incorporated western educational methods and a secular curriculum. Initially Lilienthal attempted to persuade Jewish leaders that by supporting this project the Jewish community could improve their lot, but when he discovered that the intention of the Tsar was to undermine the Talmud he left the country. These new schools were established in 1844 but they attracted a small enrolment and the Russian government eventually abandoned its plans to eliminate traditional Jewish education.

In the same year Nicholas I abolished the *kehillot* and put Jewry under the authority of the police as well as municipal government. Despite this policy it was impossible for the Russian administration to carry out the functions of the *kehillot*, and it was recognized that a Jewish body was needed to recruit students for state military schools and to collect taxes. Between 1850 and 1851 the government attempted to forbid Jewish dress, men's sidecurls, and the ritual of shaving women's hair. In 1851 a plan was initiated to categorize all Jews in the country along economic lines. Those who were considered useful subjects included craftsmen, farmers, and wealthy merchants, whereas the vast majority of Jews were liable to further restrictions. After the Crimean War of 1853–6, Alexander II (1855–81) emancipated the serfs, modernized the judiciary and established a system of local self-government. In addition he allowed certain groups, including wealthy merchants, university graduates, certified artisans, discharged soldiers and all holders of diplomas, to reside outside the Pale of Settlement. As a result Jewish communities appeared in St Petersburg and Moscow. Furthermore a limited number of Jews were allowed to enter the legal profession and participate in district councils. Government-sponsored Jewish schools also attracted more Jewish students, and in the 1860s and 1870s emancipated Jews began to take an active role in the professions and in Russian economic life.

The emergence of Jewish thought in the Enlightenment

The roots of Jewish thought during the Enlightenment go back to seventeenth-century Holland where a number of Jewish thinkers attempted to view the Jewish tradition in the light of the new scientific conception of the world. Uriel Acosta (1590–1640), for example, argued that the Torah was probably not of divine origin since it contained many features contrary to natural law. The greatest of these Dutch Jewish thinkers was Baruch Spinoza (1632–77) who published a treatise, *Tractatus Theological-Politicus*, in which he rejected the medieval synthesis of faith and reason. In the first section of this work Spinoza maintained that the prophets possessed moral insight rather than theoretical truth. Rejecting the Maimonidean belief that the Bible contains a hidden esoteric meaning, Spinoza argued that the Hebrew Scriptures were intended for the masses. God, he continued, is conceived as a lawgiver to appeal to the multitude; the function of Biblical law was to ensure social stability. In addition Spinoza asserted that God cannot be known through miraculous occurrences but only from the order of nature and from clear self-evident ideas. As far as the Torah is concerned, it was not composed in its entirety by Moses – the historical books were compilations assembled by many generations. Ezra, he believed, was responsible for harmonizing the discrepancies found in Scripture.

For Spinoza the function of religion was to provide a framework for ethical action. Philosophy on the other hand is concerned with truth, and philosophers should be free to engage in philosophical speculation unconstrained by religious opinions. It is a usurpation of the social contrct and a violation of the rights of man to legislate belief. On the basis of this view Spinoza propounded a metaphysical system based on a pantheistic conception of nature. Beginning with the belief in an infinite, unlimited, self-caused Substance which he conceived as God or nature, Spinoza maintained that Substance possesses a theoretical infinity of attributes, only two of which – extension and thought – are apprehended by human beings. God or nature can also be seen as a whole made up of finite, individual entities. In this way God exists in all things as their universal essence; they exist in God as modifications.

This philosophical scheme was based on Spinoza's concept of three grades of knowledge: the lowest form depends on sense perception; the second grade consists of systematic knowledge such as mathematics; the highest level is intuitive reason based on scientific and logical thinking which can comprehend the interconnection of the whole. The person who reaches this final stage is able to apprehend reality as a unity and attain an active love of God through knowledge. According to Spinoza, God is the sum of the laws in nature – He is totally immanent. Further, Spinoza argued that God is not in-corporeal; instead He is the totality of all bodies in the universe. On this view creation is ruled out and the whole is free only to the degree that it is self-caused. When one submits to the logical and necessary interconnection of reality, it is possible to attain tranquillity and a liberation from trivial concerns.

Such rational reflection on theological matters provided the background to the philosophical enquiries of the greatest Jewish thinker of the Enlightenment, Moses Mendelssohn (1729–86). Born in Dessau, Mendelssohn travelled to Berlin as a young student where he pursued secular as well as religious studies and befriended leading figures of the German Enlightenment, such as Gotthold Ephraim Lessing (1729–81). Under Lessing's influence, Mendelssohn published a number of theological studies in which he argued for the existence of God and creation, and he propounded the view that human reason is able to discover the reality of God, divine providence and the immortality of the soul. When challenged by a Christian apologist to explain why he remained loyal to the Jewish faith, Mendelssohn published a defence of the Jewish religion, *Jerusalem, or on Religious Power and Judaism*, in 1783. In this study Mendelssohn contended that no religious institution should use coercion; neither the Church nor the state, he believed, has the right to impose its religious views on the individual. Addressing the question as to whether the Mosaic law sanctions such coercion, Mendelssohn stressed that Judaism does not coerce the mind through dogma: 'The Israelites possess a Divine legislation – laws, commandments, statutes, rules of conduct, instruction in God's will and in what they are to do to attain temporal and eternal salvation. Moses, in a miraculous and supernatural way, revealed to them these laws and commandments, but not dogmas.'

The distinction Mendelssohn drew between natural religion and the Jewish faith was based on three types of truth: logically necessary truth, contingent truths such as the laws of nature, and temporal truths that occur in history. All human beings, he argued, have the innate capacity to discover the existence of God, providence and the hereafter. But Judaism is uniquely different from other religions in that it contains a revealed law. The Jewish people did not hear God proclaim that He is an eternal, necessary, omnipotent and omniscient being who rewards and punishes mankind; instead divine commandments were revealed to God's chosen people. The purpose of this legal code was to make Israel into a priest people. 'These descendants', he wrote, 'were chosen by providence to be a nation of priests, that is, a nation which, through its constitution and institutions, through its laws and conduct, and throughout all changes of life and fortune, was to call wholesome and unadulterated ideas of God and His attributes continuously to the attention of the rest of mankind.'

For Mendelssohn Jewish law does not give power to the authorities to persecute individuals for holding false doctrines. Yet Jews, he argued, should not absolve themselves from following God's law: 'Adopt the mores and constitution of the country in which you find yourself', he declared, 'but be steadfast in upholding the religion of your fathers, too . . . I cannot see how those who were born into the household of Jacob can in good conscience exempt themselves from the observance of the law.' Thus despite Mendelssohn's recognition of the common links between Judaism and other faiths, he followed the traditions of his ancestors and advocated the retention of the distinctive features of the Jewish faith. By combining philosophical theism and Jewish traditionalism, Mendelssohn attempted to transcend the constrictions of ghetto life and enter the mainstream of western European culture as an observant Jew.

To bring about the modernization of Jewish life, Mendelssohn also translated the Pentateuch into German so that Jews would be able to learn the language of the country in which they lived, and he spearheaded a commentary on Scripture (the Biur) which combined Jewish scholarship with secular thought. Following Mendelssohn's example, a number of Prussian followers known as the *maskilim* fostered a Jewish Enlightenment – the Haskalah – which encouraged Jews to abandon medieval patterns of life and thought. The *maskilim* also attempted to reform Jewish education by widening the curriculum to include secular subjects; to further this end they wrote textbooks in Hebrew and established Jewish schools. The *maskilim* also produced the first Jewish literary magazine, *The Gatherer*, in 1783. Contributors to this publication wrote poems and fables in the classical style of Biblical Hebrew and produced studies of Biblical exegesis, Hebrew linguistics and Jewish history.

By the 1820s the centre of this movement had shifted to the Austrian empire. A new journal, *First Fruits of the Times*, was published in Vienna between 1821 and 1832 and was followed between 1833 and 1856 by a Hebrew journal, *Vineyard of Delight*, devoted to modern Jewish scholarship. In the 1840s the Haskalah spread to Russia where writers made important contributions to Hebrew literature and translated textbooks and European fiction into Hebrew. During the reign of Alexander II, Hebrew weeklies appeared and the Society for the Promotion of Culture Among the Jews of Russia was established in 1863. In the next two decades *maskilim* produced works of social and literary criticism. These thinkers, however, were not typical of the Jewish masses. Many lived isolated lives because of their support of the Austrian and Russian governments' efforts to reform Jewish life. In addition, they were virulently critical of traditional rabbinic Judaism and so were regarded with suspicion and hostility by the religious establishment which endeavoured to perpetuate the faith of their fathers.

12

The Rise of Reform Judaism

The Enlightenment brought about major changes in Jewish life. No longer were Jews insulated from non-Jewish currents of culture and thought, and this transformation of Jewish existence led many Jews to seek a modernization of Jewish worship. The earliest reformers engaged in liturgical revision but quickly the spirit of reform spread to other areas of Jewish life; eventually modernists convened a succession of rabbinical conferences in order to formulate a common policy. Such a radical approach to the Jewish tradition provoked a hostile response from a number of leading Orthodox rabbis, a reaction which stimulated the creation of the neo-Orthodox movement. Such opposition however did not stem the tide – the development of the Scientific Study of Judaism (*Wissenschaft des Judentums*) and the positive historical school inspired many reformers who were sympathetic to modern culture and learning.

The beginnings of Reform Judaism

At the beginning of the nineteenth century the Jewish financier and communal leader Israel Jacobson (1768–1828) initiated a programme of reform. He founded a boarding school for boys in Seesen, Westphalia, in 1801, and subsequently established other schools throughout the kingdom. In these new foundations general subjects were taught by Christian teachers while a Jewish instructor gave lessons about Judaism. The consistory under Jacobson's leadership also introduced external reforms to the Jewish worship service including choral singing, hymns and addresses, and prayers in German. In 1810 Jacobson built the first Reform temple next to the school which was dedicated in the presence of Christian clergy and dignitaries. In his address at the dedication ceremony, Jacobson proclaimed:

> Our ritual is still weighed down with religious customs which must be rightly offensive to reason as well as to our Christian friends. It desecrates the holiness of our religion and dishonours the reasonable man to place too great a value upon such customs; on the other hand he is greatly honoured if he can encourage himself and his friends to realize their dispensability.

After Napoleon's defeat Jacobson moved to Berlin where he attempted to put these principles into practice by founding the Berlin temple.

In Hamburg in 1817 a Reform temple was opened in which a number of innovations were made to the liturgy including prayers and sermons in German as well as choral singing and organ music. To defend these alterations Hamburg reformers cited the Talmud in support of their actions. In 1819 the community issued its own prayerbook which omitted repetitions of prayers as well as medieval poems and changed some of the traditional prayers related to Jewish nationalism and the messianic redemption. Israel Jacobson, to whom this prayerbook was dedicated, was instrumental in obtaining a number of rabbinic opinions in support of the temple. The Hungarian rabbi, Aaron Chorin (1766–1844), for example, declared that it was not only permissible but obligatory to free the liturgy from its adhesions, to hold the service in a language understandable to the worshipper, and to accompany it with organ and song. Not surprisingly such innovations provoked the Orthodox establishment to issue a proclamation condemning the Hamburg reformers. Eleazer Fleckeles of the Beth Din of Prague stated: 'These people [of the Hamburg temple] really have no religion at all. it is their entire desire to parade before the Christians as being more learned than their brothers. Basically, they are neither Christians nor Jews.' In a personal attack on Aaron Chorin, Rabbi Eliezer of Triesch in Moravia declared: 'We know this rabbi Aaron Chorin. He is a man of mediocre knowledge in Talmud and commentaries, and far be it from us to lean on his pronouncements.'

The central aim of these early reformers was to adapt Jewish worship to contemporary aesthetic standards. For these innovators, the informality of the traditional service seemed foreign and undignified, and they therefore insisted on greater decorum, more unison in prayer, a choir, hymns and musical responses as well as alterations in prayers and the length of the service. Yet for some Jews influenced by the Romantic movement these modifications were insufficient. Two of Moses Mendelssohn's daughters, for example, became Christian converts as did Henriette Herz (1764–1847) and Rahel Varnhagen (1771–1883) whose literary salons in Berlin were attended by leading German intellectuals. These women longed for a faith which would provide sublime devotion and mystical bliss.

Such Romantic concern also generated a new intellectual development within post-Enlightenment Jewry: the establishment of a Society for the Culture and Academic study of Judaism (*Verein fur Kultur und Wissenschaft des Judentums*). This discipline encouraged the systematic study of history and a respect for historical fact. The purpose of this new approach to the past was to gain a true understanding of the origins of the Jewish tradition in the history of western civilization, and in this quest the philosophy of Hegel had a profound impact. In 1824, however, the society collapsed and several of its members such as the poet Henrich Heine and the historian of law Eduard Gans converted to Christianity to advance their careers.

In response to these developments a number of Orthodox Jews asserted that any alteration to the tradition was a violation of the Jewish heritage. For these traditionalists the written and oral Torah constituted an infallible chain of divinely revealed truth. The most prominent of these scholars was Samson Raphael Hirsch (1808–88) who was educated at a German gymnasium and the University of Bonn. At the age of twenty-two Hirsch was appointed as Chief Rabbi of the Duchy of Oldenburg. In 1836 he published *The Nineteen Letters on Judaism*, a defence of Orthodoxy in the form of essays by a young rabbi to a friend who questioned the importance of remaining a Jew. The work commenced with a typical critique of Judaism of this period: 'While the best of mankind climbed to the summit of culture, prosperity, and wealth, the Jewish people remained poor in everything that makes human beings great and noble and that beautifies and dignifies our lives.'

In response to such a criticism, Hirsch replied that the purpose of human life is not to attain personal happiness and perfection; rather humans should strive to serve God by obeying His will. To serve as an example of such devotion, the Jewish people was formed so that through its way of life all people would come to know that true happiness lies in obeying God. Thus the people of Israel were given the Promised Land in order to be able to keep God's law. When the Jewish nation was exiled, they were able to fulfil this mission by remaining loyal to God and to the Torah despite constant persecution and suffering. According to Hirsch the purpose of God's commands is not to repress physical gratification or material prosperity. Rather the aim of observing God's law is to lead a religious life thereby bearing witness to the messianic ideal of universal brotherhood. In this light Reform Judaism was castigated for abandoning this sacred duty. For Hirsch citizenship rights are of minor importance since Jewry is united by a bond of obedience to God's laws until the time when the 'Almighty shall see fit in His inscrutable wisdom to unite again his scattered servants in one land, and the Torah shall be the guiding principle of a state, a model of the meaning of Divine revelation and the mission of humanity.'

The growth of the Reform movement

Despite Hirsch's criticisms of reforming tendencies, a number of German rabbis who had been influenced by the Enlightenment began to re-evaluate the Jewish tradition. In this undertaking the achievements of Jewish scholars such as Leopold Zunz (1794–1886), who engaged in the scientific study of Judaism, had a profound impact. As this new movement began to grow, Orthodox authorities vigorously attacked its leadership and ideals. In 1838 for example when Abraham Geiger was appointed as second rabbi of Breslau, the Chief Rabbi of the city, Solomon Tiktin, denounced him as a radical. According to Tiktin, anyone who did not subscribe to the inviolable and absolute truth of tradition could not serve with him.

Tiktin's allies joined in this protest and declared Geiger unfit for the position. In 1842 Tiktin published a tract in which he insisted on the validity of Jewish law and the authority of the rabbinic tradition. In response Geiger's supporters produced a defence of religious reform: *Rabbinic Responses on the Compatibility of Free Investigation with the Exercise of Rabbinic Functions*. The bitterness evoked by this controversy was reflected in the writing of one of Geiger's supporters, the Chief Rabbi of Treves (Trier), Joseph Kahn (1809–75): 'We must publicly express our contempt for those who, like Tiktin and company', he wrote, 'blindly damn and ban, and in just indignation we must brand them as men who "some day will have to account for their deeds" ', so that, 'they should hear and fear and not sin any more'.

During this period Reform Judaism spread to other countries such as England, where the West London Synagogue was founded at the beginning of the 1840s. But it was in Frankfurt that Reform became most radical. In 1842 the Society of the Friends of Reform was founded and published and proclamation justifying their innovative approach to tradition. In the declaration of their principles, the society declared that they recognized the possibility of unlimited progress in the Jewish faith and rejected the authority of the legal code as well as the belief in messianic redemption. Furthermore, members of the society considered circumcision a barbaric rite which should be eliminated from Judaism. Aware of the danger this group posed to the tradition, Solomon Rapoport, Rabbi of Prague (1790–1867), warned against associating with any members of this new movement: 'We must strictly insist and warn our coreligionists not to have any social contacts with the members of this Reform association, and especially not to enter into matrimonial union with them.'

A similar group, the Association for the Reform of Judaism, was founded in Berlin in 1844 and under the leadership of Samuel Holdheim (1806–60) called for major changes in the Jewish tradition. The Association produced a prayerbook in German which contained very little Hebrew and abolished such customs as praying with covered heads and the blowing of the *shofar*. In their proclamation, the Berlin group decreed:

> We can no longer recognize a code as an unchangeable law-book which maintains with unbending insistence that Judaism's task is expressed by forms which originated in a time which is forever past and which will never return . . . we are stirred by the trumpet sound of our own time. It calls us to be of the last of a great inheritance in this old form, and at the same time, the first who, with unswerving courage are bound together as brothers in word and deed, shall lay the cornerstone of a new edifice.

In 1844 the first Reform synod took place at Brunswick in which the participants advocated the formulation of a Jewish creed and the modification of Sabbath and dietary laws as well as the traditional liturgy. This consultation was followed by another conference in 1845 in Frankfurt which recommended that petitions for the return to Israel and the restoration of the Jewish state be omitted from the prayerbook. At this meeting one of the more conservative rabbis, Zacharias Frankel of Dresden (1801–75), expressed his dissatisfaction with the decision of the synod to regard the use of Hebrew in worship as advisable rather than necessary and resigned from the Assembly. Subsequently Frankel became head of a Jewish theological seminary in Breslau which was based on free enquiry combined with a commitment to the Jewish tradition. In 1846 a third synod took place at Breslau and discussed Sabbath observance. Though these reformers upheld the rabbinic ordinances against work on the Sabbath, they stated that the Talmudic injunctions regarding the boundary for walking on the Sabbath were no longer binding. Further, they stipulated that the second day observance of festivals should be eliminated.

The revolution of 1848 and its aftermath brought about the cessation of these conferences, and nearly a generation passed before reformers met again to formulate a common policy. In 1868 twenty-four rabbis led by Ludwig Phillipson (1811–89) and Abraham Geiger (1810–74) assembled in Cassel to lay the foundations for a synodal conference of rabbis, scholars and communal leaders. In the following year over eighty congregations were represented when this gathering met in Leipzig under the leadership of Professor Moritz Lazarus (1824–1903). Two years later another synod took place in Augsburg which dealt with pressing theological and practical problems. In a statement produced at this synod, the participants outlined the principles and tasks of Reform Judaism. First, they pointed out that in the past Judaism went through different phases of development; Reform, they believed, marks a new and important beginning. Though the essence and mission of Judaism remain constant, many ceremonies need to be regenerated and the obsolete and antiquated must be set aside. To accomplish this task of renewal, the synod itself saw itself as a vehicle of change. Basing its reforming zeal on a quest for truth, the reformers declared: 'It [the synod] intends to labour with clear purpose so that the reform of Judaism for which we have striven for several decades should be secured in the spirit of harmony.'

The development of Reform Judaism in the United States

In the seventeenth and eighteenth centuries a number of Sephardic Jews emigrated to the colonies of the New World. After 1815 the Jewish pouplation of North America substantially increased as immigrants from Europe sought refuge from discrimination and persecution. The first signs of Reform appeared in 1824 when a small group of congregants in Charleston, South Carolina, attempted to introduce some of the reforms of Germany's Hamburg temple into synagogue worship. According to one of these early reformers, Isaac Harby (1788–1828), the desire of the Charleston Reform community was 'to take away everything that might excite the disgust of the well-informed Israelite'. In the period preceding and following the revolution of 1848, there was an outpouring of Jews including some reformers from Germany to the United States; many of these immigrants settled in New York. By 1842 there were three German congregations in New York City, and three years later Congregation Emanuel was organized and introduced various reforms in worship. Among these German newcomers were several Reform rabbis who had taken part in the early European Reform synods and were anxious to initiate a policy of Reform in this new setting.

Prominent among these early reformers were David Einhorn of Har Sinai congregation in Baltimore and Samuel Adler and Gustave Gottheil of Temple Emanuel in New York, but it was not until Isaac Mayer Wise (1819–1900) exercised his leadership and organizing skills that Reform Judaism in America reached maturity. Born in Bohemia, Wise came to the United States in 1846 to accept a rabbinic post in Albany, New York, where his efforts at reform evoked a violent reaction. At a service on the New Year, he was physically assaulted by one of his opponents. 'At the conclusion of the song', he wrote,

> I stopped before the ark in order to take out the scrolls of the Law as usual, and to offer prayer. Spaniel (a member of the congregation) stepped in my way, and without saying a word, smote me with his fist so that my cap fell from my head. This was the signal for an uproar the like of which I have never experienced.

Subsequently Wise moved to Cincinnati, Ohio, where he published a new Reform prayerbook, *Minhag Amerika*, as well as several Jewish newspapers. Wise also directed his energies to convening an American synod; it was Wise's intention that American Jewry unite organizationally and spiritually to meet the challenges of life in the United States. After several abortive attempts at rabbinic union, the first Conference of American Reform Rabbis took place in Philadelphia in 1869; this was followed in 1873 by the founding of the Union of American Hebrew Congregations comprising lay and rabbinical representatives. Two years later Wise established the Hebrew Union College, the first Reform rabbinical seminary on American soil. But the principles of American Reform Judaism were not explicitly set out until 1885 when a gathering of Reform rabbis met in Pittsburgh. Their deliberations under the chairmanship of Kaufmann Kohler (1843–1926) resulted in the adoption of a formal list of principles, the Pittsburgh Platform. In his address to the conference, Kohler declared that their purpose was to show that Judaism must be modernized in order to embrace the findings of scientific research as well as the fields of comparative religion and Biblical criticism. The Platform itself began with the statement that Judaism presents the highest conception of God. In this connection the conference spoke of the Bible as the most potent instrument of religious and moral instruction; for these reformers Scripture was also seen as compatible with the findings of science: 'We hold that the modern discoveries of scientific researches in the domains of nature and history are not antagonistic to the doctrines of Judaism, the Bible reflecting the primitive ideas of its own age and at times clothing its conception of Divine providence and justice dealing with man in miraculous narratives.'

The participants further decreed that they recognized as binding only the moral commandments as well as those rituals which they viewed as spiritually uplifting. Laws regulating diet, priestly purity and dress were rejected as anachronistic. The belief in a personal Messiah was also eliminated and replaced by a messianic hope for the establishment of a kingdom of justice and peace for humanity. The reformers also asserted that Judaism is a progressive religion 'ever striving to be in accord with the postulates of reason'. Regarding the afterlife, the participants subscribed to a belief in the immortality of the soul rather than the traditional doctrines of bodily resurrection and reward and punishment in the hereafter: 'We reject as ideas not rooted in Judaism the belief both in bodily resurrection and in *Gehinnom* and *Eden*, as abodes for everlasting punishment and reward.' As a conclusion to this document the delegates proclaimed their commitment to engage in social action. This statement of religious beliefs together with the rabbinical and congregational organizations of Reform Judaism founded in the late nineteenth century provided a framework for the growth and development of Reform Judaism in the next century.

Jewish thought in the Age of Reform

In the mid 1800s a number of German rabbis who were influenced by the cause of Reform sought to re-evaluate the course of Jewish history. One of the most important of these reformers was Abraham Geiger who combined a commitment to the scientific study of Judaism with a rabbinical career. Born in Frankfurt, Geiger studied at the universities of Heidelberg and Bonn; In 1832 he served as rabbi in Wiesbaden where he edited the *Scientific Journal for Jewish Theology*. In 1838 he was appointed rabbi in Breslau where he published studies on a variety of Jewish subjects as well as a book on the ancient text and translations of the Bible. In this work Geiger maintained that post-Biblical Jewish movements shaped the canonized version of Scripture. Although Geiger did not write a systematic Jewish theology, his approach was based on a programme to reformulate Judaism to achieve theological clarity according to the scientific spirit of the time. For Geiger religion was rooted in man's recognition of finitude and the question for the infinite. Judaism, he believed, is 'a faith founded on the trust in one who guides the universe and in the task imposed upon us to practice justice and mercy, a fact that becomes manifest in acts that fulfil this demand, and that is clothed in uplifting ritual forms designed to awaken such sentiments.' Unlike the Greeks who believed in fate, the Jewish faith conceives spiritual perfection as the ultimate aim of human striving. According to Geiger this vision which reached its climax in the prophetic tradition should be distinguished from earlier, more primitive religious practices such as animal sacrifice which had been discarded in the course of Jewish history. Similarly he argued that the Biblical concept of nationhood is not needed in the modern world.

For Geiger the evolution of Jewish history divided into four stages of development. First in the age of revelation, the idea of Judaism was seen as a moral, spiritual concept capable of continual development. In the second stage of Jewish history – the age of tradition – the Bible was continually reshaped and reinterpreted. The third stage – the age of legalism – which occurred after the completion of the Talmud, formalized the tradition so as to ensure its continuance. Finally, in the age of critical study, legalism was transcended through historical research. Yet, though the *halachah* was not considered binding in the fourth stage, this does not imply that Judaism is cut off from the past; on the contrary historical studies can revitalize the heritage. Those aspects of the Jewish tradition which are to be eliminated should be regarded as medieval abnormalities resulting from restraints – they are not connected to the core of the Jewish faith.

In Geiger's view, anti-Jewish sentiment was the result of the Church's belief that Judaism had been superseded by Christianity. But for Geiger Christianity was seen as the inferior religion since the doctrine of the Incarnation compromised the original purity of the Jewish concept of God. Further Geiger asserted that the concept of original sin undermines the Biblical view that human beings are capable of moral improvement. Geiger also pointed out that the validity of Judaism does not rest on a historical figure like Jesus, nor does the Jewish faith denigrate earthly life as does Christianity. Finally Geiger emphasized that Judaism does not contain fixed dogma which constrain free enquiry. For these reasons Geiger believed that Judaism rather than the Christian faith is the ideal religious system for the modern age. Within this framework emancipation was of vital consequence since it was only in an age of scientific investigation that Judaism could find its true nature. Historical knowledge would provide a basis for determining what is anachronistic in the tradition and should be discarded.

Heinrich Graetz (1817–91) was another major thinker who was concerned with the scientific study of Judaism. In the 1840s Graetz espoused Zacharias Frankel's approach to Jewish civilization; in an essay written in 1846 he asserted that the essence of Judaism resided not only in a theoretical conception of the Jewish faith but also in the features of Jewish existence that reformers had rejected. Adapting Hegelian notions, Graetz believed that all aspects of the Jewish tradition are the result of the unfolding of Judaism as a religious system. For Graetz this was not a logical but rather a historical process, and in his investigations he attempted to illustrate how Jewish beliefs and practices evolved throughout history. Judaism, he argued, cannot be reduced to an abstract definition; rather the Jewish tradition is historically based and can be divided into three stages. The first period began with the conquest of the land and ended with the destruction of the first Temple in 586 BC. The second stage stook place after the Babylonian exile and lasted until the destruction of the second Temple in AD 70. During this cycle of history the struggle against Greek paganism culminated in the emergence of the Pharisees who introduced doctrines concerning the afterlife into Jewish thought. For Graetz the third stage was the diaspora period in which Jews attempted to attain intellectual self-perfection and rationalize their religious faith. This scheme of Jewish history was elaborated in Graetz's *History of the Jews* published between 1853 and 1876.

Just as Geiger and Graetz had been influenced by German philosophy, so other Jewish writers sought to integrate German philosophical thought into their conceptions of Judaism. In 1841 the Reform rabbi, Solomon Formstecher (1801–89), published *The Religion of the Spirit*. In this study, which was influenced by the work of the philosopher Freidrich Wilhelm Joseph von Schelling, Formstecher argued that ultimate reality is the Divine World Soul, a cosmic unity manifesting itself both in nature and in spirit. For Formstecher nature is an organic hierarchy of events and forces which reaches self-consciousness in the realm of spirit. As the highest form of consciousness spirit can be known through its various manifestations, but Formstecher was anxious to point out that such conceptions are symbols and do not describe God's essence. The Divine Soul as it is in itself is unknowable. On the basis of this metaphysical scheme Formstecher distinguished between the religion of nature and the religion of spirit. The religion of nature refers to paganism which deifies nature; the religion of spirit identifies God not only with nature but also with the ethical good. In the history of religion, Judaism was the first religion of spirit, but within the tradition there has been a gradual development. In the early stages of Jewish history, truth was understood through the medium of statehood, and then by a theocracy of religious law. But once emancipation had taken place, it became possible for Jews to realize their mission of establishing a universal ethical religion of spirit for all people.

Like Formstecher, the Reform rabbi Samuel Hirsch (1815–89), utilized German idealism in the presentation of his conception of the Jewish heritage. In *The Religious Philosophy of the Jews*, published in 1842, Hirsch adopted Hegel's view that human beings become free by seeing themselves as distinct persons, but he rejected the Hebrew notion that sin can be overcome through rational self-determination. For Hirsch sin is a moral rather than an intellectual state; it can only be eliminated through ethical action. Thus the essential feature of religion is not the eventual self-realization of God, but the actualization of moral freedom in which natural sensuality is subordinated to ethical duty. In this light Hirsch conceived of religion as either passive or active. In passive religions such as paganism, believers are dominated by their sensual side, and nature is understood as a divine force. But in active religions the devout can attain self-chosen freedom. During the patriarchal period Judaism possessed the insight of active religion; miracles and prophecies were necessary to eliminate paganism from the faith. Yet the need for such miraculous occurrences has ceased; the only miracle is the survival of the Jewish nation. On this basis Hirsch believed that there is no evolution of truth in Judaism though development does take place in the ethical sphere. The purpose of education is to encourage Jews to choose virtue rather than sinfulness and to act as God's suffering servants so as to demonstrate the impotency of evil.

Similar to these Reform rabbis, Solomon Ludwig Steinheim (1789–1866), who was a physician and poet, published *Revelation and the Doctrine of the Synagogue* in the mid-nineteenth century. According to Steinheim, Judaism should not be confused with philosophical reflection. Not only did Steinheim criticize Formstecher and Hirsch for their reliance on German philosophy, he also disagreed with Mendelssohn's conviction that natural religion is the source of theoretical truth. For Steinheim the Bible contains beliefs contrary to ancient Greek philosophy as well as modern thought. Adopting Kant's belief that things-in-themselves cannot be known through human knowledge, Steinheim argued that reason is limited in its scope and must be supplemented by revelation. In propounding this thesis, Steinheim advanced the view that natural religion is based on the assumption that everything has a cause as well as the belief that nothing can come from nothing. These concepts, he argued, are incompatible: the first belief implies that God is the First Cause, whereas the second belief rules out the need for God. The only way out of this dilemma is through the Biblical view that the creation of the universe was due to the will of God. Belief in such a creative act qualifies determinism and provides a basis for moral freedom. For Steinheim the mission of the Jews in the past was to refute natural religion; in contemporary society philosophical rationalism must be overcome as well. Steinheim's anti-rationalism thus reverses the direction of Jewish philosophical thought in a post-Maimonidean age.

13
Jewish Life in the Nineteenth and Early Twentieth Centuries

By the second half of the nineteenth century Jewish existence had been transformed by the forces of emancipation. Some reformers believed that in such enlightened conditions anti-Jewish sentiment would disappear. Yet in the last decades of the century hostility towards the Jewish community intensified, resulting in the emergence of Jewish longing for a homeland. The foundation of the Zionist movement gave voice to such nationalistic aspirations and paved the way for the creation of the state of Israel in the next century. For many Jews America was also seen as a refuge from persecution, and at the end of the nineteenth century there was a mass migration of European Jews to the New World which brought about a resurgence of Jewish life and thought.

The rise of anti-Semitism

By the last decades of the nineteenth century the European Jewish community had attained a high degree of emancipation. Nevertheless political conditions in Europe after 1870 brought about considerable disruption; several proud and independent nations emerged and fought against indigenous minority groups which threatened their homogeneity. Living in such conditions Jews were regarded as aliens and unassimilable. Symptomatic of such attitudes was the invention of the term anti-Semitism by the German journalist Wilhelm Marr in the 1870s. Previously Jewish persecution was based largely on religious grounds but Marr's concept of anti-Semitism focused on biological descent; anti-Semitism was thus a racist policy which significantly differed from previous dislike of the Jews and Judaism. For Marr, the Jews have 'corrupted all standards, have banned all idealism from society, dominate commerce, push themselves ever more in state services, rule the theatre, form a social and political phalanx'. According to Marr there is a continuous struggle in contemporary society between these Semitic aliens and native Teutonic stock.

Anti-Jewish feelings intensified in the 1870s in Germany as a result of economic and cultural upheaval. The political liberalism of previous decades had enabled Jews to benefit from economic activities, and in reaction conservatives blamed the Jewish community for the ills of society. In 1878 Adolf Stocker founded a Christian Social Party on the basis of an anti-Semitic platform. By accusing the press and the financial institutions of being controlled by Jewish interests, many artisans, shopkeepers, clerks and professionals were attracted to his political movement. Such allegations were also supported by German nationalists who emphasized that Jews would need to assimilate to German life before they could be accepted as Germans. Other nationalists adopted a more radical position; in 1881 for example Eugen Duhring argued that the Jewish type constituted a biological threat to the German nation. In the same year anti-Semites presented a petition of 225,000 signatures to stop all Jewish immigration; this was followed in 1882 by an international anti-Semitic congress. In the next decade anti-Semitic parties elected sixteen deputies to the German *Reichstag*. At the end of the century anti-Semitism was utilized by Karl Lueger to foster the creation of the first political party in Europe which obtained power on the basis of anti-Jewish feeling.

During this period French anti-Semitism was also used by the monarchy and clergy who were unhappy with the liberal ideas of the French Revolution. Such anti-Semitism reached a climax with the Dreyfus affair. Accused of treason, Alfred Dreyfus was banished from the army and sentenced to life imprisonment in 1894. Subsequently however it was discovered that forged evidence had been used to implicate Dreyfus and a scandal ensued which divided public opinion. Those opposed to Dreyfus believed that he was part of a Jewish conspiracy to undermine the military and discredit France; his supporters viewed the court martial of Dreyfus as an injustice which threatened the stability of French life. Eventually Dreyfus was pardoned, but for many Jews this episode illustrated that despite the forces of emancipation, anti-Semitism was deeply rooted in European society. In a tract written after the Dreyfus affair, Theodor Herzl (1860–1905) came to the conclusion that Jews would never be accepted in countries where they lived. 'In vain we are loyal patriots', he wrote,

> our loyalty in some places running to extremes; in vain do we make the same sacrifices of life and property as our fellow citizens; in vain do we strive to increase the fame of our native land in science and art, or her wealth by trade and commerce. In countries where we have lived for centuries we are still cried down as strangers.

In Russia anti-Semitism became an official policy of the state. After Alexander II was assassinated in 1881, a succession of pogroms against the Jewish population took place in the southern Ukraine. Jewish property was looted and destroyed, and in 1882 the minister of the interior decreed a series of laws which curtailed Jewish residence in the Pale of Settlement. In the later 1880s quotas were imposed on the admittance of Jews to Russian schools, universities and professions. In addition more than 20,000 Jews were expelled from Moscow in 1891–2. In 1903 a violent pogrom was unleashed on the Jews of Kishinev. In the next year Jews were accused of helping the enemy in the war against Japan and armed gangs attacked Jews in various towns and cities. Though these outbursts ceased in 1907 a right-wing political party, the Union of the Russian People, initiated a campaign of anti-Semitic propaganda. In 1911 Mendel Beilis, a Jew from Kiev, was accused of ritual murder but was exonerated in 1913.

Such manifestations of anti-Jewish sentiment were based on the belief that the Jewish people constituted a dangerous racial group. Ideologues argued that the Semitic mentality was egoistic, materialistic, economic-minded, cowardly and culturally degenerate. In this context a number of writers propagated racist theories. In *The Foundations of the Nineteenth Century*, published at the turn of the century, Houston Stewart Chamberlain maintained that the antiquity and the mobility of the Jewish nation illustrated that the confrontation between superior Aryans and parasitic Semites is the central theme of history. Earlier, in the 1880s, the *Protocols of the Elders of Zion* were believed to be the minutes of a clandestine world government. In this document the elders were depicted as attempting to strengthen their hold over the European economy, the press, and the parties opposed to the Tsar as well as other autocratic regimes.

The Zionist movement

The pogroms of 1881–2 forced many Jews to emigrate; most went to the United States but a sizeable number were drawn to Palestine. In the Pale of Settlement nationalist zealots organized Zionist groups (Lovers of Zion) which collected money and organized courses in Hebrew and Jewish history. In 1882 several thousand Jews left for Palestine where they worked as shopkeepers and artisans; other Jewish immigrants, known as Bilu (from the Hebrew 'house of Jacob, let us go') combined Marxist ideals with Jewish nationalist fervour and worked as farmers and labourers. During this period Leon Pinsker (1821–91), an eminent Russian physician, published an influential tract, *Autoemancipation*, in which he argued that the liberation of Jewry could only be secured by the establishment of a Jewish homeland. Nations, he wrote, live side by side in a state of relative peace, which is based chiefly on fundamental equality between them. But it is different with the people of Israel. This people is not counted among the nations, because when it was exiled from its land it lost the essential attributes of nationality by which one nation is distinguished from another.

By the 1890s the idea of Jewish nationalism had spread to other countries in Europe. Foremost among its proponents was Theodore Herzl who made contact with the Lovers of Zion. In 1887 the first Zionist congress took place in Basle which called for a national home for Jews based on international law. At this congress Herzl stated that emancipation of the Jews had been an illusion: Jews were everywhere objects of contempt and hatred. The only solution to the Jewish problem, he argued, was the re-establishment of a Jewish homeland in Palestine. In the same year the Zionist Organization was created with branches in Europe and America. After establishing these basic institutions of the Zionist movement, Herzl embarked on diplomatic negotiations. In 1898 he met with Kaiser Wilhelm II who promised he would take up the matter with the Sultan. When nothing came of this, Herzl himself attempted to arrange an interview, and in 1901 a meeting with the Sultan took place. In return for a charter of Jewish settlement in Palestine, Herzl suggested that wealthy Jewish bankers might be willing to pay off the Turkish debt. In the following year the Sultan agreed to approve a plan of Jewish settlement throughout the Ottoman empire, but not a corporate Jewish homeland in Palestine.

Unwilling to abandon a diplomatic approach, Herzl sought to

cultivate contacts in England such as Lord Nathan Rothschild (1840–1915) who arranged an interview for him with Joseph Chamberlain, the Secretary of State for Colonial Affairs. During their conversation Herzl suggested that El Arish in the Sinai Peninsula might be a feasible area of settlement. Though this plan was discussed at the highest political levels, it never reached fruition. In 1903 Herzl was summoned to London for a second talk with Chamberlain after his return from Africa. 'On my travels', Chamberlain stated, 'I saw a country for you: Uganda. On the coast it is hot, but in the interior the climate is excellent for Europeans. You can plant cotton and sugar. I thought to myself: That's just the country for Dr. Herzl. But he must have Palestine and will move only in its vicinity.' Aware of increasing persecution in Russia, Herzl was uncertain whether to wait for Palestine and asked for time to consider the offer. After a trip to the Pale of Settlement where he encountered poverty and deprivation, Herzl reluctantly agreed to Chamberlain's proposal in August 1903 for a place of temporary asylum. At the next Zionist conference in Basle this plan was presented for ratification. When Chamberlain's scheme was explained, it was emphasized that Uganda was not meant to serve as a permanent solution, but rather as a temporary residence. When the resolution was passed by a small margin, the delegates from eastern Europe walked out of the auditorium. During the next few days the Zionist movement was threatened by schism; at the end of the proceedings the Russian Jews set off for Kharkov where they convened their own conference committing themselves to the idea of Palestine. In England public opinion was opposed to the transference of Uganda to the Jews, and the offer was eventually withdrawn. In the following year Herzl died, and the Zionist movement was led by a new President, David Wolffsohn (1856–1914), who attempted to heal the rifts between competing factions. Under his leadership Orthodox Jews joined the Zionist Organization as members of the Mizrachi Party; socialist Jews also became members through the Labour Zionist Party. In the 1907 congress during Wolffsohn's presidency a resolution was passed which pledged the movement to the quest for a charter, the physical settlement of Palestine and the revival of the Hebrew language.

During the next decade the major developments in the Zionist movement took place in Israel, and by the beginning of the twentieth century a sizeable number of Jews had migrated to Palestine. Most of these pioneers lived in cities but a small minority worked on farm colonies under the control of the Palestine Jewish Colonization Association. In 1904 when a second wave of immigrants departed for the Holy Land, most of these settlers were determined to become farmers. Prominent among these newcomers was Aaron David Gordon (1856–1922) who declared: 'too long have the hands been the hands of Esau, and the voice the voice of Jacob. It is time for Jacob to use his hands too.' Socialist ideas were espoused by many, such as Nachman Syrkin (1867–1924), who founded the Poale Zion Party, and Ber Borochov (1881–1917), the founder of the radical Hapoel Hatzair Party. Both of these leaders maintained that Zionism and socialism were compatible ideologies.

Among those who were attracted to such socialist policies was David Ben Gurion (1886–1973), the future Prime Minister, who wrote of his first night in Palestine: 'I did not sleep. I was among the rich shell of corn. Above were massed clusters of stars clear against the deep blue firmament. . . . My dreams had become a reality.' Those who came in this second wave organized trade unions, edited their own newspapers and attempted to establish their own collective settlements. In addition these settlers were determined to create Hebraic culture for the country: they put their children in Hebrew language schools and used Hebrew in their daily life. The philologist Ben Yehudah (1858–1922) produced a Hebrew dictionary and such writers as Ahad Ha'am (1856–1927), Reuben Brainin (1862–1939) and Chaim Nachman Bialik (1873–1934) contributed to the development of Hebrew literature. By 1917 the Jewish community numbered approximately 90,000.

Emigration to the United States and the impact of the First World War

By 1880 there were about 250,000 Jews in the United States; after the pogroms of 1881–2 the Jewish community increased enormously. Approximately 2,750,000 eastern European Jews emigrated between 1881 and 1914; about 350,000 settled in continental Europe; 200,000 went to England; 40,000 emigrated to South Africa; 115,000 to Argentina; 100,000 to Canada; and nearly 2,000,000 to the United States. This massive influx of immigrants strongly affected the composition of American Jewry. Initially Sephardic Jews dominated Jewish life in the coastal towns of the New World. Jews of German origin who emigrated in the nineteenth century settled throughout the country; many worked as businessmen in midwestern, southern and west coast cities. These German Jews quickly assimilated and Americanized their religious traditions. The majority of eastern

European Jews who arrived at the end of the century settled in the north-east. In the lower East Side of New York City settlers engaged in various manual trades such as the garment industry. Crowded together in tenements these newcomers worked in unhealthy surroundings, but after 1900 trade unions brought about enormous improvements in working conditions. In this milieu these immigrants created a wide range of societies which supported synagogues, provided insurance for sickness and burial, and supported educational programmes. In this environment Yiddish flourished resulting in the efflorescence of Yiddish language, theatre and journalism. Yet despite the vibrancy of this immigrant community, many Jews who prospered fled to middle-class neighbourhoods.

Between 1881 and 1914 the American Jewish population was divided between native-born Jews of German origin and eastern European immigrants. Those German Jews who had already settled in the new country found their eastern European co-religionists too remote and unworldly. As a result a number of acculturated German Jews attempted to defend Jewish interests and advance the process of assimilation. In 1902 they revived the Jewish Theological Seminary in New York in order to train modern rabbis in line with the modernized traditional stance of Zecharias Frankel. Under the leadership of Solomon Schechter (1850–1915) this rabbinical seminary became the centre for Conservative Judaism which advocated a scientific approach to the Jewish faith as well as an adherence to the Jewish heritage. This movement had considerable appeal for many eastern European Jews who desired to combine dedication to the Jewish faith with an openness to their new surroundings. German Jews also founded settlements for immigrants as well as a number of Jewish charities. In 1906 German Jews also established the American Jewish Committee in order to influence the government on behalf of persecuted Jews who lived in foreign countries. The German Jewish community was also instrumental in the creation of the Anti-Defamation League under the auspices of the B'nai B'rith to counter anti-Semitism in the United States. German Jews were also active in encouraging Zionist initiatives which attracted native-born advocates such as Louis Brandeis who maintained that a dedication to Zionist ideals could be combined with loyalty to one's own country.

The development of Jewish life in the United States was interrupted by the First World War. During the war Jews fought on the side of the Allies and the Central Powers. In Russia the Tsar was overthrown in March 1917 after two years of fighting, and the provisional government abolished all legal discriminations against the Jewish community. In November the military and political situation deteriorated and a second revolution was carried out by the Bolsheviks; Lenin sued for peace, and in March 1918 a treaty was signed with Germany that gave the Germans control over Estonia, Latvia, Lithuania, Poland and the Ukraine. After America entered the war an armistice was declared on 11 November 1918; in the east, however, fighting continued. When the Germans withdrew from the Ukraine, a number of groups fought for control. In this situation the Red Army attempted to eliminate anti-Jewish feeling in its ranks, but other troops massacred the Jewish population. By 1920 when the fighting ceased, between 100,000 and 150,000 Jews had been killed.

After the war Jewish immigration to the United States increased but was curtailed by restrictive laws passed in 1921 and 1924. Other western countries also followed similar policies. This cessation of Jewish immigration led to the decline of the Jewish working class and the erosion of Yiddish culture. The Jewish community became increasingly middle class and prosperous and a number of Jews attained positions of importance in politics, the arts, music, science and literature. World War I also profoundly altered European centres of Jewish population: over 3,000,000 Jews lived in reconstituted Poland; 445,000 in Hungary; 850,000 in expanded Romania; 95,000 in Latvia; 115,000 in Lithuania; 375,000 in Czechoslovakia; 191,000 in Austria; 68,000 in Yugoslavia; 48,000 in Bulgaria; and 73,000 in Greece. In these countries the war had taken a significant toll – property was destroyed, large markets were replaced by small economic units and high protective tariffs were introduced. In all these cases governments were anxious to foster middle-class interests at the expense of minority groups.

In this situation Jews were unable to find political allies and became increasingly vulnerable. In 1919 Jewish delegates attended the Paris peace talks to insure that political treaties would guarantee the rights of minority groups, but their efforts were largely unsuccessful. In Lithuania, Poland, Czechoslovakia, Hungary and Romania most Jews steadfastly adhered to the Jewish faith and were regarded as outsiders. In universities and the professions quotas were strictly applied; Jews were excluded from state bureaucracies; and anti-Semitic policies were advocated by various political parties. Yet despite such anti-Jewish sentiment Jewish life flourished and Jewish political parties founded Hebrew and Yiddish schools competing with one another for support. Eastern European Jewry was also enriched by such institutions as the Yivo Institute of Jewish Research founded in Vilna in 1925 as well as the establishment of the Jewish youth movements and *yeshivot*.

In post-revolutionary Russia Jewish organizations except for synagogue committees were eliminated and poor Jews living in villages were deprived of civil rights. In the 1920s all *yeshivot* were closed and the printing of religious books ceased. Such anti-Semitism however did not hinder Jews from settling in Russian cities where they worked as managers and bureaucrats. A significant number attended institutions of higher education in order to obtain professional qualifications, and in 1921 the New Economic Policy encouraged Jews to establish farming villages in various parts of the Soviet Union; in the 1920s Birobidzhan was set aside for Jewish colonization. But in 1928 this policy was revoked, and as a result of industrialization many Jews worked instead as labourers, technicians, scientists and engineers. During this period the communist government established Yiddish-speaking workers' councils, schools, scholarly institutes, publishing houses and theatres. In such a climate anti-Semitism was officially prohibited. Yet in subsequent years Jewish institutions and cultural programmes were dismantled and Jews were removed from the party and governmental positions.

Jewry in Palestine, Africa, Asia and Germany

After World War I Jews in Palestine organized a National Assembly and an Executive Council. By 1929 the Jewish community (*yishuv*) numbered 160,000 with 110 agricultural settlements; in the next ten years the community increased to 500,000 with 233 agricultural communities. About a quarter of this population lived in co-operatives. Tel Aviv had 150,000 settlers, Jerusalem 90,000 and Haifa 60,000. Industrialization was initiated by the Palestinian Electric Corporation and developed by the Histradrut (the General Federation of Hebrew Workers). In 1925 the Hebrew University was opened. During this period Palestine was only 160 miles long and 70 miles wide; this territory contained about one million Arabs consisting of peasants (*fellahin*) and a number of landowners in addition to the Jewish pouplation. In 1929 the Arab community rioted following a dispute concerning Jewish access to the western wall of the ancient Temple. This conflict caused the British to curtail Jewish immigration as well as the purchase of Arab land.

By the late 1920s Labour Zionism had become a dominant force in Palestinian Jewish life; in 1930 various socialist and Labour groups joined together in the Israel Labour Party. Within the Zionist movement a right-wing segment criticized the President of the World Zionist Organization, Chaim Weizmann (1874–1952), who was committed to co-operating with the British. Vladimir Jabotinsky (1880–1940), leader of the Union of Zionist Revisionists, stressed that the central aim of Zionists was the establishment of an independent state in the whole of Palestine. After several Zionist congresses, the Revisionist movement formed its own organization and withdrew from the militia of the *yishuv* (the Haganah) to form its own military force. In 1936 the Arabs, supported by Syria, Iraq and Egypt, commenced an offensive against Jews, the British and moderate Arabs. In 1937 a British Royal Commission proposed that Palestine be partitioned into a Jewish and Arab state with a British zone; this recommendation was accepted by the Zionists but rejected by the Arabs. Eventually the British government published a White Paper in 1939 which rejected the concept of partition, limited Jewish immigration to 75,000 and decreed that Palestine would become independent in ten years.

While these events were taking place in Palestine, Jews in North Africa flourished as a result of French influence. In the 1860s the Alliance Israelite began to establish modern French-language schools for these communities and such progressive attitudes continued into the twentieth century. In India the long-established Jewish communities continued until the modern period. Modern Jewry was active in Alexandria and Cairo under British rule. The Jews of Iraq also prospered and played an important role in educational and economic life. At the beginning of the nineteenth century Jews in the Caucasus, Georgia and Bukhara were incorporated into the Russian empire and continued their religious traditions. In Turkey Sephardic Jews developed a distinctive culture based on Ladino, a Jewish Spanish dialect. The Jews of Persia lived under oppressive conditions throughout the nineteenth century, but a revival of Judaio-Persian literature took place at the end of the century. In the 1920s Persia was modernized and the Jewish community began to establish cultural and educational institutions.

After the First World War Germany flourished as a federal republic, but the depression of 1930–2 brought about massive unemployment. As a consequence extremist parties gained considerable support forcing the government to rule by presidential decree. After several unsuccessful conservative coalitions, the president, Field Marshal Paul von Hindenburg, appointed the leader of the Nationalist Socialist Worker's Party (the Nazi Party), Adolf Hilter

(1889–1945), as chancellor. The ideology of the Nazi party was based on German nationalism, anti-capitalism and anti-Semitism. According to Hitler, the Jews were responsible for Germany's defeat in the war as well as the economic and cultural decline of the post-war period. In addition the Bolshevik victory in Russia was portrayed as part of a Jewish plot for world domination. To combat the plans of international Jewry, Hitler believed it was necessary for Germany to gain control over a vast empire in which Aryan supremacy could be ensured.

Once the Nazis gained control of the government, they pursued these racist objectives by curtailing civil liberties. In 1933 all political parties were eliminated; strikes were forbidden; and trade unions were dissolved. The arrest of dissident scholars and scientists was followed by a purge of the party's radicals. During the next few years Jews were eliminated from the civil service, the legal and medical professions, and cultural and educational institutions. In September 1935 the Nuremburg Laws made Jews into second-class inhabitants, and all marriage and sexual liaisons were described as crimes against the state. In 1938 Jewish communal bodies were put under the control of the Gestapo, and Jews were forced to register their property. Later in the year the Nazi party organized an onslaught against the Jewish population in which Jews were murdered and Jewish property was destroyed. This event known as *Kristallnacht* was a prelude to the Holocaust which brought about a new stage of modern Jewish history.

14
Holocaust and Aftermath

After the conquest of Poland in 1939, Germany occupied Denmark and Norway, the Netherlands, Belgium and France. In the spring of 1941, Hitler strengthened the Italian forces and extended their control over the Balkans and North Africa. In June of the same year Germany launched an attack on Russia, and by the end of the year most of the Ukraine had been captured. In December 1941 Germany and Italy declared war against the United States, and in the following year the invasion of Russia was recommenced. Throughout the war Hitler attempted to realize his plan of eliminating the Jews, but when Hitler was defeated the state of Israel became the focus of Jewish aspirations for Jews worldwide.

The beginnings of the Holocaust

With the first phase of war, pressure on Jews in Germany increased. From September 1939 Jews had to be off the streets by 8.00 pm; their movements were restricted; they were banned from various types of transport and deprived of the use of the telephone. From December 1939 Jewish rations were cut and Jews were restricted to specific shopping hours. The Nazis' plan for the elimination of the Jews proceeded in stages. Initially thousands of Jews were deported or put into forced labour camps which frequently led to their death. But in 1941 when the invasion of Russia was imminent, rumours began to circulate that Hitler had entrusted Reinhard Heydrich with the preparation of a Final Solution to the Jewish problem. On 30 July 1940 Hermann Goering, who was in charge of the German economy, had ordered Reinhard Heydrich to 'take all preparatory measures . . .

required for the final solution of the Jewish question in the European territories under German influence'. Heydrich himself revealed the Final Solution to staff members at a conference on 20 January 1942 in the office of the International Criminal Police Commission in Berlin. The war with Russia, he explained, made the plan of deporting all Jews an impossibility. The only alternative was extermination: the Jews who survived the hardships of the camps 'must be given treatment accordingly, for these people, representing a natural selection, are to be regarded as the germ-cell of a new Jewish development, should they be allowed to go free.'

The first stage of the Nazis' plan for European Jewry had already begun with the invasion of Poland. In September 1939 Hitler decided to incorporate much of Poland into Germany, and move more than 600,000 Jews into a central area (the 'General Government'). When the Jewish population was ghettoized into what Hitler referred to as a huge Polish labour camp, a massive work programme was initiated. Here Jews worked all day, seven days a week, dressed in rags and fed on bread, soup and potatoes. This slave-labour operation was a form of murder; the phrase 'destruction through work' was used repeatedly in discussions between Georg Thierack, Joseph Goebbels and Heinrich Himmler in September 1942. According to Rudolf Hess, the commandant at Auschwitz, by the end of 1944 about 400,000 slaves worked in the German armaments industry: 'In enterprises with particularly severe working conditions', he stated, 'every month one-fifth died or were, because of inability to work, sent back by the enterprises to the camps in order to be exterminated.' These workers had no names, only numbers tattooed on their bodies; if one died a replacement was sought without any inquest into the cause of death. Yet working Jews to their graves was not sufficient for the Nazi regime; what was needed was a plan of mass extermination which began with the invasion of Russia in 1941. This was designed to destroy the centre of what was described by the Nazis as the 'Jewish–Bolshevik conspiracy'.

At first mobile killing battalions of 500–900 men (the *Einsatz-gruppen*) under the supervision of Heydrich began the slaughter of Russian Jewry. Of the 4,500,000 Jews who resided in Soviet territory, more than half fled before the German invasion; those who remained were concentrated in large cities making it easier for Heydrich's troops to carry out their task. Throughout the country the *Einsatz-gruppen* moved into Russian towns, sought out the rabbi or Jewish council and obtained a list of all Jewish inhabitants. The Jews were then rounded up in market places, crowded into trains, buses and trucks and taken to the woods where mass graves had been dug. They were then machine-gunned to death. A typical example of such killing was depicted by a civilian works engineer in the 1945 Nuremburg trials:

> people were closely wedged together, lying on top of each other so that only their heads were visible. Nearly all had blood running over their shoulders from their heads. Some of the people shot were still moving. Some lifted their arms and turned their heads to show that they were still alive. The pit was already two-thirds full. I estimated that it held a thousand people.

In this slaughter some Jews attempted to escape the onslaught by hiding under floorboards and cellars, but they were buried alive or blasted out with grenades. A few girls offered themselves to stay alive; they were used during the night but killed the next morning. In the initial sweep between October and December 1941, these troops killed over 300,000 Jews; in a second stage that lasted throughout 1942 over 900,000 were murdered.

The death camps

Other methods were also employed by the Nazis. Mobile gas vans were sent to each battalion of the *Einsatzgruppen*. Meanwhile these mobile killing operations were being supplemented by the use of fixed centres, the death camps. Six of these were at Chelmno and Auschwitz in the Polish territories, and at Treblinka, Sobibor, Majdanek and Belzec in the Polish 'General Government'. Construction of this mass-murder industry began in 1941. Two civilians from Hamburg went to Auschwitz to teach the staff how to use Zyklon-B gas. In September 1941 the first gassing took place in Auschwitz Block II; then work began on Birkenau, the central killing centre in Auschwitz. The first death camp to be completed was Chelmno near Lödz which started functioning in December 1941. Subsequently Belzec became operational and the building of Sobibor began in March 1942. At the same time Majdanek and Treblinka were transformed into death centres. At this time Goebbels noted: 'A judgement is being visited on the Jews . . . the prophecy which the Führer made about them for having brought on a new world war is beginning to come true in the most terrible manner.'

The eradication of the Jews in western Europe (as opposed to the destruction of Polish and Russian Jewry) was the private preserve of Adolf Eichmann. In 1942 he decided to send 100,000 Jews from the

Greater Reich (Germany, Austria and Czechoslovakia) to Poland where they were gassed at Belzec and Majdanek. By the end of 1943 the majority of Jews from the Greater Reich were killed: 180,000 from Germany; 60,000 from Austria; and 243,000 from Czechoslovakia. The deportation of Jews in countries west and south of Poland was on an equally massive scale. Out of a population of 140,000 Dutch Jews, 110,000 were deported to Auschwitz and Sobibor to be exterminated between 1941 and 1942. During this period 25,000 Belgian Jews, 50,000 Yugoslav Jews and 80,000 Greek Jews perished in the death camps. Until the summer of 1942 Jewish deportees from central and western Europe were divided equally between Auschwitz and the other death camps, but in August 1942 Himmler decided that Auschwitz should become the central extermination centre for western Europe. At its fullest capacity it held 140,000 inmates and its five crematoria could burn 10,000 bodies each day. Those who escaped the gassing engaged in bricklaying for twelve to fourteen hours a day surviving on a watery turnip soup until they became living corpses.

Though nearly all of European Jewry succumbed to Nazi terror without resistance, there were some Jews who revolted against the Germans. In the summer of 1942 a young Zionist, Mordecai Anielewicz, persuaded the Jewish leaders of the Warsaw ghetto that resistance offered the only possibility of survival. Underground shelters and bunkers were constructed; money was raised from Jewish capitalists; revolvers and grenades were purchased. By the autumn of 1942 the Jewish resistance had become a powerful force. By January of the next year Himmler visited the Warsaw ghetto and issued the order for a final eradication of the remaining Jews; in April, SS Major-General Jürgen Stroop arrived to put this operation into effect. When the SS troops numbering 2,000 moved into position, they were attacked from rooftops. In response the Nazis bombarded buildings and systematically levelled the places where Jews were hiding. In the sewers and shelters the Jews continued their resistance: Jewish patrols disguised in German uniforms ventured out to capture arms and rations; grenades and molotov cocktails were tossed at German troops and tanks. The SS retaliated with dynamite and gas shells, flooded the sewers and released police dogs. One of the Jewish fighters, Ziviah Lubetkin, described the last days of this struggle:

Our comrades entrenched themselves near the entrance and waited with their weapons ready for the Germans. Finally the Germans began to send gas into the bunker. They let in a small quantity of gas, then stopped, trying to break their spirit with a prolonged suffocation. A terrible death faced the 120. Aryeh Wilner was the first to cry out: 'Come let us destroy ourselves. Let's not fall into their hands alive!' The suicides began.

In the face of such a powerful enemy the Jewish community in Europe was doomed to massive destruction. Nearly 9 million Jews were resident in European countries under German control. Of those it is estimated that the Nazis killed about 6 million. In Poland more than 90 per cent were killed (3,300,000). The same percentage of the Jewish population died in the Baltic States, Germany and Austria. More than 70 per cent were murdered in the Bohemian protectorate, Slovakia, Greece and the Netherlands. More than 50 per cent were killed in White Russia, the Ukraine, Belgium, Yugoslavia, Romania and Norway. The six major death camps constituted the main areas of killing: over 2,000,000 died at Auschwitz; 1,380,000 at Majdanek; 800,000 at Treblinka; 600,000 at Belzec; 340,000 at Chelmno; and 250,000 at Sobibor. In this way Hitler attempted to destroy what he believed was a unified Jewish community which threatened the Nazi masterplan.

The state of Israel

The Holocaust and the establishment of the state of Israel were organically related events – the death of millions of Jews in the Second World War profoundly affected Jewry throughout the world. Some traditional Jews believed that the Holocaust was a punishment upon the community because of its sins but would be followed by the founding of a Jewish state; others thought the creation of Israel was the consequence of Jewish suffering. Whatever the cause Hitler's policy unintentionally assisted the Jewish community in Palestine: 60,000 Jews initially left Germany for Israel and contributed substantially to the growth and development of the homeland. In addition, from the beginning of the war in 1939, the creation of a Jewish state became the primary aim of Zionists. In order to achieve this objective the Jewish community had to persuade the allies of the virtues of their plan. As far as the British were concerned, though the Balfour Declaration of 1917 supported the establishment of a Jewish homeland in Palestine, the 1939 White Paper effectively rejected this proposal and projected a future in which there would be no predominantly Jewish presence.

During the war and afterwards, the British steadfastly maintained this policy and prevented illegal immigrants from entering the Holy Land. In the Jews' struggle against the British, Menachem Begin, the leader of the Revisionists' military arm (the Irgun), played an important role. Similarly an extremist group called the Stern Gang, which broke away from the Irgun, carried on a campaign against British domination. On 6 November 1944 the Stern Gang murdered Lord Moyne, the British Minister for Middle East Affairs. The official Zionist military force, the Haganah, was appalled by this action and launched an offensive against the Sternists and the Irgun. Yet despite this internal conflict these various Jewish factions eventually joined forces in forming a united resistance movement.

In this struggle two episodes involving Menachem Begin were instrumental in forcing Britain to capitulate. On 29 June 1946 the British arrested over 2,000 Jewish activists; in response Begin convinced the Haganah to blow up the King David Hotel in Jerusalem where part of the British administration was housed. At the end of July an explosion took place killing twenty-eight British, forty-one Arabs and seventeen Jews plus five others. Subsequently the British government proposed a tripartite division of Palestine, but both Arabs and Jews rejected the scheme. On 14 February the British Foreign Secretary Ernest Bevin handed over the Palestinian problem to the United Nations though Britain did not immediately withdraw from the country. In April 1947 three members of the Irgun were arrested and hanged for attacking the prison in Acre and freeing 251 prisoners. In retaliation Begin gave instructions to hang two British soldiers. In response anti-Jewish riots took place in various English cities, which helped to persuade the British to leave Palestine as soon as possible.

Once the British announced their intention, President Harry Truman argued for the creation of a Jewish state. In May 1947 the United Nations discussed the Palestinian problem. Two reports were issued by a special committee: a minority recommended a federated bi-national state; the majority advocated a new plan of partition in which there would be a Jewish and an Arab state as well as an international zone in Jerusalem. This latter proposal was endorsed by the General Assembly of the United Nations on 29 November 1947. Once the UN plan for partition was endorsed, the Arabs began to attack Jewish settlements. Azzam Pasha, Secretary-General of the Arab League, declared: 'This will be a war of extermination and a momentous massacre.' By March 1948 over 1,000 Jews had been killed, but in the next month David Ben Gurion ordered the Haganah to link up all the Jewish enclaves and consolidate the territory given to Israel under the UN partition plan. On 14 May 1948 Ben-Gurion read out the Scroll of Independence: 'By virtue of our national and intrinsic right and on the strength of the resolution of the United Nations General Assembly, we hereby declare the establishment of a Jewish State in Palestine which shall be known as the State of Israel.'

Immediately a government was formed Egyptian air raids began. A truce lasting a month was formalized on 11 June during which time the Arabs reinforced their armies. When the fighting began again on 9 July, the Israelis appeared to be in control – they took Lydda, Ramleh and Nazareth as well as large territories beyond the partition borders. Though the Arabs agreed to a truce, there were outbursts of violence, and in October the Israelis launched an offensive which resulted in the capture of Beersheba. On 12 January 1949 armistice talks were held and later signed with Egypt, the Lebanon, Transjordan and Syria. During this period more than 650,000 Arab inhabitants of Palestine escaped from Israeli-held territory: 280,000 to the West Bank; 70,000 to Transjordan; 100,000 to Lebanon; 4,000 to Iraq; 75,000 to Syria; 7,000 to Egypt; and 190,000 to the Gaza Strip.

Because of these Palestinian refugees the Arabs regarded the armistice as merely a temporary truce. Under President Nasser of Egypt, a plan for the elimination of the Jewish state was put into operation. From 1956 President Gamal Abdel Nasser refused Israeli ships access to the Gulf of Aqaba; in April he signed a pact with Saudi Arabia and Yemen; in July he seized the Suez Canal; in October he formed a military command with Jordan and Syria. In response Israel launched a strike on 29 October conquering Sinai and opening the sea route to Aqaba. In an agreement which ended the fighting, Israel undertook to withdraw from Sinai provided that Egypt did not remilitarize it and UN forces constituted a *cordon sanitaire*. This arrangement existed for a decade though armed struggle between both sides continued. In 1967 Nasser began another offensive against Israel. On 15 May he moved 100,000 troops into the Sinai and ordered the UN forces to leave. He then blockaded Aqaba by closing the Tiran Straits to Israeli shipping, and signed a military agreement with King Hussein of Jordan. On 5 June the Israelis launched a pre-emptive strike devastating the Egyptian air force on the ground. Jordan and Syria then entered the war on Egypt's side. Two days later Israel captured the Old City of Jerusalem and on the following day the West Bank. During the next two days Israel attacked the Golan Heights and reoccupied Sinai.

The Six Day War was a major victory for the Israelis but did not bring security to the Jewish state. In July 1972 President Anwar Sadat of Egypt expelled Egypt's Soviet advisers, dispensed with Nasser's alliances with other Arab states, and on Yom Kippur, 6 October 1973, he attacked Israel. The Egyptian and Syrian forces broke through Israeli lines and serious losses were inflicted on Israeli planes and armour. On 9 October the Syrian advance was halted, and the next day the American President Richard Nixon began an airlift of weapons. Two days later the Israelis mounted a counter-attack on Egypt – this was a turning point in the conflict and a ceasefire came into force on 24 October 1973. During this period and for the next few years the Israeli government was led by a Labour-dominated coalition, but in May 1977 the Likud Party led by Menachem Begin came to power. On 9 November 1977 President Sadat offered to negotiate peace terms with Israel which were formalized at Camp David – the American presidential summer home – on 5 September 1978. Under the terms of this agreement, Egypt recognized Israel's right to exist, and provided guarantees for Israel's southern border; in return Israel gave back Sinai, undertook to negotiate away much of the West Bank, and made concessions over Jerusalem in exchange for a complementary treaty with the Palestinians and other Arab peoples. These latter terms however were not realized since the plan was rejected by the Palestinian Arabs.

In the 1980s Israel attempted to combat the menace of the Palestine Liberation Organization which continually threatened Israeli security. From 6 June 1982 the Israel Defence Forces launched an offensive against the PLO in southern Lebanon; this occupation involved heavy bombing which resulted in massive Arab casualties. In addition Muslim refugees were slaughtered by Christian Falangist Arabs in the Sabra and Shatilla refugee camps on 16 September 1982. Both the invasion of Lebanon and this massacre provoked discord between Israel and her allies as well as controversy in Israel. Yet despite these events, Israel held fast to its purpose of providing a homeland for all Jews. In the light of the Holocaust Jews worldwide remained committed to the belief that the state of Israel is the only guarantee against another Final Solution being imposed on the Jewish people.

Jewry after the Holocaust

The Holocaust significantly changed the nature of Jewry in the modern world. Before the war there were about 10 million Jews; in the 1980s the Jewish community had not recovered from the losses of the Nazi period. Out of a total of 13,500,000 Jews, approximately 3,500,000 live in Israel, but the largest Jewish community is in America: 5,750,000 live in the United States, 310,000 in Canada, 250,000 in Argentina, 130,000 in Brazil, 40,000 in Mexico and smaller populations in other South American countries. The next largest community is in Soviet Russia comprising about 1,750,000. Some eastern European countries also have a sizeable number of Jews such as Hungary with 75,000 and Romania with 30,000 (out of a population of 130,000 in Marxist states). In western Europe there are some 1,250,000 Jews: 670,000 in France, 360,000 in Britain, 42,000 in West Germany, 41,000 in Belgium, 35,000 in Italy, 28,000 in the Netherlands and 21,000 in Switzerland. On the African continent, 105,000 Jews reside in South Africa, 17,000 in Morocco and about 5,000 in Ethiopia. In Asia there are 35,000 Jews in Iran and 21,000 in Turkey. The Australian and New Zealand communities consist of about 75,000.

These various Jewish populations have had a complex history since the war. In many cases Jewry was reduced to only a fraction of its size before the Holocaust. The Jewish community of Salonika, for example, was 60,000 in 1939 but only 1,500 in the 1980s; Vienna shrank from 200,000 to less than 8,000; Berlin Jewry fell from approximately 175,000 to about 6,000; the Jews in Poland dwindled from 3,300,000 to about 5,000. Yet in other parts of the world Jewish numbers have increased as a result of immigration. In France Sephardic immigrants from the Muslim world swelled the Jewish population and intensified Jewish identification. Britain also welcomed a large number of newcomers after the war which increased the community and added to its cultural development. But it was in the United States particularly that the Jewish community grew in size and importance.

Before the war the American Jewish population was diverse and vibrant, and refugees from Nazi Europe increased its dynamism. These immigrants included adherents of more developed forms of European liberalism as well as Hasidim with strong folk traditions. As Jewish numbers increased, earlier religious groupings gained strength and influence. On the left of the religious spectrum the Reform movement gradually became more favourable to Zionism and once the state of Israel became a reality previous Reform antipathy to a Jewish homeland largely disappeared. In the last few decades the Jewish Institute of Religion founded by Stephen Wise in 1922 has merged with the Hebrew Union College and campuses have been established in California and Jerusalem. In matters of ritual

Reform Judaism has moved towards a more traditional stance, though recently reformers took the radical step of ordaining women to the rabbinate and redefined Jewish identity to include children of Jewish fathers.

In the Conservative movement tension between liberals and traditionalists was expressed in the 1960s and 1970s concerning the ordination of women which has now become official policy. In addition it was from the ranks of Conservative Jews that Reconstructionist Judaism emerged; this new branch was founded by Mordecai Kaplan who adopted a radical approach to the tradition which envisaged Judaism as a civilization. Rejecting belief in a personal God, Kaplan argued that the Jewish heritage should be perpetuated with the synagogue as the centre of Jewish life. Within the Orthodox fold internal divisions were also evident. Yeshivah University in New York and the Hebrew Theological College of Chicago produced rabbinical graduates who belonged mainly to the Rabbinical Council of America, whereas Orthodox rabbis of a more traditional orientation were generally members of the Aggudas Ha-Rabbonim founded by Yiddish-speaking immigrant rabbis at the turn of the century. The divisions within the Orthodox camp reflect differing attitudes to Americanization and co-operation with other Jews, yet despite this diversity the majority of American Orthodox Jewry are unified today in their commitment to the state of Israel.

In contrast with Jewish life in the United States, Jewish activities in the Soviet Union have been officially curtailed by the government. During the war anti-Semitism existed in the Red Army, and as the war ended many Jews were removed from government departments. In September 1948 an article in Pravda denounced Israel as a bourgeois tool of American capitalism; the Jewish anti-Fascist committee was eliminated; and Yiddish schools were closed. This was followed by an attack on Jewish writers, painters, musicians and intellectuals. The campaign extended to Czechoslovakia, and on 20 November 1952 the Czech Communist Party General Secretary as well as other communist leaders including eleven Jews were accused of a Trotskyite–Titoist–Zionist conspiracy and executed. In 1953 nine doctors including six Jews were accused of plotting to poison Joseph Stalin in conjunction with British, American and Zionist agents. This trial was to have been a prelude to the deportation of Jews to Siberia but Stalin died before the doctors were tried. Stalin's successor Nikita Khrushchev changed the orientation of anti-Jewish propaganda from spying to economic criminality; many Jews were convicted and sentenced to death. Furthermore, during Khrushchev's reign the number of synagogues was reduced from 450 to sixty and he permitted the publication of the anti-Semitic tract, *Judaism without Embellishment*. After Khrushchev's fall there was a brief respite, but following the Six Day War in 1967 the campaign against Jews was resumed. In 1971 Leonid Brezhnev decided to allow a large number of Jews to leave the Soviet Union, and during the next decade 250,000 emigrated. But accompanying this large-scale exodus there was an increase in trials of Jews and the procedure for obtaining an exit visa became more complicated. In the 1980s even fewer visas were granted as the Soviet campaign against Zionism intensified.

Parallel with Soviet anti-Semitism was the propaganda disseminated in the Arab world. Arab polemics against the Jews were based in part on the *Protocols of Zion* which circulated widely in Arab countries. In 1958, for example, President Nasser told an Indian journalist: 'It is very important that you should read it. I will give you a copy. It proves beyond a shadow of a doubt that three hundred Zionists, each of whom knows all the others, govern the fate of the European continent and that they elect their successors from their entourage.' Extracts and summaries from this anti-Semitic work were used in Arab school textbooks and in training manuals for the Arab military forces. In addition blood-libel material appeared in 1962 as a government publication of the United Arab Republic entitled *Talmudic Human Sacrifice*. Recently Ayatollah Khomeini in Iran has portrayed Zionism as an emanation of Satan. Such anti-Jewish material from the Soviet bloc and the Arab states contributed to the United Nations' decision to condemn Zionism. In the 1975 session of the United Nations General Assembly President Idi Amin of Uganda denounced the 'Zionist–American conspiracy' against the Arab world and called for the expulsion of Israel from the United Nations. Though this was not carried through, on 17 October the Third Committee of the General Assembly passed a motion condemning Zionism as a form of racism, and in November the General Assembly endorsed the resolution. Thus the spectre of anti-Semitism, which led to the destruction of 6 million Jews in the Holocaust, has again emerged in modern society.

15
Modern Jewish Thought

In the modern period Jewish writers have wrestled with issues relating to Jewish existence and the nature of God's activity. In the light of Jewish emancipation questions were posed about the relationship between Judaism and science, the position of the Jew in contemporary society and the nature of a Jewish homeland. Further, Jewish thinkers also attempted to make sense of the Holocaust in theological terms. As in the past, Jewish theology in the modern world has attempted to utilize the tradition in forging a living faith in touch with contemporary currents of thought.

Jewish nationalism

In the mid-nineteenth century metaphysical idealism pervaded the work of Jewish thinkers such as Formstecher, Hirsch and Steinheim. But for several Jewish writers this idealist approach was inadequate and their ideas paved the way for the Jewish nationalist movement at the end of the century. The German Jewish philosopher Moses Hess (1812–75), for example, argued in *Rome and Jerusalem* that Jewish nationhood provides the setting for the realization of Judaism's ethical ideals. According to Hess this view was anticipated in the Mosaic legislation as well as the prophetic literature which foresaw a model society in Israel which would be a light to all nations. For Hess the economic and social conditions of the diaspora prevent Jews from exercising such a mission. What is needed is a Jewish commonwealth. In advocating such an ideal Hess argued that a Jewish homeland in Palestine would bring about the unification of ethics and life and could serve as a model for the oppressed peoples of Asia and Africa.

In establishing such a state, eastern European Jews would be the main volunteers. In propounding this thesis, Hess criticized the Reform movement for its preoccupation with other-worldly goals. Accommodation with Christianity, he maintained, betrayed the Jewish heritage and could never gain the respect of German Christians. Orthodox Judaism on the other hand could become fertile once it was translated to the Holy Land.

Paralleling Hess's views the eastern European ideologue of Jewish nationalism, Peretz Smolenskin (1840–85), maintained that German Reform Judaism brought about division in the Jewish world. Judaism, he argued, was more than a religious association and the Jews should be seen as a nation like all the nations. Though the Jewish people lack territory, government and a spoken language, they are a spiritual nation sustained by the Torah. For Smolenskin the Torah was grounded in the 'Spiritual Absolute' but nevertheless constituted an evolving cultural heritage adaptable to changed circumstances. According to Smolenskin Reform Judaism had abandoned two forces for Jewish unity – the Hebrew language and the concept of a redemption of the Jewish people. Hebrew, he asserted, must remain the medium for Torah study as well as for Jewish scholarship. Moreover, he insisted that belief in messianic redemption is a central feature of the Jewish religious system. Though these views were originally based on the assumption that Jews would remain a nation in the diaspora, he eventually despaired of the future of Jewry outside Israel and embraced Zionism as a blueprint for Jewish survival.

In their studies Hess and Smolenskin argued that anti-Jewish sentiment is not an antiquated prejudice; for Leon Pinsker (1821–91) and Theodore Herzl (1860–1905) this recognition led to the ideology of Jewish nationalism. In *Autoemancipation*, Pinsker portrayed anti-Semitism as an irrational fear of the stranger. Because Jews are seen as a people without a home, their successes evoke jealousy and resentment and their powerlessness makes them an easy target. For Herzl the indirect cause of Jew-hatred was the medieval segregation of the Jews which impelled them to develop financial resources. When the ghettos were eliminated, such economic acumen enabled them to cope successfully with the gentile population. In *The Jewish State*, Herzl argued that economic prosperity encouraged Christians to fear the power of Jewish financiers. Further he stressed that the growth of socialist and radical ideologies in the Jewish community intensified prejudice. Thus, he concluded, it was impossible for Jews to live a secure life in the diaspora.

For some Jewish theorists such a conception of Jewish nationalism was simply an imitation of current European political formulae. What they sought instead was a cultural nationalism which could amalgamate traditional Judaism with secular values as advocated by a number of influential European writers committed to the betterment of society. Foremost among these cultural Zionists was Asher Ginsberg, known as Ahad Ha-Am, who believed that the Jewish national movement would provide a framework for coming to terms with the post-ghetto environment. Hibbat Zion (Love of Zion), he maintained, is not a part of the Jewish heritage; it is the whole of Judaism: 'It stands for a Judaism which shall have as its focal point the ideal of our nation's unity, its renaissance, and its free development through the expression of universal human values in terms of its own distinctive spirit.' Moreover, Ahad Ha-Am asserted that only in the land of Israel could Judaism recover its inner freedom. In such a spiritual setting Jews would be freed from the constricting demands of the non-Jewish world.

According to Ahad Ha-Am the national character of Judaism was more important than religious belief. Jewish commitment was based on communal responsibility. Judaism, he wrote, imposed itself upon Jews without their knowledge or consent. 'Why are we Jews?' he asked. 'It is within us', he stated. 'It is one of our laws of nature. It has an existence and a constancy of its own, like a mother's love for her children, like a man's love of his homeland.' Jewish identity is thus not rooted in theological speculation; it is grounded in Jewish civilization. The Jewish religion is therefore a product of the nation's response to historical circumstances. Prophetic monotheism for example was accepted by Jews during the Babylonian captivity because it enabled the people to reject the view that their captivity was a punishment inflicted by the Babylonian gods. Similarly during the medieval period ritual law prevented Jewry from being assimilated and kept alive the belief in a final ingathering of the exiles. Zionism too is a further instance of the belief that the nation will survive.

Unlike Ahad Ha-Am the Russian historian Simon Dubnow (1860–1941) argued that it is possible for the Jewish people to be a nation even without a homeland. According to Dubnow nationhood consists of common memories, kinship and a shared identity. Like Smolenskin he believed that a nation can endure without land, language and a statehood. Jewry, he explained, evolved through various successive states: from its tribal origins it became a political entity and eventually adjusted to the loss of a country. Yet in its history there had been important Jewish centres outside Israel. In this light the Jews are a nation without boundaries. Thus, he argued, the *kahal* system of government which had developed in eastern Europe should be reconstituted in the diaspora into a communal body embracing all branches of Judaism.

At the end of the nineteenth century some Jewish thinkers rejected the ideology of cultural Zionists. Michah Joseph Berdichevsky (1865–1921), for example, dismissed Ahad Ha-Am's blend of traditionalism and modernity. For Berdichevsky the Jewish people need to be liberated from Judaism. 'Among us', he wrote, 'man is crushed by traditional customs, laws, doctrines and judgements, for many things are bequeathed to us by our ancestors which deaden the soul.' The past must be overcome so that individuals are able to attain self-fulfilment. There must be a reformulation of values. Bold steps are required to transcend Jewish intellectualism and submission to God – what is needed is a wholeness of life involving physical activity and a love of nature. The duty of present-day Jewry, he argued, was to emulate the heroism of past generations and create a Hebrew humanism.

Such a heroic style of Jewish existence was elaborated by Nahman Syrkin (1868–1924) who proposed the creation of a Jewish common-wealth based on socialist principles. Judaism could only survive if eastern European Jews refused to imitate western bourgeois values. Zionism, he argued, was capable of creating the utopian ideal of a socialist state whose values are grounded in the Biblical concept of justice. For Syrkin a socialist Jewish homeland would be a realization of the messianic vision. Other socialist scholars advanced a form of Zionism based on the dialectical materialism of Karl Marx. According to Ber Borochov (1881–1917) the socialization of the means of production would not solve the Jewish problem because the Jewish proletariat was marginal in the diaspora. Neither would emigration provide a basis for Jewish survival since anti-Semitism would continue to be a constant factor in Jewish life. The only solution was to create a base in Palestine that would result in a Jewish socialist structure. The evolution of socialist Jewish existence, he believed, would be an inevitable outcome of the dialectical laws of history.

Twentieth-century European thought

At the beginning of the twentieth century the German liberal rabbi, Leo Baeck (1873–1956), exerted an important influence on Jewish theology. In *The Essence of Judaism*, Baeck argued that Judaism represents a classical type of religion embodying ethical optimism and a commitment to human freedom. In other writings Baeck stated that certain forms of Christianity influenced by Paul emphasize faith at the expense of works; this attitude, he maintained, leads to a passive indifference to the struggle against evil. Judaism however focuses on the ethical life as a response to divine mystery. In apprehending God's commandments, the Jew becomes aware that he is obligated to create a better world. Israel, he wrote, must constantly apply God's demands to changing circumstances. Another Jewish thinker of this period, Aaron David Gordon (1856–1922), visualized a means for Jewish redemption in the agricultural settlements of the Holy Land. For Gordon authentic religiosity is expressed through a bond between man and nature; in this fashion Jewry is able to experience moral rebirth in Palestine which would make the Jewish people an 'incarnation' of ideal humanity. A similar mystical outlook was expressed by another settler in Palestine, Chief Rabbi Abraham Isaac Kook (1865–1935) who argued that there is no segregation between religious and secular life. Drawing on the Kabbalah, Kook maintained that Jews have the task of transmuting earthly aspects of existence to a higher realm. For Kook Israel has the capacity to reach a state of holiness. The renewal of Jewish life in the land of Israel, he believed, was a crucial stage in mankind's spiritual progress.

Another seminal thinker of the early twentieth century was the German philosopher Hermann Cohen (1842–1918) who attempted to harmonize certain aspects of Jewish belief with Kantian idealism in presenting a defence of Jewish ethical monotheism. In *Religion of Reason Out of the Sources of Judaism* Cohen argued that God is the source of everything in the phenomenal world; in Kantian terms this means that the idea of God is the precondition for causality. For Cohen the universe is eternal rather than created at a single point in time – thus there is renewal in the world as the Jewish prayerbook proclaims: 'God renews daily the work of creation.' Revelation also is not tied to a particular historical occurrence. According to Cohen, revelation refers to man's capacity to reason. In this regard Cohen asserted that the spirit of holiness denotes the moral quality shared by God and human beings. God's holiness is the archetype of ethical action – man's holiness lies in his quest to emulate God's nature by performing ethical actions. This link between the human and the Divine is referred to by the term 'correlation'.

Ethical monotheism, Cohen believed, correlated God and man in three unique ways which are superior to philosophy. First, monotheism first discovered the concept of the fellow man (*mitmensch*) in contrast to the other man (*neben*); this distinction implies an awareness of common humanity. Here religion can attain what philosophical ethics cannot achieve from its own resources: the idea of the God of social love who serves as an archetype for righteousness and compassion. Secondly, it is religion rather than philosophy which correlates God and man through the process of atonement for wrongdoing. The rituals and practices of Yom Kippur, for example, serve as a means for self-purification which makes man worthy of divine forgiveness. The third correlation is based on the prophetic ideal of humanity with transcends philosophical ethics by postulating a future of peace and brotherhood. For Cohen immortality in a non-supernatural sense is related to this messianic vision; it consists of the continuation of the individual in the continuity of people and humanity.

Another European theologian of this period, Franz Rosenzweig (1886–1929), explored in *The Star of Redemption* the ways in which theology complements philosophy. In this work Rosenzweig contended that in revelation God confronts man; what is revealed is God's presence, and through the experience of divine love human beings are commanded to love God in return. In propounding this view Rosenzweig distinguished between commandments, which are directed to individuals, and laws for humanity – revelation results in commandments rather than laws. This relationship between God and man is supplemented by creation which relates the individual to the world. Creation, Rosenzweig argued, establishes the dependence that all creatures have on God's power. A third relationship is provided by redemption which links man and the world. For Rosenzweig, through redemption it is possible to overcome isolation because of God's command to love one's neighbour. Throughout history redemption has pervaded the world through acts of loving kindness, bringing about the unification of the world and man with the Divine. These three themes – revelation, creation and redemption – are thus viewed as fundamental aspects of God's plan of cosmic restoration.

Rosenzweig was also concerned with the relationship between Christianity and Judaism with regard to God's kingdom. For Rosenzweig both traditions represent authentic communities of love through which the Divine manifests His presence in the world. Judaism is the 'eternal life'; Christianity constitutes the 'eternal way'. The Jewish tradition commemorates the cycle of creation–revelation–redemption and thereby places the Jewish people outside time in anticipation of humanity's ultimate redemption. The Jewish task is 'to be' rather than 'to missionize'. Christianity on the other hand bears witness to divine truth through proselytizing gentiles in order to bring humanity into its covenant for the eventual redemption of the world. Thus the two religions have complementary roles in the unfolding of God's eternal plan.

A contemporary of Rosenzweig, the German theologian Martin Buber (1878–1965), exerted an important influence on Jewish thought with the publication of *I and Thou*. In this work Buber stated that there are two primary attitudes that individuals can take in relation to the world. The I–It relationship is based on a detachment of the self from the others in which knowledge is objectified. But in the posture of I–Thou there is an encounter between two subjects in which each stands over against the other. Such an attitude is characterized by total presentness: the I addresses the Thou spontaneously and intensely. In a relationship of I–It, however, there is predetermination and control. In presenting this thesis, Buber stressed that he can offer no description of the I–Thou posture; it can only be pointed to. The attitude of I–Thou is a basic dimension of human existence in the world and a key to the concept of 'relation'; it has the character of a dialogue and can only be properly understood through personal experience.

According to Buber, both modes of being are necessary: individuals must move back and forth between the two attitudes. From I–It comes a refinement of knowledge and understanding necessary for dealing with the world. Yet in modern society I–It is eclipsing the I–Thou encounter. This is tragic, Buber believed, since a fulfilled human life requires the experience of I–Thou. What is required in modern society is a restored balance between I–Thou and I–It. Buber linked this discussion to God who is the 'Eternal Thou'. For Buber, God is the only Thou who can never become an It. He is the unifying ground for particular Thous which makes possible all relationships. And, conversely, it is through the encounter with all things that God is met. As Buber explained:

> Every particular *Thou* is a glimpse through to the eternal *Thou*: by means of every particular *Thou* the primary word addresses the eternal *Thou*. Through this mediation of the *Thou* of all beings fulfilment, and non-fulfilment, of relations comes to them: the inborn *Thou* is realised in each relation and consummated in none. It is consummated only in the direct relation with the *Thou* that by its nature cannot become *It*.

Contributions to American Jewish religious thought

Turning to the work of Jewish theologians in America, the writings of Mordecai Kaplan (1881–1983) have had a significant impact. In *Judaism as a Civilization*, Kaplan argued that Jews in the past believed in a supernatural God who revealed Himself to the Jewish people and provided a means for salvation. Today however this religious view has disintegrated for several reasons. First, many Jews in modern society tend to look to the improvement of their life in this world as a central goal rather than to an other-worldly concept of salvation. A second feature seriously affecting traditional Jewish life has been a tendency to adopt the scientific approach as the best method of ascertaining truth. Thirdly, there has been a shift in the modern perception of moral responsibility. In the past moral values were grounded in God's will, yet today there is increasing emphasis upon man as the standard of values. Finally the traditional account of the origin of the Jewish people has become more difficult to sustain. Scholarly research has revealed that the Biblical account of Israel's beginnings is a construct of a popular and uncritical imagination.

The effect of these influences on contemporary Judaism, Kaplan argued, has deprived the Torah of its pivotal influence on Jewish life. The scientific habit of mind is incompatible with the view that God has revealed His will fully and absolutely to His chosen people. The modern view of Scripture is that it is the result of a long historical process – its teachings are no more than a reflection of the moral and spiritual attainments of its authors. Such a perception of the Torah inevitably undermines the belief in its immutability. Thus, Kaplan asserted, without the belief in the supernatural origin of Scripture the very ground is removed from the entire structure of rabbinic thought, and he maintained it is therefore no longer possible to believe in a transcendent God who acts in history. This however does not mean that the idea of God must be abandoned. On the contrary, Kaplan insisted that God is an immanent reality that impinges on every aspect of human existence. The idea of God must be revised – the belief in a supernatural deity must be superseded by a conception of God as man's will to live.

Kaplan was persuaded that such a non-supernatural orientation to religion can provide the basis for a spiritual life. Judaism, he believed, is essentially the concretization of the collective self-consciousness of the community. The Jewish faith is a civilization which is manifest in sancta. Such sancta commemorate what the Jewish people hold most sacred and provide continuity through history as well as fortify the collective conscience. Conceived in this way, the Jewish faith includes history, literature, language, social organization, sanctions, standards of conduct, social and spiritual ideas and aesthetic values. By concentrating on Judaism as a civilization, Kaplan was able to activate Jewish concern and commitment to peoplehood and tradition in his presentation of the nature of the Jewish faith.

Another Jewish theologian of importance was Abraham Joshua Heschel (1907–72) who in various writings was concerned with faith and its antecedents – the experiences, insights, emotions, attitudes and acts out of which faith arises. According to Heschel certain experiences and acts that are commonly regarded as aspects of faith are also antecedents of faith. Wonder before the sublime mystery of nature, for example, is not in itself an aspect of the Jewish faith. Such wonder many occur prior to the emergence of faith; it can ignite the flame of faith. Realities through which God is revealed, like nature and tradition, may be considered sources of faith even prior to the perception of God's presence insofar as they occasion the perception and response to God. Such wonder then can be considered an antecedent of the Jewish faith. When faith in God emerges, what were antecedents of faith become aspects of the life of faith.

Again, other expressions which Heschel claimed give rise to faith such as indebtedness, praise and *mitzvah* might at first be considered aspects rather than antecedents of faith. Unlike wonder which is a response to nature, indebtedness is a response to God. For Heschel indebtedness is an antecedent of faith because a sense of indebtedness can be felt even prior to a recognition of God. In such cases indebtedness is an antecedent of faith in that it prepares us to see the source of our ultimate indebtedness. After faith itself emerges the sense of indebtedness continues. In this fashion what was an antecedent of faith becomes one of its central features. Regarding praise Heschel asserted that the praise which precedes faith is a moment of responding to God – it is an experience of faith that precedes the loyalty of faith. In this respect praise is both an antecedent and an aspect of faith. But this does not imply that there is no form of prayer that might precede the initial act of faith. The prayer of empathy which attempts to feel the meaning of ritual words may be a prayer for the ability to praise and believe in God. Thus by empathizing with the words, we can arrive at the kind of prayer that is a form of faith. Such prayers involve the remembrance of sacred events which can inspire faith. Once faith emerges, the ritual prayer continues to nourish the life of faith. In this sense ritual prayer, like other *mitzvot*, functions as both antecedent and aspect of faith – it is the beginning of faith that leads to religious fidelity.

Within the ranks of Reform Jewry Jacob Petuchowski, in *Heirs of the Pharisees*, presents a vigorous and illuminating defence of contemporary Judaism. According to this study, Reform Jews are legitimate heirs of the Pharisees; linked to the Biblical tradition, they are descended from the scholars and sages who began their activity during the second Temple period. These scholars, Petuchowski believes, initiated a process of continuous reform by adapting Scriptural ordinances to the changing circumstances of everyday life – a process which Reform Judaism should carry on today.

Throughout this study Petuchowski affirms that Reform Judaism is a valid form of Judaism. Contemporary Reform Jews, he believes, should refuse to accept the lowest common denominator as the ideal; instead they should be tradition-oriented. But this does not mean they should unquestionably accept the system of Orthodox Judaism. On the contrary, the tradition must be modified to meet the spiritual needs of modern Jewish men and women. 'It must be left to the individual', he writes, 'to decide which of the commandments he accepts as binding for himself.' In order to make such a choice, Reform Jews should have at their disposal a knowledge of the legal tradition from which such selection can be made. In this light, he argues, a Reform Jewish education should be more intensive than an Orthodox one since only an informed Jew can make an educated choice. According to Petuchowski such a selection can be made by posing four basic questions about the tradition: (1) what, in a given case, has been the direction of the millennial tradition?; (2) in what manner can I best realize the traditional teaching in my life and in the situation I find myself?; (3) what is the voice of my own conscience?: (4) what is my responsibility to the covenant community? On the basis of these criteria, Petuchowski thinks it is possible for a knowledgeable Reform Jew to construct a personal code of Jewish practice: 'The four criteria in their aggregate', he asserts, 'represent the yardstick which the modern Jew must apply to the inherited tradition.'

Holocaust theology

Recently a number of Jewish theologians have grappled with the question of whether it is possible to believe in God after the Holocaust. In *The Face of God after Auschwitz*, the British

theologian Ignaz Maybaum contends the Jews died in the concentration camps for the sins of mankind as God's suffering servant and
sacrificial lamb. For Maybaum, Auschwitz is the analogue of
Golgotha, and he sees the Nazis as instruments of God's will. On the
analogy of Nebuchadnezzar who in Jeremiah 27:6 is described as
God's servant, Maybaum maintains that Hitler played a divinely
instrumental role (like Satan who in the Bible is a servant and
messenger of God) in the purification of a sinful world. God is
pictured at Auschwitz in the role of a surgeon performing a necessary
operation, cutting out a part of Israel for the renewal of the body of
mankind.

Jews therefore suffer in order to bring about the rule of God over
the world and its peoples; their God-appointed mission is to serve the
course of historical progress and bring mankind into a new era. Only
a part, though admittedly a traumatically large part, of the Jewish
people were exterminated. The planned genocide did not succeed,
and Maybaum emphasizes that the remnant that was saved has been
selected by God as a perennial witness to His presence in the world
and in the historical process. Of the sacrificial victims of Auschwitz he
states categorically: 'Their death purged Western civilisation so that it
can again become a place where man can live, do justly, love mercy
and walk humbly with God.'

A second approach to the Holocaust is to see in the death camps a
manifestation of God's will that His chosen people survive. Such a
paradoxical view is most representatively expressed by the Reform
theologian Emile Fackenheim in a series of publications in which he
asserts that God revealed Himself to Israel out of the furnaces and
through the ashes of the victims of Auschwitz. Through the
Holocaust, he believes, God issued the 614th commandment: 'Jews
are forbbiden to grant a posthumous victory to Hitler.' According to
Fackenheim the commitment of faith is not called into question by
any event of history, including the Holocaust. Thus Fackenheim urges
Jews to hold fast to the traditional covenant God who is present in
and the Lord of history. What is at risk, he argues, is the continuation
of Judaism itself. Therefore, for the sake of Jewish survival, he asserts
that 'we are forbidden . . . to deny or despair of God however much
we may have to contend with him or with belief in Him, lest Judaism
perish.'

Though not an answer to the Holocaust, the state of Israel is for
Fackenheim a response to Auschwitz, and the Six Day War is
regarded as a moment of Divine revelation and redemption. 'Israel',
he writes, 'is collectively what every survivor is individually, a No to

the demons of Auschwitz, a Yes to Jewish survival and security and thus a testimony to life against death on behalf of all mankind.'

A third approach to the Holocaust is to reject any kind of explanation; instead the events of the Holocaust are seen as part of God's inscrutable plan. In *Faith After The Holocaust* the Orthodox scholar Eliezer Berkovits argues that the modern Jewish response to the destruction of 6 million Jews should be modelled on Job's example. We must believe in God, he maintains, because Job believed. If there is no answer to the question for any understanding of God's silence in the face of the Nazi genocide, 'it is better to be without it than in the sham of . . . the humbug of a disbelief encouraged by people who have eaten their fill at the tables of a satiated society.' At Auschwitz God was hidden, yet according to Berkovits, in His hiddenness He was actually present. As Hidden God (*El Mistater*), God is Saviour; in the apparent void He is the Redeemer of Israel.

How this is to be understood is shrouded in mystery. Berkovits writes that if Jewish faith is to be meaningful in the post-Holocaust age, the Jew must make room for the impenetrable darkness of the death camps within religious belief: 'The darkness wil remain, but in its "light" he will make his affirmations. The inexplicable will not be explained, yet it will become a positive influence in the formulation of that which is to be acknowledged . . . perhaps in the awful misery of man will be revealed to us the awesome mystery of God.' The Holocaust is thus part of God's incomprehensible plan, defying rational justification and transcending human understanding.

A final approach to the Holocaust replaces the redeeming God of Biblical faith with an entirely different concept. According to Richard Rubenstein, Auschwitz is the utter and decisive refutation of the traditional affirmation of a providential God who acts in history and watches over the Jewish people whom he has selected from all nations. In *After Auschwitz* Rubenstein argues that the Auschwitz experience has resulted in a rejection of the traditional theology of history which must be replaced by a positive affirmation of the value of human life in and for itself without any special theological relationship. Joy and fulfilment are to be sought in this life rather than in a mystical future or eschaton. This, he insists, involves a return to ancient Canaanite paganism. Thus he writes that we should attempt to establish contact with those powers of life and death which engendered men's feelings about Baal, Astarte and Anath. This would not mean literally a return to the actual worship of these deities, but simply that earth's fruitfulness, its vicissitudes and its engendering power will once again become the central spiritual realities of Jewish life.

According to Rubenstein God is the ultimate Nothing, and it is to this divine nothing that man and the world are ultimately to return. There is no hope of salvation for mankind; man's ultimate destiny is to be returned to divine nothingness. In this context Auschwitz fits into the archaic religious consciousness and observance of the universal natural cycle of death and rebirth. The mass slaughter of European Jewry was followed by a rebirth of the Jewish people in the land of Israel.

Inconclusion: the Future

Over the last 200 years Jewry has entered the mainstream of western society – no longer are Jews restricted to a ghetto existence. Such a transformation of Jewish life has profoundly altered the nature of the Jewish faith. In the past Judaism was essentially a unified structure embracing different interpretations of the same tradition. But the modern period has witnessed the fragmentation of the Jewish community into a variety of sub-groups ranging from ultra-Orthodox Hasidism to progressive Reform Judaism. In addition, the events of this century – including the Holocaust, the emergence of the state of Israel, the persecution of Jews in the Soviet Union and Arab lands, and the continuing conflict in the Middle East – have intensified the complications regarding the future of Judaism and the Jewish people. After nearly 4,000 years of history, the Jewish nation today faces new difficulties.

First, and arguably most importantly, Jews ask themselves what they should make of the greatest tragedy of modern Jewish history – the destruction of 6 million of their number by the Nazis. If the God of Israel is an all-powerful, omniscient, benevolent Father who loves His children, how could He have allowed such an event to take place? If there is a divine providential scheme, what is the purpose of this slaughter of the chosen people? These haunting questions will not disappear, and even if some theologians wish to suspend judgement about the horrific experiences of the death camps, individual Jews will not find it so easy to escape from this theological dilemma. Some Jews in contemporary society have simply abandoned their belief in God; others have substituted the state of Israel as the source of salvation. Yet whatever the response there is a vitally important theological task to be undertaken if the Jewish faith is to continue as a vibrant force in the future. Within the Biblical and rabbinic heritage, the belief in a merciful and compassionate Deity is of fundamental significance. The Holocaust challenges such a religious commitment: Jewish theologians must grapple with the religious perplexities of the death camps if Judaism is to survive as a coherent religious tradition.

Related to the problem of religious belief is the dilemma of halachic observance. Today Orthodoxy claims the largest number of adherents. Yet the majority of those who profess allegiance to Orthodox Judaism do not live by the code of Jewish law. Instead each individual Jew feels free to write his own *Shulchan Arukh*. This is so also within the other branches of Judaism. For most Jews the halachic tradition has lost its hold on Jewish consciousness – the bulk of rituals and observances appear anachronistic and burdensome. In previous centuries this was not the case; despite the divisions within the Jewish world – between Sadducees and Pharisees, rabbinates and Karaites, Hasidim and mitnagdim – all Jews accepted the binding authority of the law contained in the Torah. The 613 Biblical commandments were universally viewed as given by God to Moses on Mt Sinai and understood as binding for all time. Thus food regulations, stipulations regarding ritual purity, the moral code, as well as all other commandments served as the framework for an authentic Jewish way of life. Throughout Jewish history the validity of the written Torah was never questioned. In contemporary society, however, most Jews of all religious positions have ceased to regard the legal heritage in this light. Instead individual Jews including those of the Orthodox persuasion feel at liberty to choose which laws have a personal spiritual significance. Such an anarchic approach to the halachic tradition highlights the fact that Jewish law no longer serves as a cohesive force for contemporary Jewry. In short, many modern Jews no longer believe in the doctrine of Torah MiSinai which previously served as a cardinal principle of the Jewish faith. Instead they subscribe only to a limited number of legal precepts which for one reason or another they find meaningful. Such a lack of uniformity of Jewish practice means that there is a vast gulf between the requirements of halachic observance and the actual lifestyle of the majority of Jews both in Israel and the diaspora.

In this connection there is also considerable confusion about the status of the Pentateuch. According to Orthodox belief the Five Books of Moses were revealed to Moses on Mt Sinai. This act of revelation provided the basis for the legal system as well as Jewish theology. Many modern Orthodox adherents pay lip-service to this conviction but in their daily lives illustrate that such a belief has little if any relevance. They fail to live up to the halachic requirements as prescribed in Scripture and are agnostic about the nature and activity of God. The gap between traditional belief and contemporary views of the Torah is even greater in the non-Orthodox branches of Judaism. Here there is a general acceptance of the findings of Biblical criticism – the Five Books of Moses are perceived as divinely inspired but at the same time the product of human reflection. Thus the Pentateuch is viewed as a unified text, combining centuries of tradition, in which a variety of individual sources were woven together by a number of editors. Such a non-fundamentalist approach, which takes account of recent scholarly developments in the field of Biblical studies, rules out the traditional belief in the infallibility of Scripture and in this way provides a rationale for halachic change. Arguably in many cases Jewish law needs to undergo radical transformation. But how is such a departure from tradition to be justified? Frequently Conservative, Reconstructionalist and Reform scholars cite various criteria which can be implemented in deciding which laws should be retained, discarded or changed. Yet such decision-making is ultimately subjective, and there are no clear guidelines for altering the legal and theological features of the Biblical narrative. Even more perplexing is the question of what elements of Scripture are of divine origin. By what criteria is one to determine which elements of the Pentateuch were revealed to Moses? The lack of satisfactory answers to this question points to the religious chaos that exists in the various branches of non-Orthodox Judaism. Thus in contemporary society many Orthodox Jews who express allegiance to the Torah do not live according to the tenets or the tradition while non-Orthodox Jews are uncertain which aspects of Scripture should be revered. In both cases the Torah has for most Jews ceased to be, in the words of the psalmist, 'A tree of life to those who hold fast to it.'

Not only is there uncertainty in the Jewish world about practice and belief, there is also a great deal of confusion about Jewish identity. Are the Jews a nation, a civilization or a religious community? In the past it was relatively easy to answer this question – Jewry was united by a common heritage and way of life. Jews constituted an identifiable religious grouping sharing ancient folkways. No longer is this the case. Contemporary Jewish existence is pluralistic and most Jews are secularized and assimilated. This disordered situation is further complicated by the fact that the Reform movement has recently altered the sociological definition of Jewish status. Previously all branches of Judaism held the view that a person was Jewish if he or she had a Jewish mother; in other words, Jewishness was seen as dependent on maternal descent. However in 1983 the Central Conference of American Rabbis decreed that a child of either a Jewish mother or a Jewish father should be regarded as Jewish. By expanding the determination of Jewishness to include children of both matrilineal and patrilineal descent the Reform movement defined as Jews individuals whom the other branches of Judaism regard as gentiles; this means that neither these persons nor their descendants can be accepted as Jews by the non-Reform religious establishment.

A similar situation applies to Reform converts and their offspring who, according to Orthodox Judaism, are non-Jews. The Orthodox movement has debarred such individuals from access to Jewish privileges, and has exerted pressure on the government of Israel not to allow Reform converts the right to return to the Holy Land as Jewish citizens. A final complication concerning Jewish status concerns the re-marriage of female Jews who, though civilly divorced, have failed to obtain a Jewish bill of divorce (*get*). Orthodoxy does not recognize their divorces as valid and any subsequent liaison, even when accompanied by a non-Orthodox Jewish marriage ceremony or civil marriage, is regarded as adulterous. Further, the children of such unions are stigmatized as bastards (*mamzerim*) and barred from marrying other Jews unless they also are *mamzerim*. These problems, produced by deviations from traditional Jewish practice, present contemporary Jewry with enormous perplexities and highlight the fissures separating the various Jewish religious groupings. How a commitment to Jewish peoplehood (*klal Yisrael*) can be sustained when religious organizations are so deeply divided about such fundamental aspects of Jewish identity is a deeply troubling question for present and future generations.

Another serious dilemma facing the Jewish community concerns the position of women. This issue has become one of the most pressing problems in the Jewish world today as many Jewish women are attempting to reshape their personal lives as well as public institutions in the light of modern feminism. According to these women, Jewish law discriminates against them by exempting them from the obligation to observe positive time-bound commandments as well as from participating in public prayer, Torah reading and traditional study. Moreover such discrimination, they argue, extends to a variety of other areas of Jewish life: marriage, divorce, sexuality outside marriage, procreation, abortion and rape. Such criticism has evoked various responses from the different wings of the religious establishment. At one end of the spectrum, Orthodox spokesmen have rejected the feminists' call for Jewish law to accommodate their demands for equal status. The *halachah*, they argue, has its own ideal role for women, and the values of the non-Jewish world – on which it is alleged feminism is based – constitute no cause for change.

At the opposite end of the spectrum, Reform exponents insist that Jewish law is fundamentally opposed to the realities of contemporary life and must therefore be rejected. Between these two poles Conservative scholars argue that change in Jewish law to accommodate the demands of Jewish feminism should be possible since Conservative Judaism sees the *halachah* as evolving historically. In this vein some Conservative rabbis have suggested that minority opinions preserved in the Talmud and afterwards can function as legitimate sources for altering the legal system. There is thus a wide range of opinion in contemporary Jewry about the status of women. In all likelihood the women's movement will continue to press for full participation in Jewish life; the way in which these demands are either accepted or rejected will no doubt have serious implications for the Jewish religion in the future.

Despite the divisions in the Jewish community, Jewry is united in its allegiance to the state of Israel. For most Jews worldwide the establishment of a Jewish homeland is a sign of hope in the face of the Holocaust. Yet here too there are real dilemmas for the Jewish community regarding a number of central issues. First there is the problem of Israeli identity. Is being an Israeli sufficient to define Jewishness – and if so, what is one to say about non-Jews living in Israel? A second dilemma concerns the relationship between Jews living in the diaspora and those who reside in Israel. Previously many Zionists argued that it was necessary to live in the Holy Land in order to live a fully Jewish life, but is such a position valid in the modern world? There are many diaspora Jews who, though loyal to the state of Israel, would reject such a contention.

Another crucial concern is related to the role of Jewish values in the state. A number of early Zionists were convinced that the Jewish nation should embody traditional Jewish ideals. But is such a vision feasible in the Middle East today? Does it make sense for Judaism to be the established religion of the state? And what of minority groups, such as Conservative and Reform Jews – should they be granted full recognition as authentic expressions of the Jewish faith? Again, there is considerable uncertainty about the nature of the policies of the state – should they embody Jewish values, and if so how would this affect both domestic and foreign policies? Further, there is the question whether the state should encourage Jewish observance or allow citizens to make their own decisions about religion. Finally, Jews in the diaspora need to ask themselves whether they owe a special loyalty to Israel regardless of her policies. Is the correct attitude to support Israel right or wrong, or should the actions of the country be evaluated in the light of Jewish ethical categories and humanitarian concerns?

Today Jews are also faced with the issue of religious pluralism. What should the relationship be between Judaism and other faiths? In the medieval world the general view of Jewish thinkers was that Islam was not to be classified as idolatry, but there was considerable debate about the status of Christianity. By the time of the Enlightenment it was widely held that Christians and Muslims were in no way to be included in the harsh condemnation of heathens in classical sources, but Far Eastern religions such as Hinduism were regarded as idolatrous. In contemporary society there are some traditionalists who hold an exclusivist view of Judaism. The Jewish religion, they believe, is absolutely true since at Mt Sinai God revealed His Holy Torah to Moses. Sinaitic revelation is viewed as a unique divine act which provides a secure foundation for the sacred traditions of Israel. In this light other religions are regarded as false – such an understanding assumes that throughout the history of the world human beings have mistakenly assumed that they have had an encounter with the Divine. Yet in fact, God made Himself known only to His chosen people.

Some progressive Jewish thinkers have criticized this point of view. For these writers God is seen as the providential Lord of history, and they question the conviction that God hid His presence and withheld His revelation from all mankind with the exception of the Jews. To allow humanity to wallow in darkness and ignorance weighed down by false notions of divine disclosure, they argue, is hardly what we would expect from a loving, compassionate and caring God. According to these thinkers, what is much more likely is that in the past God revealed Himself not only to the Jews but to others as well. Some of these theologians desire to preserve the centrality of the Jewish faith while giving credence to the claims of other faiths that they have had an encounter with the Divine. Other more radical thinkers take this position one stage further; they contend that in each and every generation and to all the peoples of the world God has disclosed Himself in numerous ways. Thus neither in Judaism – nor for that matter in any other religion – has God revealed Himself absolutely and completely. Whatever one makes of this view, there is no doubt that the Jewish community will need to respond to the issue of religious pluralism as Jews gain a greater awareness of other faiths. What they learn and experience may well affect their understanding of their own heritage.

All of these dilemmas about the nature of contemporary Judaism are in varying degrees related to the fundamental issue of assimilation. Prior to the Enlightenment Jews did not have full citizenship rights of the countries in which they lived. Nevertheless they were able to regulate their own affairs through an organized structure of self-government. Within such a context Jewish law served as the basis of communal life, and rabbis were able to exert power and authority in the community. But as a result of political emancipation, Jews entered the mainstream of modern life taking on all the responsibilities of citizenship. The rabbinical establishment thereby lost its status and control, and the halachic system became voluntary. In addition, Jews took advantage of widening social advantages: they were free to choose where to live, whom to marry, and what career to follow. By gaining access to secular educational institutions, the influence of the surrounding culture also pervaded all aspects of Jewish life. As a consequence Jewry in modern society is fragmented and secularized; intermarriage is on the increase.

As Jews stand on the threshold of the twenty-first century, answers must urgently be found to the perplexing problems now facing the Jewish people. Orthodox Jewish theology, traditional Jewish practice, the divine status of the Torah, the ancient definition of Jewishness, the age-old role of women, the political state of Israel and the primacy of the Jewish faith are all being questioned. The writing is on the wall. If the Jewish people are not to become extinct like the Sumerians, Akkadians and Assyrians of the ancient world these problems must be confronted. What is at stake is no less than the survival of the Jewish heritage.

Further Reading

General

P. Johnson, *A History of the Jews* (Weidenfeld and Nicolson, 1987).
H. H. Ben-Sasson (ed.), *A History of the Jewish People* (Harvard University Press, 1976).
R. Seltzer, *Jewish People, Jewish Thought: The Jewish Experience in History* (Collier Macmillan, 1980).
L. Trepp, *A History of the Jewish Experience* (Behrman House Inc., 1973).
J. G. Williams, *Judaism* (Quest Books, 1980).
N. de Lange, *Judaism* (Oxford University Press, 1986).
A. L. Sachar, *A History of the Jews* (Alfred A. Knopf, 1973).
M. L. Margolis and A. Marx, *A History of the Jewish People* (Harper and Row, 1965).
C. Roth, *A History of the Jews* (Schocken, 1973).
I. Epstein, *Judaism* (Penguin, 1975).
S. W. Baron, *A Social and Religious History of the Jews* (Columbia University Press, 1952–76).
Encyclopedia Judaica (Keter Publishing House Ltd., 1972).

Chapter 1 The Ancient Near Eastern Background

H. Frankfort (ed.), *Before Philosophy* (Penguin, 1964).
S. H. Hooke, *Middle Eastern Mythology* (Penguin, 1981).
W. Beyerlin (ed.), *Near Eastern Texts Relating to the Old Testament* (SCM Press, 1978).
J. Pritchard (ed.), *The Ancient Near East: An Anthology of Texts and Pictures* (Princeton University Press, vol. 1, 1958, vol. 2, 1975).
D. Winton Thomas, *Documents From Old Testament Times* (Harper and Row, 1976).

Chapter 2 Patriarchy to Monarchy

J. Drane, *The Old Testament Story* (Lion Publishing, 1983).
M. Grant, *The History of Ancient Israel* (Scribner's, 1984).
G. W. Anderson, *The History and Religion of Israel* (Oxford University Press, 1966).
J. Bright, *A History of Israel* (Westminster Press, 1972).
K. M. Kenyon, *The Bible and Recent Archaeology* (John Knox Press, 1978).

Chapter 3 Kings and Prophets

J. Lindblom, *Prophecy in Ancient Israel* (Basil Blackwell, 1962).
G. Von Rad, *The Message of the Prophets* (SCM Press, 1968).
B. W. Anderson, *The Eighth Century Prophets* (SPCK, 1979).
J. Gray, *The Biblical Doctrine of the Reign of God* (T. and T. Clark, 1979).
B. Vawter, *The Conscience of Israel* (Sheed and Ward, 1961).

Chapter 4 Captivity and Return

P. R. Ackroyd, *Exile and Restoration* (SCM Press, 1968).
P. R. Ackroyd, *Israel under Babylon and Persia* (Oxford University Press, 1970).
Y. Kaufmann, *The Babylonian Captivity and Deutero-Isaiah* (Union of American Hebrew Congregations, 1970).
J. Blenkinsopp, *Prophecy and Canon: A Contribution to the Study of Jewish Origins* (University of Notre Dame Press, 1977).
M. Hengel, *Judaism and Hellenism: Studies in Their Encounter in Palestine During the Early Hellenic Period* (Fortress Press, 1974).

Chapter 5 Rebellion and Dispersion

C. H. Dodd, *The Bible and the Greeks* (Hodder and Stoughton, 1935).
S. Sandmel, *Judaism and Christian Beginnings* (Oxford University Press, 1978).
E. Schürer, *The History of the Jewish People in the Age of Jesus Christ* (T. and T. Clark, 1973).
V. Tcherikover, *Hellenistic Civilisation and the Jews* (Jewish Publication Society of America, 1959).
S. Zeitlin, *The Rise and Fall of the Judean State*, vols 1–3 (Jewish Publication Society of America, 1962–8).

Chapter 6 Rabbinic Judaism

C. G. Montefiore and H. Loewe, *A Rabbinic Anthology* (Schocken, 1974).
M. Mielziner, *Introduction to the Talmud* (Bloch, 1968).
A. Cohen, *Everyman's Talmud* (Schocken, 1975).
S. Schechter, *Aspects of Rabbinic Theology* (Schocken, 1961).
H. Strack, *Introduction to the Talmud and Midrash* (Jewish Publication Society of America, 1931).

Chapter 7 The Emergence of Medieval Jewry

I. Abrahams, *Jewish Life in the Middle Ages* (Athenaeum, 1969).
J. Parkes, *The Jew in the Medieval Community: A Study of His Political and Economic Situation* (Hermon Press, 1976).
J. R. Marcus (ed.), *The Jew in the Medieval World* (Harper and Row, 1965).
A. Sharf, *Byzantine Jewry: From Justinian to the Fourth Crusade* (Routledge and Kegan Paul, 1971).
J. Trachtenberg, *Jewish Magic and Superstition* (Jewish Publication Society of America, 1961).

Chapter 8 Medieval Jewish Philosophy and Theology

I. Husik, *A History of Medieval Jewish Philosophy* (Jewish Publication Society of America, 1958).
S. Katz (ed.), *Jewish Philosophers* (Jewish Publishing Co., 1975).
J. L. Blau, *The Story of Jewish Philosophy* (Random House, 1962).
L. Jacobs, *A Jewish Theology* (Darton, Longman and Todd, 1973).
J. B. Agus, *The Evolution of Jewish Thought, From Biblical Times to the Opening of the Modern Era* (Abelard-Schuman, 1959).

Chapter 9 Medieval Jewish Mysticism

G. Scholem, *Major Trends in Jewish Mysticism* (Schocken, 1954).
G. Scholem, *Kabbalah* (Quadrangle, 1974).
I. Abelson, *Jewish Mysticism* (Harmon Press, 1969).
J. Dan, *Jewish Mysticism and Jewish Ethics* (Washington University Press, 1986).
J. Dan and F. Talmage (eds), *Studies in Jewish Mysticism* (Association for Jewish Studies, 1982).

Chapter 10 Judaism in the Early Modern Period

G. Scholem, *Sabbatai Sevi: The Mystical Messiah 1626–1676* (Princeton University Press, 1973).

J. Katz, *Tradition and Crisis: Jewish Society at the End of the Middle Ages* (Free Press, 1961).

S. Stern, *The Court Jew: A Contribution to the History of the Period of Absolutism in Central Europe* (Jewish Publication Society of America, 1950).

C. Roth, *The Spanish Inquisition* (W. W. Norton, 1964).

B. Weinryb, *The Jews of Poland. A Social and Economic History of the Jewish Community of Poland from 1100 to 1800* (Jewish Publication Society of America, 1973).

Chapter 11 From Hasidism to the Enlightenment

D. Ben-Amos and J. R. Mintz (eds), *In Praise of the Baal Shem Tov: The Earliest Collection of Legends About the Founder of Hasidism* (Indiana University Press, 1970).

L. S. Dawidowicz, *The Golden Tradition: Jewish Life and Thought in Eastern Europe* (Holt, Reinhardt and Winston, 1966).

S. Dubnow, *History of the Jews in Russia and Poland* (Ktav Publishing House, 1973).

A. Hertzberg, *The French Enlightenment and the Jews* (Columbia University Press, 1968).

J. Katz, *Out of the Ghetto: The Social Background of Jewish Emancipation, 1770–1870* (Harvard University Press, 1973).

Chapter 12 The Rise of Reform Judaism

D. Phillipson, *The Reform Movement in Judaism* (Ktav Publishing House, 1967).

G. W. Plaut (ed.), *The Rise of Reform Judaism: A Sourcebook of Its European Origins* (World Union of Progressive Judaism, 1963).

G. W. Plaut (ed.), *The Growth of Reform Judaism: American and European Sources* (World Union of Progressive Judaism, 1965).

D. Marmur (ed.), *Reform Judaism* (Reform Synagogues of Great Britain, 1973).

W. Jacob (ed.), *American Reform Responsa* (Central Conference of American Rabbis, 1983).

Chapter 13 Jewish Life in the Nineteenth and Early Twentieth Centuries

L. Poliakov, *The History of Anti-Semitism*, 3 vols (Vanguard Press, 1965–76).
W. Laqueur, *A History of Zionism* (Schocken, 1976).
H. M. Sachar, *The Course of Modern Jewish History* (Delta Publishing Company, 1958).
N. Glazer, *American Judaism* (University of Chicago Press, 1972).
J. Reinharz, *Fatherland or Promised Land: The Dilemma of the German Jew 1893–1914* (University of Michigan Press, 1975).

Chapter 14 Holocaust and Aftermath

L. S. Dawidowicz, *The War Against the Jews 1937–1945* (Holt, Rinehart and Winston, 1975).
N. Levin, *The Holocaust: The Destruction of European Jewry 1933–1945* (Schocken, 1973).
L. S. Dawidowicz (ed.), *A Holocaust Reader* (Behrman House, 1976).
C. C. O'Brien, *The Siege: The Saga of Israel and Zionism* (Weidenfeld and Nicolson, 1986).
N. de Lange, *Atlas of the Jewish World* (Phaidon, 1985).

Chapter 15 Modern Jewish Thought

S. H. Bergman, *An Introduction to Modern Jewish Thought* (Schocken, 1963).
N. Rotenstreich, *Jewish Philosophy in Modern Times: From Mendelssohn to Rosenzweig* (Holt, Rinehart and Winston, 1968).
J. B. Agus, *Modern Philosophies of Judaism* (Behrman House, 1971).
S. Noveck, (ed.) *Great Jewish Thinkers of the Twentieth Century* (B'nai B'rith Department of Jewish Education, 1963).
W. Kaufman, *Contemporary Jewish Philosophies* (Behrman House, Inc., 1976).

Index

Note: In this index most names of the ancient and medieval periods are entered under the first element (e.g. *Johanan* ben Zaccai), however, see *ibn* Daud, etc.

Index by Justyn Balinski